Functioning

with

Access 2013

by

Mark A. Laurent PhD

About the author: Dr. Laurent is currently an adjunct professor, teaching three levels of Access at Northlake College (Irving, Tx.). He completed his doctorate in Education, concentrating in Computer Education. As a corporate educator for over 16 years, he has an understanding how complex software appears and how confusing it can be using Functions in Access.

Published by Lulu.com, 2013.

Printed and bound in the United States by LuLu.com

Book available online at many at www.LuLu.com,

ISBN   978-1-304-50529-3

DISCLAIMER: While the author takes care to ensure the accuracy of these materials, he cannot guarantee their accuracy, and all materials are provided without any warranty whatsoever, including, but not limited to, the implied warrantees or fitness for a particular purpose. The names used in the data files in this book are fictitious and do not represent anyone.

Microsoft© and Access© are registered trademarks of Microsoft Corporation in the United States and other countries.

Copyright © 2013 by Mark A. Laurent PhD. All rights reserved. This publication is protected by Copyright, and permission should be obtained from the author prior to any prohibited reproduction or transmission in any form or by any means, electronic, mechanical, and photocopying or likewise.

Functioning with Access 2013

Functioning with Access 2013
TABLE of CONTENTS

Subject covered	Pages

Introduction — 1 – 4
Requirements (1), PBL (2), Conventions used (3),
AND criteria in queries (4), OR criteria in queries (4)

Chapter 1 - Beginning — 5 – 20
Data (5-6), Expression Builder (7-11),
Types of queries (12-13), Select query (14-16),
Make Table query (17-20)

SELECT QUERIES --

Chapter 2 - Character (Text) Functions — 21 – 46
Left (23-25), Right (26-28), Mid (29-31),
Concatenate (32-34, 40-42), Len (35), InStr (36-39),
LTrim, RTrim, Trim (40-42), Replace (43-45), SQL(46)

Chapter 3 - Math Functions — 47 – 60
Avg (49-52), Round (51-52), Fix (52), Int (52),
Count (53), Max (54), Min (55), Sum (56)

Chapter 4 - Date Functions — 61 – 86
DateDiff (62-66, 68), Format (62-64), Now (62-66),
DateAdd (67-69), DatePart (70-71), Second (72, 85),
Minute (73, 85), Hour (74, 85), Day (75, 85),
WeekDay (76-78, 86), WeekDayName (79-80),
Month (81, 86), Year (82, 86), Timer (83, 86),
VBA code (85-86)

UPDATE QUERIES --

Chapter 5 - Character (Text) Functions — 87 – 108
Left (88-91), Parameter (89, 93, 95), Right (92-94),
Mid (95-97), Replace (97-98, 104-105), Len (99, 108),
InStr (100-101, 105), Concatenate (102-104, 108),
LTrim, RTrim, Trim (102-104), UCase (106, 108),
LCase (107-108)

Chapter 6 - Math Functions — 109 – 116
Round (110-111), Fix (110-112), Int (110-111),
Math operations (+, -, /, *) (113-115)

Functioning with Access 2013
TABLE of CONTENTS

UPDATE QUERIES (continued) --------------------------------

Chapter 7 - Date Functions 117 – 122
Adding to Dates (117-118), DateAdd (119-121), DateDiff (122)

APPEND QUERIES --

Chapter 8 - Character (Text) Functions 123 – 134
Parameter (126-127), Left (126), Right (127), Mid (128), Replace (129-130), Len (131), InStr (132), LTrim, Trim (132)

Chapter 9 - Math Functions 135 – 140
Avg (136-137), Round (137), Fix (137), Int (137), Count (138-140), Max (138-140), Min (138-140), Sum (138-140)

Chapter 10 - Date Functions 141 – 150
DateDiff (142-144), Now (143), DateAdd (145-146), DatePart (147-148), Day (147-148), Month (147-148), Year (147-148), WeekDay (149-150), WeekDayName (149-150)

OTHER INFORMTION ---

Chapter 11 Parameter Queries 151 – 164
Text Functions
Left (151-153), Right (154-156), Mid (157-158), Len (159-161), InStr (162-164)

Chapter 12 Function reference, VBA help 165 – 174
Wild cards (169), Like operator (170), Input masks (171-173)

Chapter 13 -- Character set information 175 – 184

Appendix 185 – 186

Functioning with Access – 2013
Introduction

This guide was created to provide examples and insight to the Microsoft Access application. Use this guide as a supplement to a course textbook. Any Access class has established educational goals and content based upon those goals; students' expectations may not always align with these goals. Textbook selection is based upon these educational goals but the textbook may not reflect the educational needs of the student. This guide provides insight to the student enabling them to expand their knowledge beyond what any textbook may provide. "Thinking outside the textbook" may be a catch phrase used here, however the examples and explanations will help readers to go beyond even this guide.

Every aspect of Access will not be covered; the software has so many functionalities such a complete explanation is not reasonable for the scope of this guide. However, with some initial examples, the user of this book will be able to comprehend new uses of the software and feel comfortable with the application. The final goal is to enable students to utilize this guide to help them "Function with Access" in a more productive way.

Requirements

To utilize this text, the user must have Access loaded on a pc where they can create, modify and save. Each of these actions helps to test the examples and practice creating queries and updating tables. The version of Access will also determine if the functions illustrated are available, later versions of Access have more functions. This guide is written using Access 2013; however most of the functions are available in earlier Access versions. All functions were tested in Access 2013. A vast majority of the functions in this guide were available in Access 2007 and 2010 and were included in previous versions of this guide.

Problem Based Learning

Teaching adults in a web-based environment requires techniques that provide quick understanding by the participant. Teaching database software to adults who are not computer savvy requires instructional techniques that allow for variations in participants' backgrounds. A very viable method is Problem Based Learning (PBL). Students build their educational foundation and then add to it as they add specialties and expertise. Accumulation of general knowledge allows students to increase their overall wealth of knowledge. A student learning in an Internet based class does not have the same interactive opportunities as a classroom student. Classes developed for web-based training must utilize a different approach to educate the participant, such as PBL.

This guide is broken up into three types of queries: Select, Update and Append. Each of these types of queries is presented using Character, Math and Date functions. Delete queries are not covered. To delete data, create a Select query, run the query and once you are satisfied with the outcome, change the query type to Delete and run the query again. Chapter 11 presents examples of Parameter queries using Character functions. An appendix illustrates using Access Help. Some of the Help material is for programmers and does not make sense to use directly in functions. Once you have gained a better understanding of Access, the Help is more effective in guiding you.

Using this book and practicing the examples provide many problems to experience. The examples are relevant to a business situation and to home usage. A PBL approach has helped many to understand functions. The examples in this manual are solutions to student and work problems during the authors seventeen years of teaching Access and 21 years working with Access.

Functioning with Access – 2013
Introduction

Conventions used in this manual.

This guide is referred to as a text, book, manual or reference. The name of a field will be surrounded by square brackets (these characters are to the right of the "p" key). Formulas will be shown in the queries and outside of the query. The formulas will be bold to better facilitate reading. Screenshots of returned messages have been added where they were seen. The wording in this manual has been written is a non-formal style to illustrate a discussion between you and someone who is helping you do your work. Mistakes are made and corrected to help illustrate that the most obvious answer is not always the correct answer.

This book is an update to the 2010 version created in 2011. Input from my online students and fellow educators have streamlined some areas for clarity.

NOTE: When formulas are shown in the text, often a period '.' will follow. This is not to be included in the formula; it is just ending the sentence. An example follows:

Number of Books: [# of Books] +10.

Do not include the period at the end of the sentence, the code you should place in your query is

Number of Books: [# of Books] +10 otherwise you will get an error from Access.

This manual is not intended to be your only resource for information on Access. This manual is intended to supplement any other introductory book that you may have on Access. As stated above, the direction and content were derived from student questions during Face-to-Face and Online classes.

Functioning with Access – 2013
Introduction

AND & OR criteria in queries. During your creation of queries, you may need to have queries that limit the number of records being retrieved. This can be done by using **AND** along with **OR** criteria in your queries. Examples are shown below. This is presented here because it applies to all of the queries created in this book and you need to be aware of it as a tool to use in your query creation.

AND criteria in a query.

The following query is an AND criteria, it has 2 limits on the records being retrieved. These two limits are on 1 row in the criteria area which means that both conditions must be met. Here only the records where the [Last Name] is **Lawrence** AND the [First Name] is **Anderson** will be retrieved.

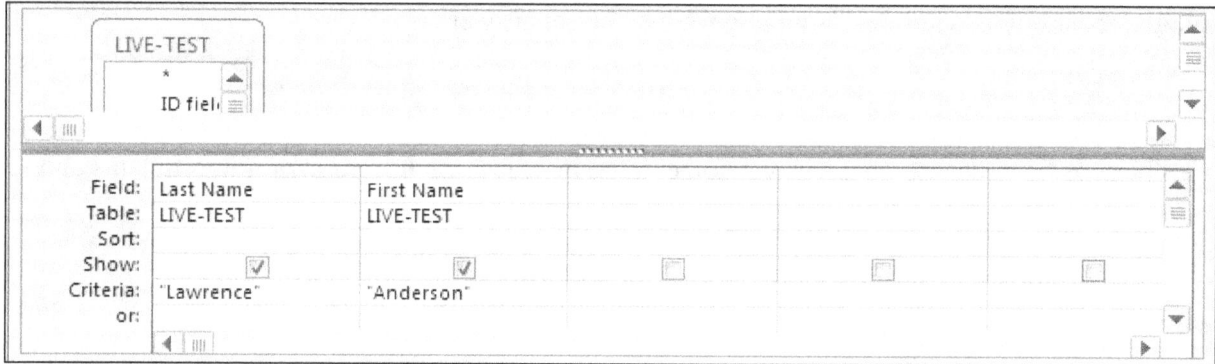

OR criteria in a query.

The following query is an OR query criteria, it has 2 limits on the records being retrieved. These two limits are on 2 rows in the criteria area which means that either of the conditions must be met. Here all records with a [Last Name] of **Lawrence** OR all the records where the [First Name] is **Mike** will be retrieved (OR queries normally return more records than AND queries).

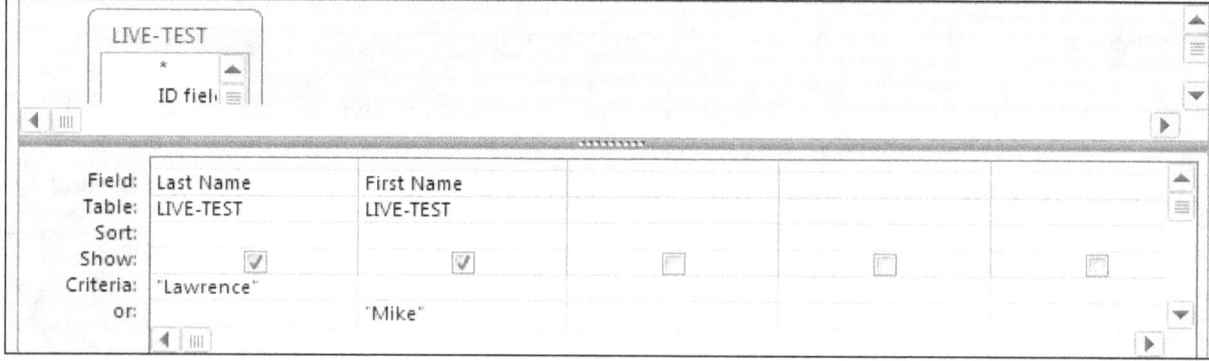

Chapter 1.

To get started, open Access and create a new database, give it any name you desire (the database used for this book is called 'Functioning-Access-2013'). Next, create the table as shown below. Name the table 'INITIAL-DATA'. Here is the table design.

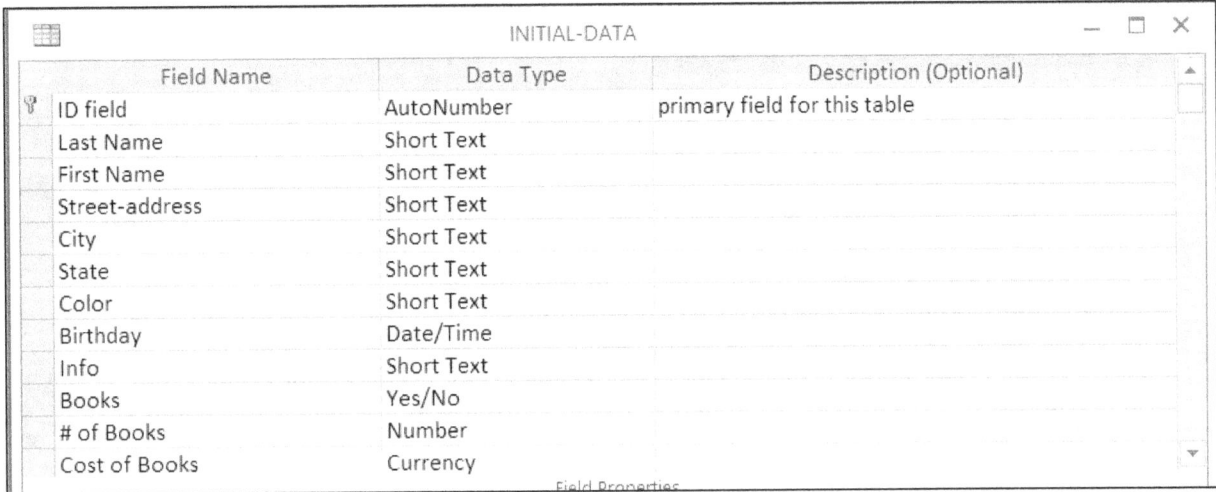

The details are as follows

ID field	Auto number – unique key field
Last Name	30 characters
First Name	20 characters
Street-address	50 characters
City	30 characters
State	15 characters
Color	15 characters
Birthday	Short date format mm/dd/yyyy
Info	50 character text for information
Books	Yes/No values accepted only
# of Books	Numeric field (long integer)
Cost of Books	Currency, 2 decimal places

This assortment of data types will provide many opportunities to use functions.

Functioning with Access – 2013
Chapter 1 – Beginning

The data to be entered into this table is shown below. Here is the data for the ID field, Last Name, First Name, Street-address, City, State, Color and Birthday fields.

ID field	Last Name	First Name	Street-address	City	State	Color
1	Cederoth	Katherine	141 Grant	Chicago	Illinois	Tan
2	Yeaoman	Mike	322 Sheffield	San Francisco	California	Orange
3	Yeaoman	Shirley	1112 Canada	San Antonio	Texas	Easter Pink
4	Dionne	Tom	Route 4, 277 West	Onarga	Wisconsin	Milatary Green
5	Lawrence	Anderson	PO box 12A79, slot 7	Grand Prarie	Texas	Burnt Orange
6	Lawrence	Motherbee	PO box 12A79, slot 8	Grand Prarie	Texas	Scarlet Red
7	Lawrence	Fatherbee	PO box 12A79, slot 9	Grand Prarie	Texas	Green
8	Lawrence	Sisterbee	PO box 12A79, slot 10	Grand Prarie	Texas	Pink
9	Deenoyer	Tony	1456 Bad Ax	St Francis	Oklahoma	Blue

Here are the values for the Birthday, Info, Books, # of Books and Cost of Books fields.

Birthday	Info	Books	# of Books	Cost of Books
6/15/1957	Moved away due to ballteam losses	✓	768	$56,788.22
12/14/1958	Married early in life .		0	$0.00
6/22/1957	Dropped out of high school, became a pilot .	✓	500	$7,788.76
12/1/1977	Works on a farm and has hopes of being a doctor .	✓	35	$678.30
3/15/1999	Young child with many toys.	✓	4	$22.30
5/15/1969	Mother of a young child.	✓	55	$5,555.55
5/22/1967	Father of a young child.	✓	44	$4,444.44
7/22/1997	Sister of a young child.	✓	7	$77.77
2/29/1996	Leap day baby, has bad attitude.	✓	34	$456.44

In the table above, for the Books field if the value is 'Yes', then the box is checked.

The queries for this book use these values unless indicated as being different.

Functioning with Access – 2013
Chapter 1 – Beginning

To get a visual representation of the functions that are available to us, we will create a new Select query using the Initial-data table. (Select Create, Query Design)

Then select the INITIAL-DATA table.

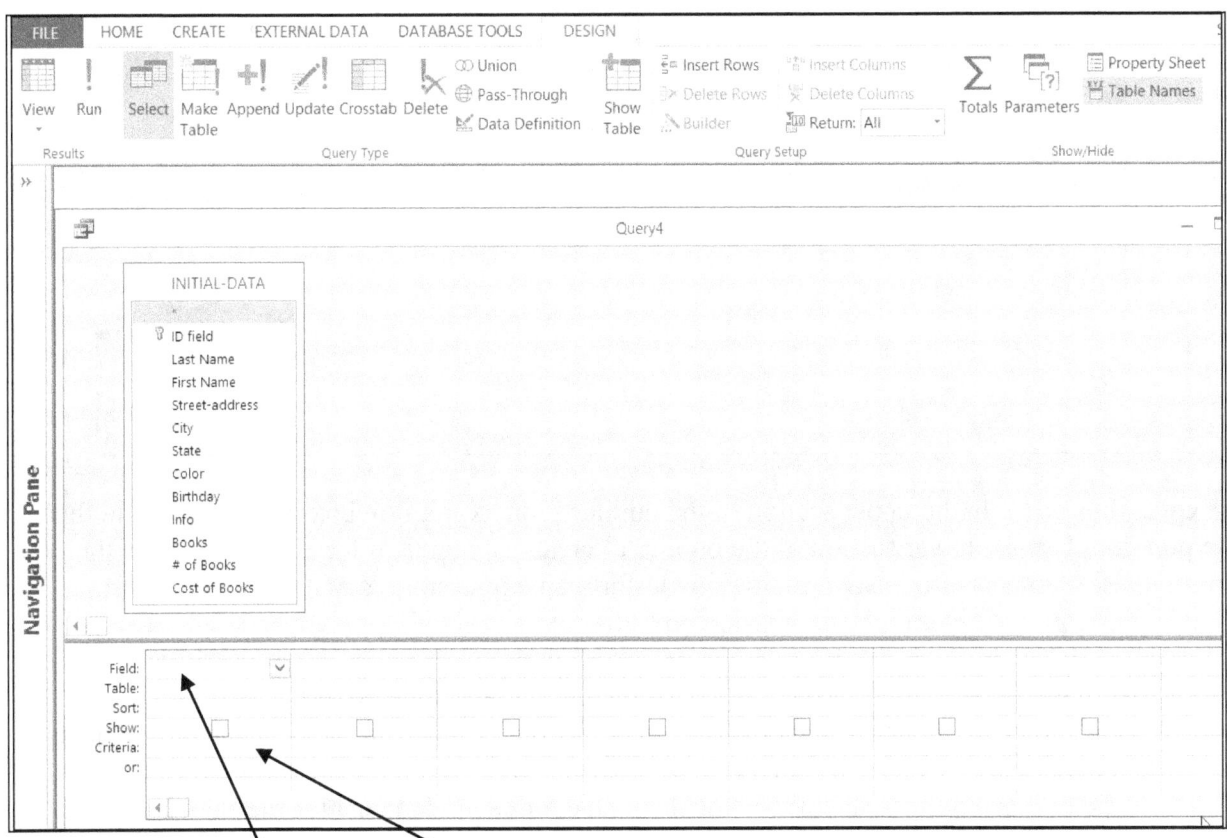

Get focus in the Field row or the Criteria row. This will enable the **Builder** selection

Now select **Builder**.

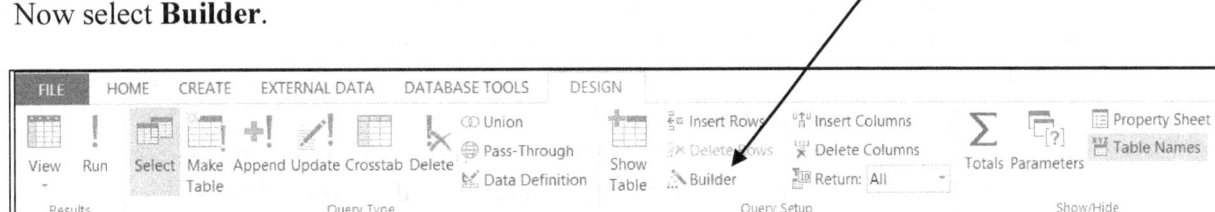

The Expression Builder has two sections, the upper section shows built expression while the lower section (made up of 3 areas) provides the components to make the expressions.

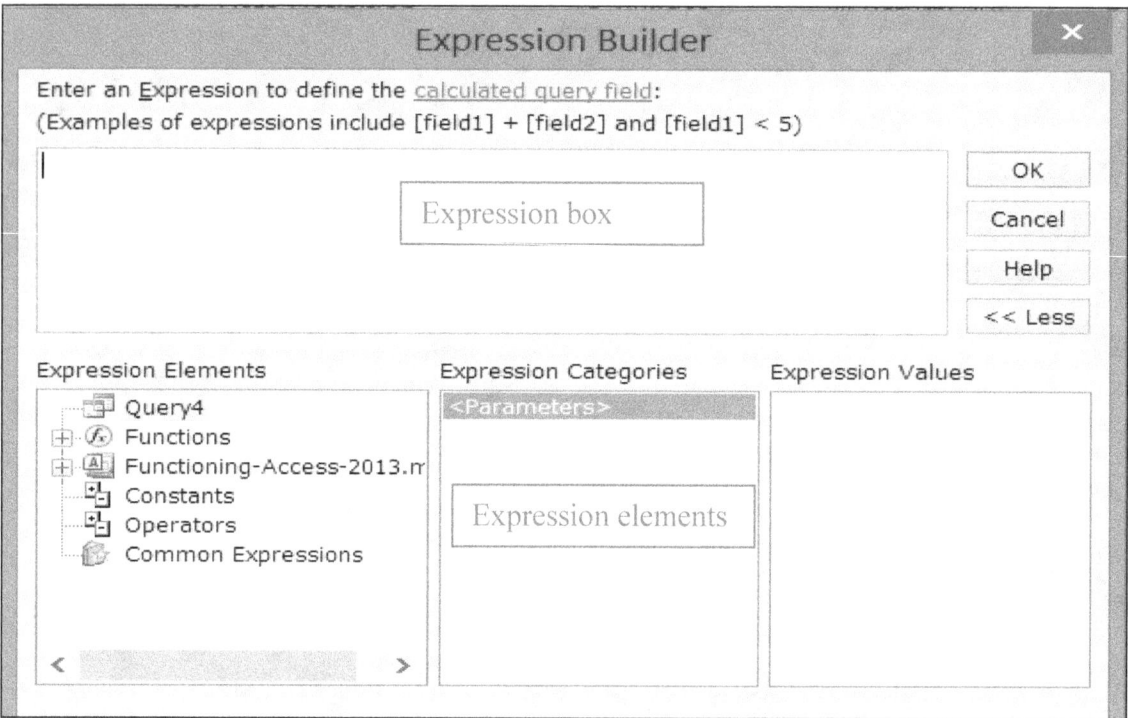

Expression box   In the upper section of the builder is an expression box where you build the expression. Use the lower section of the builder to create elements of the expression, and then paste these elements into the expression box to form an expression. You can also type parts of the expression directly into the expression box.

Expression elements   In the lower section of the builder are three boxes:
   The left box contains folders that list the table, query, form, and report database objects, built-in and user-defined functions, constants, operators, and common expressions.
   The middle box lists specific elements or categories of elements for the folder selected in the left box. For example, if you click **Built-In Functions** in the left box, the middle box lists categories of Microsoft Access functions.
   The right box lists the values, if any, for the elements you select in the left and middle boxes. For example, if you click **Built-In Functions** in the left box and a category of functions in the middle box, the right box lists all built-in functions in the selected category.
   Note: When you paste an identifier in your expression, the Expression Builder pastes only the parts of the identifier that are required in the current context. For example, if you start the Expression Builder from the property sheet of the Customers form, and then paste an identifier for the **Visible** property of the form in your expression, the Expression Builder pastes only the property name: **Visible**. If you use this expression outside the context of the form, you must include the full identifier: Forms![Customers].Visible.

Functioning with Access – 2013
Chapter 1 – Beginning

Authors guide

The previous material is from Access help. Using your mouse you can build expressions by clicking on the folders n the Leftmost box of the bottom section (Expression Elements). This method can help you create Visual Basic programming statements, which is beyond this document. This guide is to illustrate how to use some of the most commonly used functions available in Access in Queries. This knowledge and formulas can also be used in Forms and Reports.

Double click on Functions.

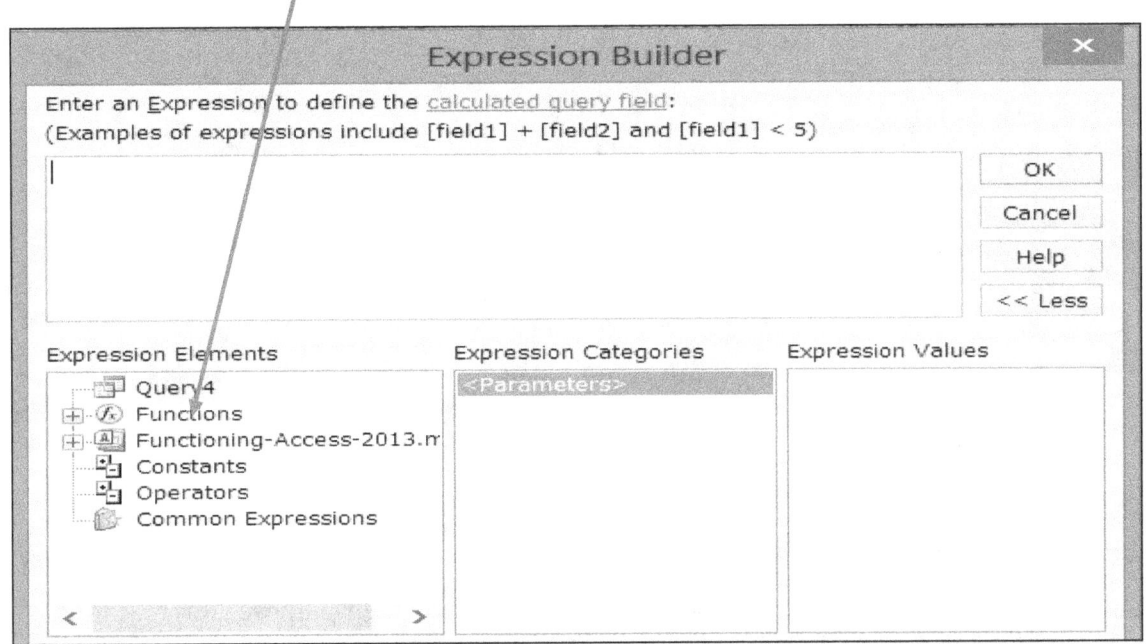

Once you click on Functions, it will open the folder revealing three selections. Select Built-In Functions.

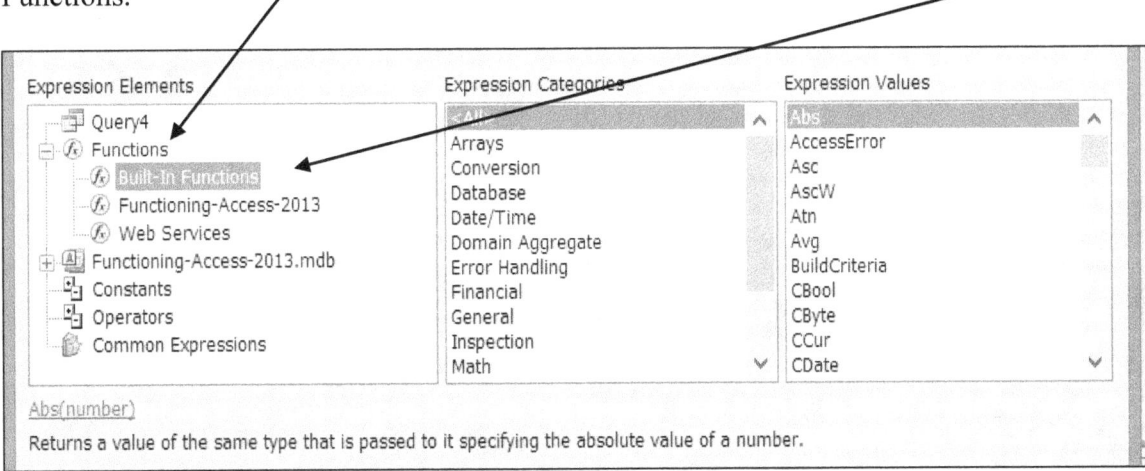

Now the right two areas are populated.

The top selection, 'Built-In Functions' is where we will be investigating. Selecting 'Built-In Functions' populates the middle and right sections with available selections. The center and right areas in the bottom of the Expression builder are filled populated.

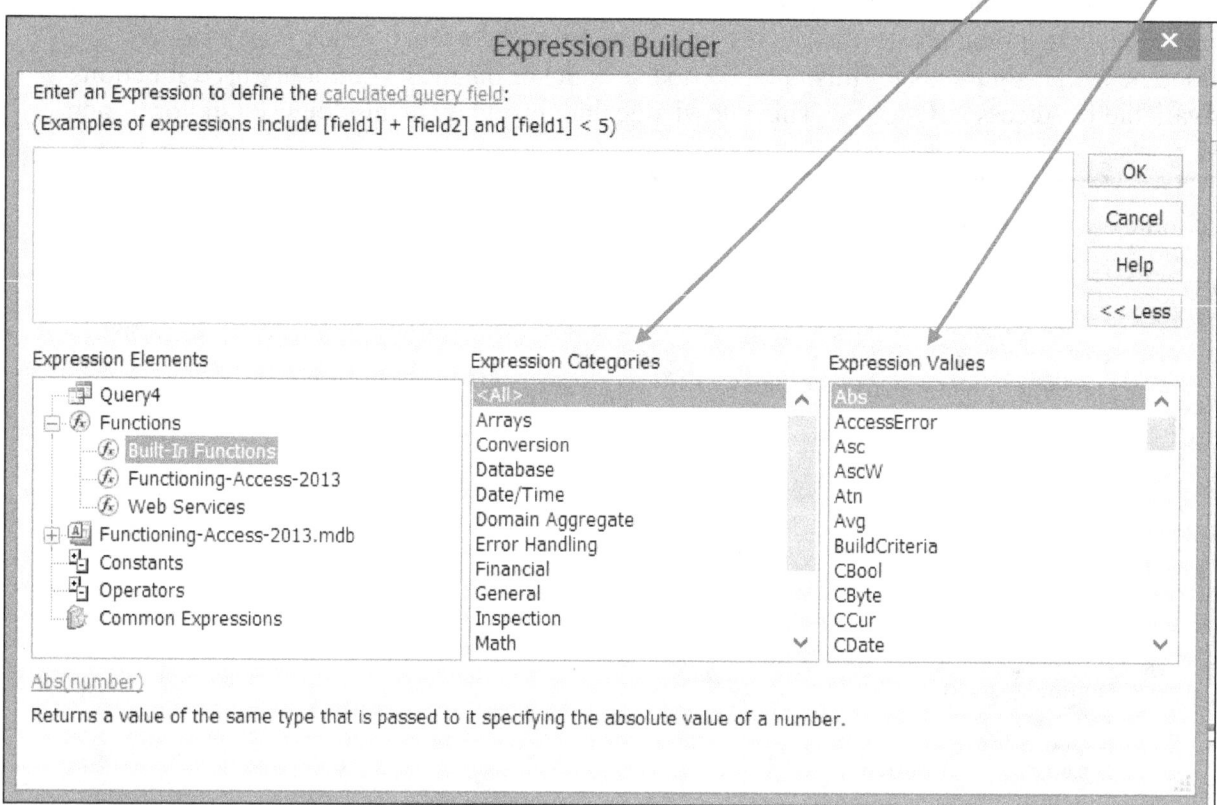

The middle section categorizes (groups) the functions based upon their purpose (for Text, Math, Messages, etc.). In the right section is where we will be focusing our investigation. Looking at just the Math functions (below), only 13 are available.

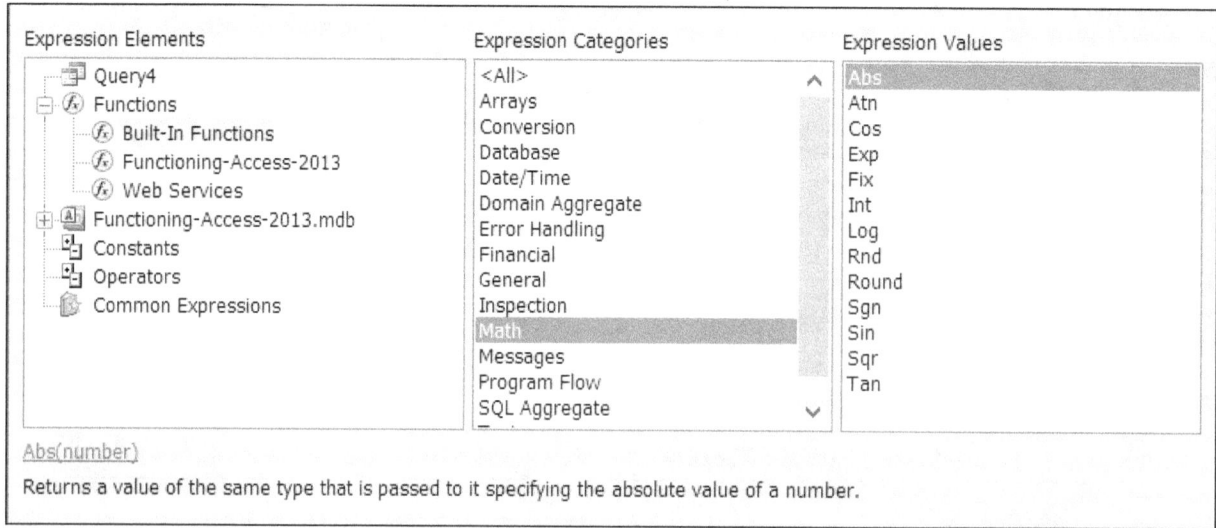

Looking at the Text functions, 40 functions are available.

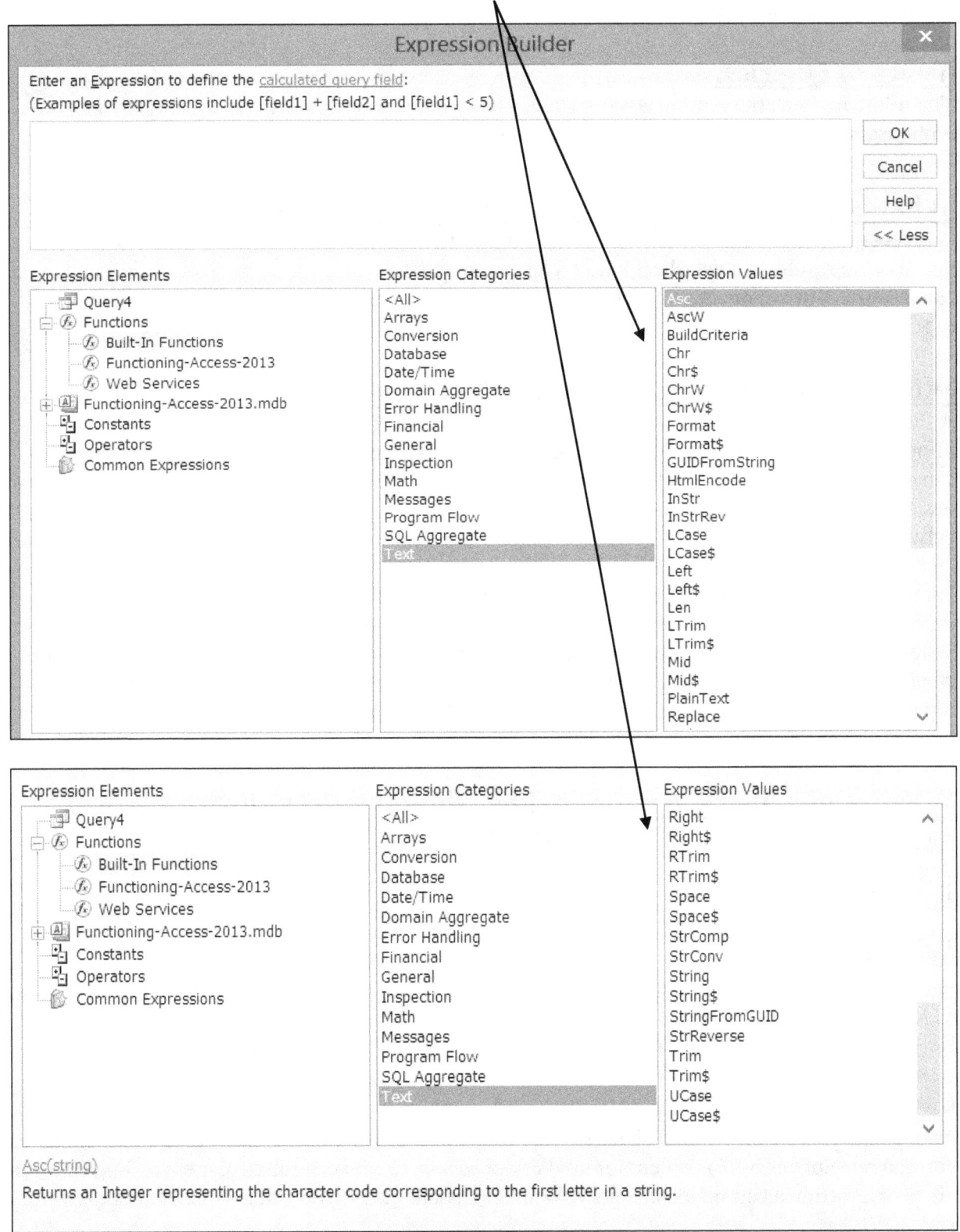

The initial queries that we will do shall include these Text functions. Later in this book, queries using other Categories are shown.

Types of Queries.
The following material is from Access Help. The remainder of this document will provide you with instructions and examples to help you comprehend what is being presented.

What is a Select query and when would you use one?
A Select query is the most common type of query. It retrieves data from one or more tables and displays the results in a datasheet where you can update the records (with some restrictions). You can also use a Select query to group records and calculate sums, counts, averages, and other types of totals.

What is a parameter query and when would you use one?
A Parameter query is a query that when run displays its own dialog box prompting you for information, such as criteria for retrieving records or a value you want to insert in a field. You can design the query to prompt you for more than one piece of information; for example, you can design it to prompt you for two dates. Microsoft Access can then retrieve all records that fall between those two dates.

Parameter queries are also handy when used as the basis for forms, reports, and data access pages. For example, you can create a 'Monthly Earnings' report based on a parameter query. When you print the report, Microsoft Access displays a dialog box asking for the month that you want the report to cover. You enter a month and Microsoft Access retrieves the appropriate report. You can also create a custom form or dialog box that prompts for a query's parameters instead of using the parameter query's dialog box.

What is an action query and when would you use one?
An Action query is a query that makes changes to many records in just one operation. There are four types of action queries: Delete, Update, Append, and Make-Table.
This topic provides examples of:

Delete query
A Delete query removes a group of records from one or more tables. For example, you could use a Delete query to remove products that are discontinued or for which there are no orders. With Delete queries, you always delete entire records, not just selected fields within records.

Update query
An Update query makes global changes to a group of records in one or more tables. For example, you can raise prices by 10 percent for all dairy products, or you can raise salaries by 5 percent for the people within a certain job category. With an Update query, you can change data in existing tables.

What is an action query and when would you use one (continued)?

Append query

An Append query adds a group of records from one or more tables to the end of one or more tables. For example, suppose that you acquire some new customers and a database containing a table of information on those customers. To avoid typing all this information in, you'd like to append the new data to your Customers table.

Append queries are also helpful for:

- Appending fields based on criteria. For example, you might want to append only the names and addresses of customers with outstanding orders.

- Appending records when some of the fields in one table don't exist in the other table. An append query will append the data in the matching fields and ignore the others.

Make-Table query

Creates a new table from all or part of the data in one or more tables. Make-Table queries are helpful for:

- Creating a table to export to other Microsoft Access databases. For example, you might want to create a table that contains several fields from your Employees table, and then export that table to a database used by your personnel department.

- Creating data access pages that display data from a specified point in time. For example, suppose you want to display a data access page on 15-May-11 that displays the first quarter's sales totals based on the data that was in the underlying tables as of 9:00 A.M. on 1-Apr-11. A data access page based on a query or SQL statement extracts the most up-to-date data from the tables (the data as of 15-May-11), rather than the records as of a specific date and time. To preserve the data exactly as it was at 9:00 A.M. on 1-Apr-11, create a Make-Table query at that point in time to retrieve the records you need and store them in a new table. Then use this table, rather than a query, as the basis for the data access page.

- **Making a backup copy of a table.**

- Creating a history table that contains old records. For example, you could create a table that stores all your old orders before deleting them from your current Orders table.

- Improving performance of forms, reports, and data access pages based on multiple-table queries or SQL statements. For example, suppose you want to print multiple reports that are based on a five-table query that includes totals. You may be able to speed things up by first creating a Make-Table query that retrieves the records you need and stores them in one table. Then you can base the reports on this table. However, the data in the table is frozen at the time you run the Make-Table query.

Select query (example).

Here is a Select query using all of the fields from the INITIAL-DATA table. Running this query will bring return of the data to the screen. This query does not alter the original data. Select queries can be made which alter the data which is presented to the user but does not alter the data in the table, this will be shown later.

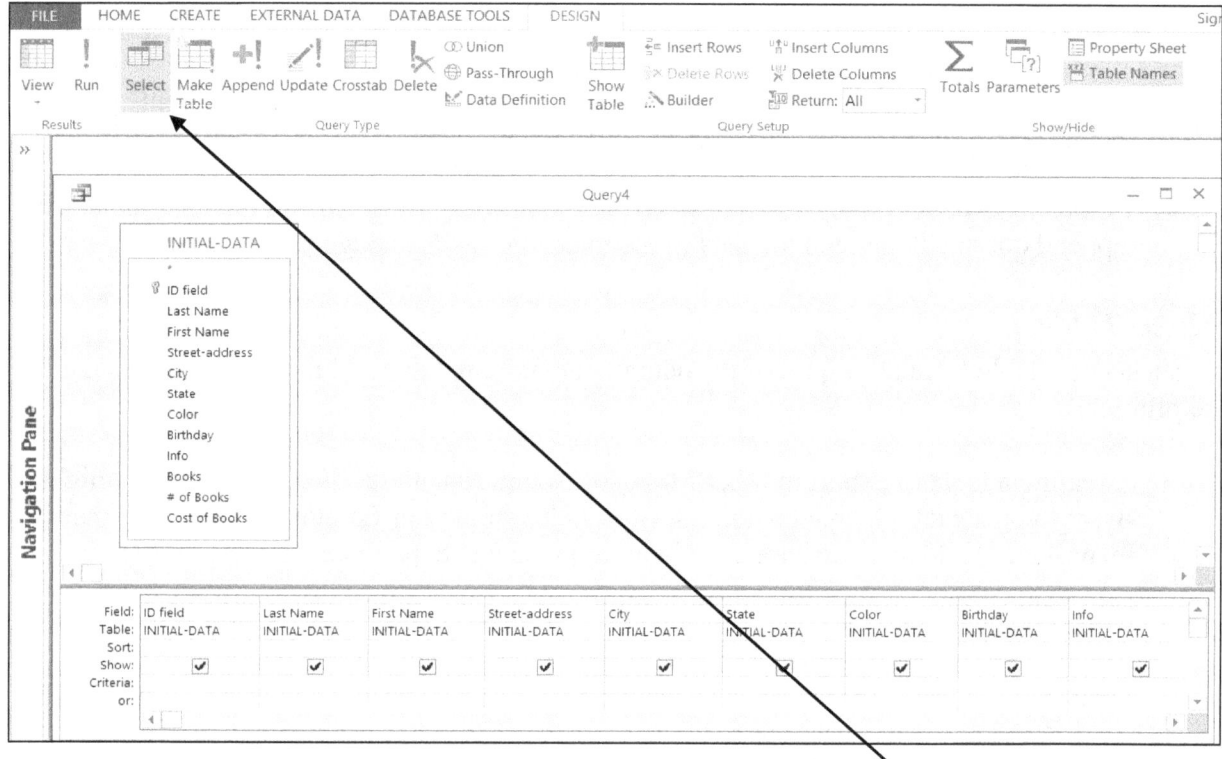

A query which returns data in the table and does not alter the data is a Select query. In the query above, all fields have been selected, the last three (Books, # of Books and Cost of Books) are not seen. They can be viewed by scrolling to the right.

When the query is 'Run', or 'Executed' (by selecting the Run button) , the data will return to the screen

(Note: some of the fields have been narrowed).

Functioning with Access – 2013
Chapter 1 – Beginning

Select query, with changes of data (on screen).

This will modify the values on the screen only, not in the table. Here are the initial values for selected fields. The next Select query will add 10 books to the [# of Books] field. To represent the [# of Books] field use square brackets [ ], like this [# of Books].

Query1					
ID field	Last Name	First Name	Birthday	# of Books	Cost of Book
1	Cederoth	Katherine	6/15/1957	768	$56,788.22
2	Yeaoman	Mike	12/14/1958	0	$0.00
3	Yeaoman	Shirley	6/22/1957	500	$7,788.76
4	Dionne	Tom	12/1/1977	35	$678.30
5	Lawrence	Anderson	3/15/1999	4	$22.30
6	Lawrence	Motherbee	5/15/1969	55	$5,555.55
7	Lawrence	Fatherbee	5/22/1967	44	$4,444.44
8	Lawrence	Sisterbee	7/22/1997	7	$77.77
9	Deenoyer	Tony	2/29/1996	34	$456.44

Here is the Select query to add 10 to [# of Books].

Field:	ID field	Last Name	First Name	Birthday	Number of Books: [# of Books]+10	Cost of Books
Table:	INITIAL-DATA	INITIAL-DATA	INITIAL-DATA	INITIAL-DATA		INITIAL-DATA
Sort:						
Show:	✓	✓	✓	✓	✓	✓
Criteria:						
or:						

Since the [# of Books] field is being used in the query, the output field name has to be changed. The name of the output field is changed to 'Number of Books'. The code to do this is **Number of Books: [# of Books] +10**. The use of the [and] characters around the field name is needed because the name of the field has spaces in it. Any time that you reference to a field in a formula or while doing a query, it is best to use the [leading and the] closing brackets.

Here is the output, the 'Number of Books' column is 10 more then the [# of Books] field.

Query1					
ID field	Last Name	First Name	Birthday	Number of Books	Cost of Book
1	Cederoth	Katherine	6/15/1957	778	$56,788.22
2	Yeaoman	Mike	12/14/1958	10	$0.00
3	Yeaoman	Shirley	6/22/1957	510	$7,788.76
4	Dionne	Tom	12/1/1977	45	$678.30
5	Lawrence	Anderson	3/15/1999	14	$22.30
6	Lawrence	Motherbee	5/15/1969	65	$5,555.55
7	Lawrence	Fatherbee	5/22/1967	54	$4,444.44
8	Lawrence	Sisterbee	7/22/1997	17	$77.77
9	Deenoyer	Tony	2/29/1996	44	$456.44

Select query, with changes of data (on screen-continued).

This Select query does not change the actual values in the table. If you return to the table, the values for [# of Books] would be the same.

Errors seen when trying to update the output may include some of the following.

This error was caused by the formula:
# of Books: [# of Books] + 10.

The format of this formula is:
   Fieldname (that you want to see on the output) **: Operator/Function**.
      Fieldname = # of Books (which is the original fieldname)
      : = this separates the fieldname and Operator/Function (this is a colon)
      Operator/Function = Fieldname, Function or Formula done in this column.

The error indicates that the formula is using the same field that it is updating in the formula. If the field value was 20, and we were adding 10 to it then the formula is giving the instructions that Field Value = Field Value + 10. This formula would be seen as (20 = 20 + 10). Access cannot do this update, it is a Circular reference.

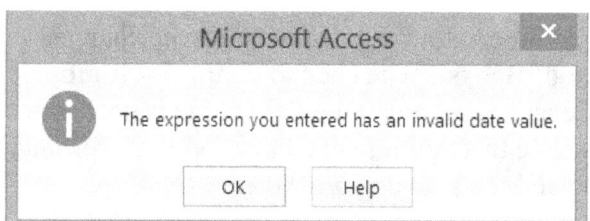

This following error is due to not placing brackets around the field name.

The formula that caused this error was:
# of Books: # of Books + 10.

This next error is caused by using too many brackets.

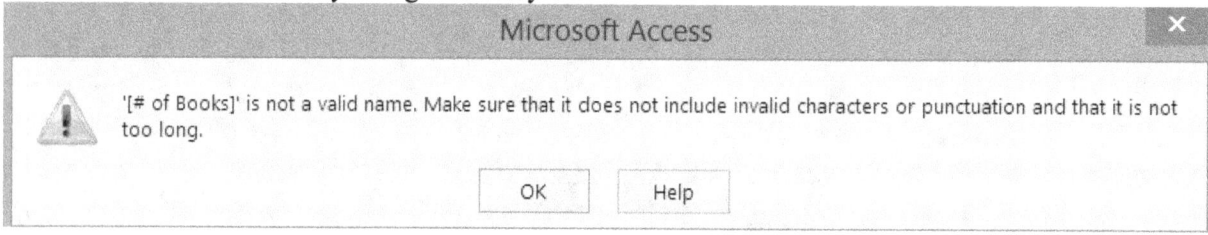

This was caused by this formula: **[# of Books]: [# of Books] + 10.**
In conclusion, Access has many RULES which are not obvious, and you must discover them.

Functioning with Access – 2013
Chapter 1 – Beginning

Make-Table query (example).

Because the RULES for Access are not obvious, a user of Access should use techniques, which will minimize the amount of rework. One-way to prevent rework is never use your original data. Making a copy of the original data and then working on the copy will give you the opportunity to problem solve and try functions/formulas.

Creating a **Make-Table** query enables you to copy your original data into another table. Then, as you work with functions and are changing data values in the copy, you still have the opportunity to start with your original data.

Creating a **Make-Table** query requires that you have a table with data.
Select Create, Query Design.

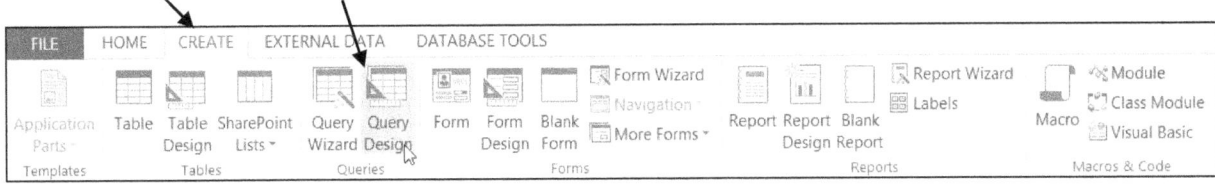

Add your table to the query, select all fields (or select *).

Make-Table query (continued).

Select the Make-Table button and answer the prompts.

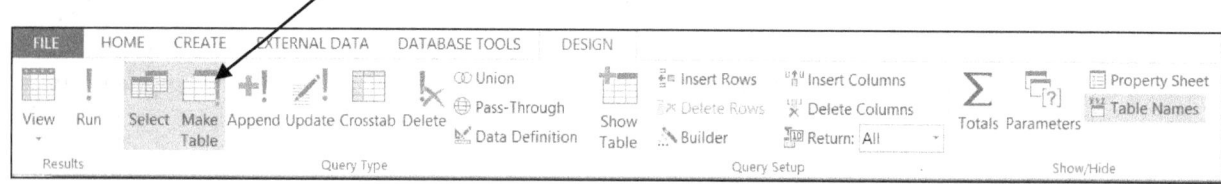

A pop up appears, asking for the name of the table this data will be placed in. In this book, one of the tables where test data will be stored while doing work will be the "LIVE-TEST" table. As the query is run, this prompt appears.

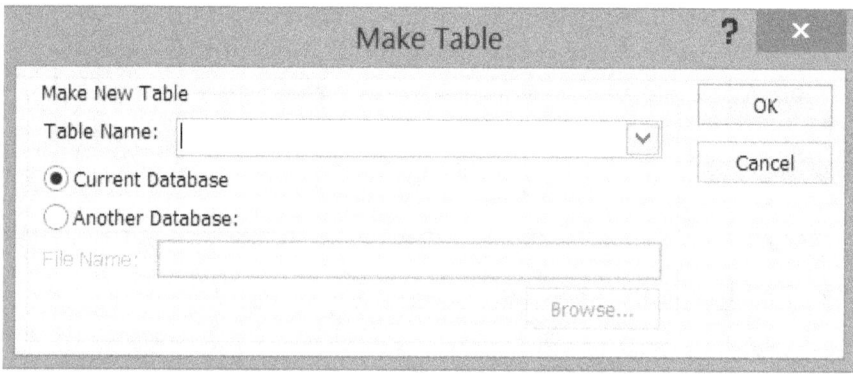

Type in the name of the new table (LIVE-TEST).

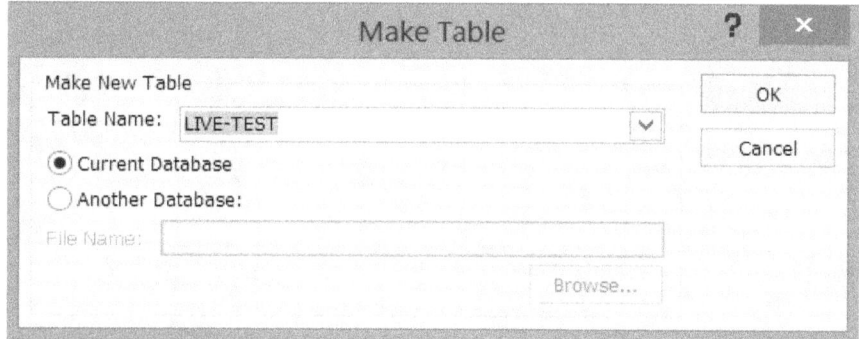

This **Make-Table** query will only be used to create the table initially and when data needs to be copied into it again from the Initial-data table. This will allow us to always restart from the same point.

The following message will appear to you when you run this query.

Make-Table query (continued).

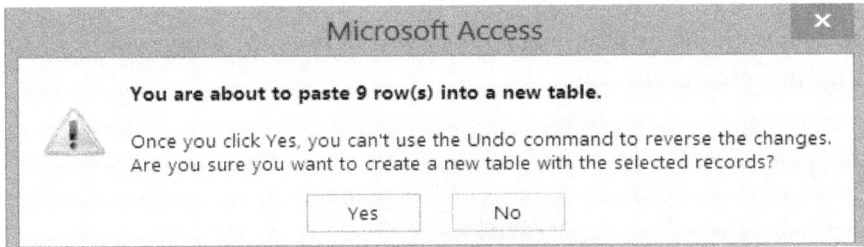

Save the query.

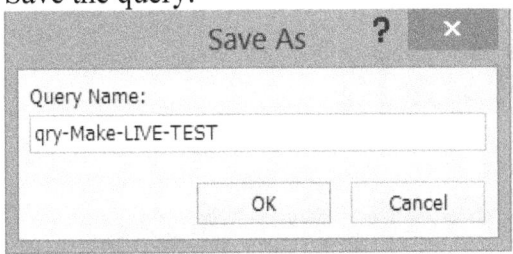

Now two tables exist in this database.
1: Initial-data (the original data that we will use)
2: LIVE-TEST (a table that will be the practice area for our work)

Now, one query, called qry-Make-LIVE-TEST, exists.

If you run the qry-Make-LIVE-TEST query again, the following message will appear

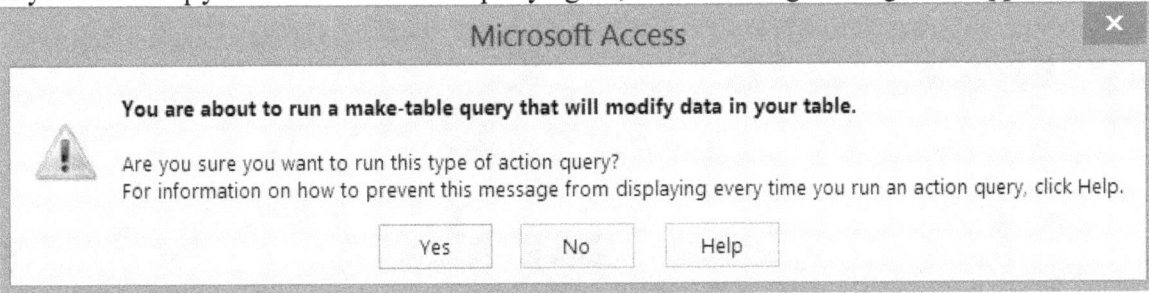

Select Yes.

Make-Table query (continued).

Select [Yes] to replace the data with the original data. This will allow practicing with functions while never diverging from the initial data.

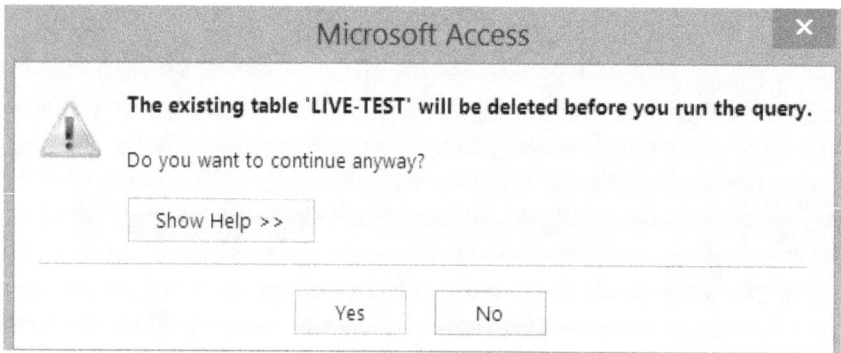

Often the reasoning behind this 'Make-table' is not understood. The ability to practice and make mistakes and start over again with the same initial data, is a technique that many students approve.

Having to retype the initial data is a repetitive action that you should not have to do. Always make backups of your data so that your efforts are toward learning, not data entry.

Chapter 2 - Text functions – Select queries.

Text (Character) functions are explained in this chapter using Select queries. These activities will bring the data back to the screen and are not intended to modify the original table. These examples are an introduction to creating queries, which can be used to audit and investigate data.

If you have a small table with fewer than 20 records, data you can update and investigate by hand. Once the number of records in a table exceeds a screen of data, using queries to test for values can make the process efficient. This chapter is useful in making the investigation of data faster and your work more effective.

Function Name	Function format	Function use – why use it?
Left	Left(field, length)	To retrieve a set number of characters from the left side of a field.
Right	Right(field, length)	To retrieve a set number of characters from the right side of a field.
Mid	Mid(field, start position, length)	To retrieve a set number of characters starting from a position in a field.
Left & Right	Left(field, length) & " " Right(field, length)	Used to bring parts of a multiple fields together, also called Concatenate.
Len	Len(field)	Used to determine how long a field is.
InStr	InStr(field, ",")	Used to determine where a character string is located in a field or character string.
LTrim	LTrim(field)	Removes leading spaces from a field.
RTrim	RTrim(field)	Removes ending spaces from a field.
Trim	Trim(field)	Removes leading or ending spaces from a field.
LCase	LCase(field)	Changes all uppercase characters to lowercase. Does not affect any none letters.
UCase	UCase(field)	Changes all lowercase characters to uppercase. Does not affect any none letters.
Replace	Replace(field, "7","8") Replace(Name, Smith, Smyth) this replaces the value Smith with the value Smyth in the field called Name.	Replaces one character string with another character string. In this example it replaces 7 with 8 in the field called field. The format is Replace(Expression(field name), Find (text value to find), Replace(what you will place into the Expression field).

Functioning with Access – 2013
Chapter 2 – Text functions – Select queries

One way to see the functions available in the software is to go through a query.
Use design view to examine any query, then press the Builder button.

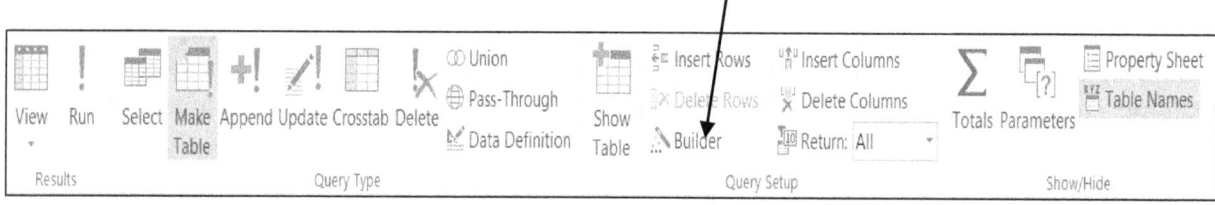

Select Text in the 2nd column and then you can select Functions in the 3rd column.

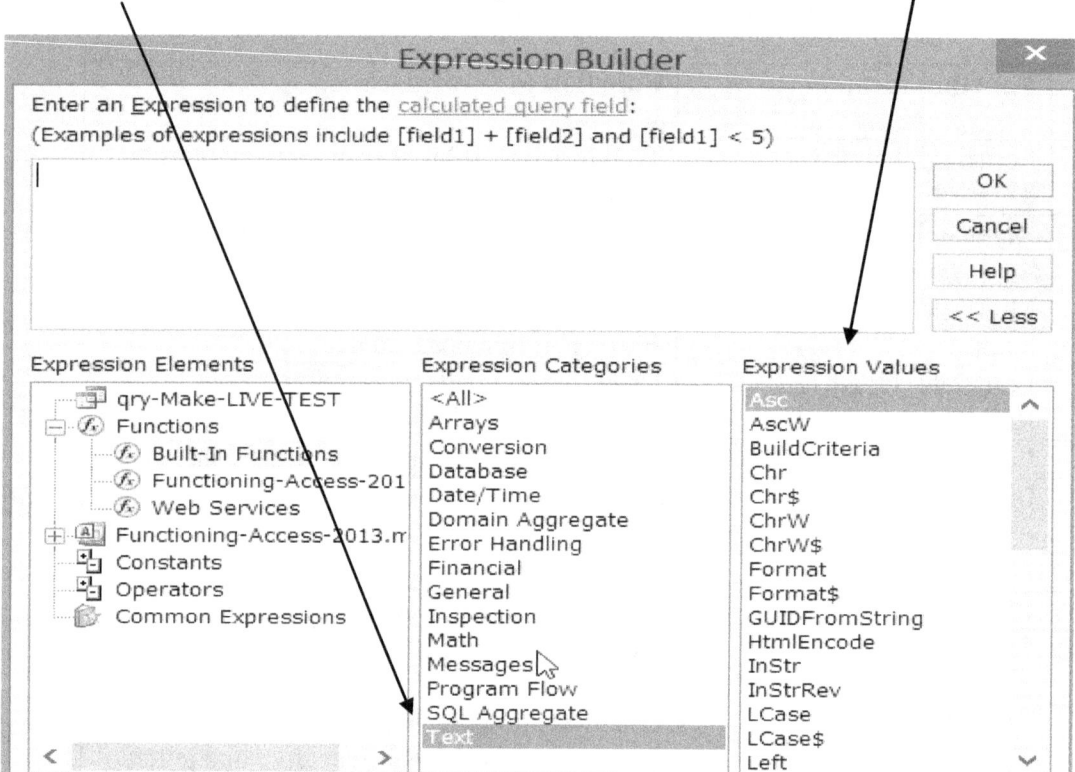

Functioning with Access – 2013
Chapter 2 – Text functions – Select queries

The Left function explained.

The 1st step is to create a new Select query. Go to the Query part of Access, create a new query, insert the LIVE-TEST table, and select the [ID field], [Last Name] and [First Name] fields. Change the text in the [Last Name] column. Type in **Last: Left([Last Name], 3)** as shown below.

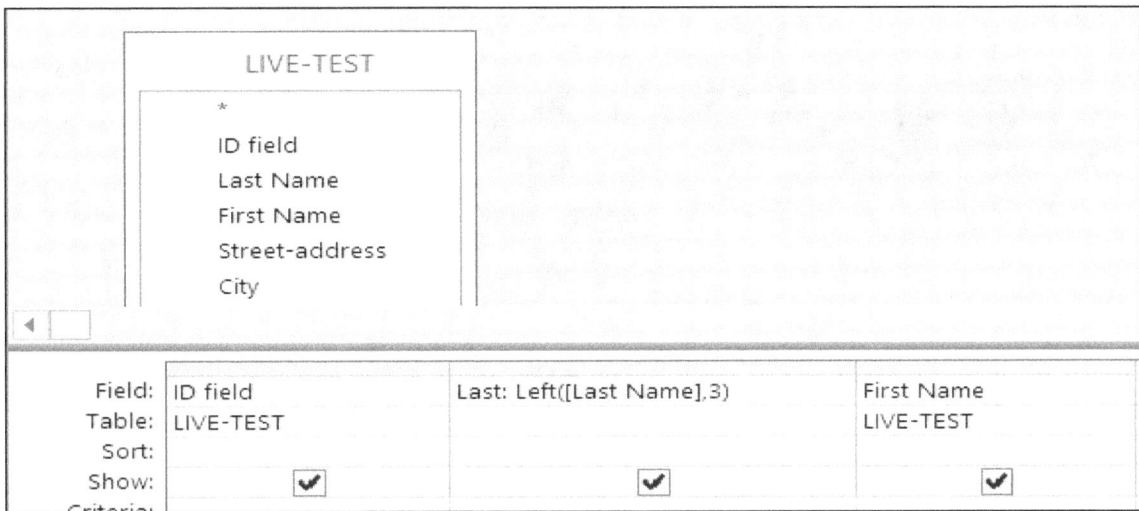

The above query will return to the screen the [ID field], the left 3 characters of the [Last Name] field (renamed as Last), and the [First Name] field. These values are returned for all records and are displayed below. Notice, the Last Name field had to be included inside of brackets.

ID field	Last	First Name
1	Ced	Katherine
2	Yea	Mike
3	Yea	Shirley
4	Dio	Tom
5	Law	Anderson
6	Law	Motherbee
7	Law	Fatherbee
8	Law	Sisterbee
9	Dee	Tony

Here the query done again and the length is changed to 6.

Field:	ID field	Last: Left([Last Name],6)	First Name
Table:	LIVE-TEST		LIVE-TEST
Sort:			
Show:	✓	✓	✓
Criteria:			

Here is the output.

ID field	Last	First Name
1	Cedero	Katherine
2	Yeaoma	Mike
3	Yeaoma	Shirley
4	Dionne	Tom
5	Lawren	Anderson
6	Lawren	Motherbee
7	Lawren	Fatherbee
8	Lawren	Sisterbee
9	Deenoy	Tony

The maximum number of characters returned will be 6, if the field does not contain that many characters then all characters will be returned.

Try this function with different values for length until you feel comfortable. This function will be used again when we do Update queries and Append queries. These two types of queries (Update and Append) can change the values of the data.

Authors guide (This material is from Access help).

Left Function

Returns a **Variant** (**String**) containing a specified number of characters from the left side of a string.

Syntax

Left(*string*, *length*)

The **Left** function syntax has these named arguments:

Part	Description
string	Required. String expression from which the leftmost characters are returned. If *string* contains Null, Null is returned.
length	Required; **Variant** (**Long**). Numeric expression indicating how many characters to return. If 0, a zero-length string ("") is returned. If greater than or equal to the number of characters in *string*, the entire string is returned.

Left(*string*, *length*)
```
AnyString = "Hello World"       ' Define string.
MyStr = Left(AnyString, 1)      ' Returns "H".
MyStr = Left(AnyString, 7)      ' Returns "Hello W".
MyStr = Left(AnyString, 20)     ' Returns "Hello World".
```

A string of characters called 'AnyString' is given a value of "Hello World"
The Left function retrieves a number of characters (1, 7 or 20)

The Left function is easy to explain; now we venture to the other side of the field and retrieve data from the right side of a field.

Access 2013 will take you to this screen (Developer Network) when you look up the Left function. Click on the Blue Left function to proceed.

The Right function explained.

The 1st step is to create a new Select query (or modify the query used for the Left function). Go to the Query part of Access, create a new query, insert the LIVE-TEST table, and select the [ID field], [Last Name] and [First Name] fields. Change the text in the [Last Name] column, type in: **Last: Right([Last Name, 3])**. This is shown below.

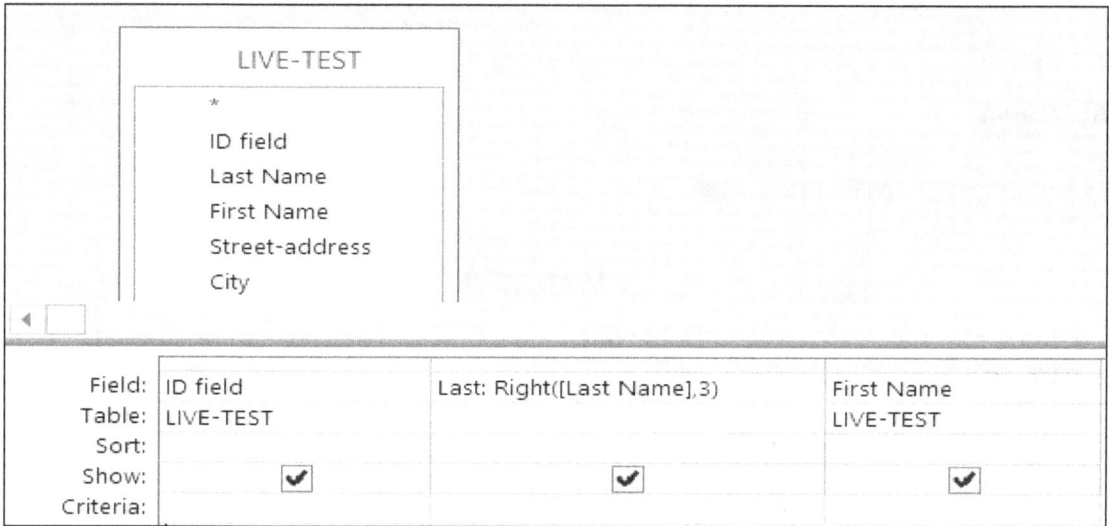

The above query will return to the screen the [ID field], the 3 rightmost characters of the [Last Name] field (renamed as Last), and the [First Name] field. These values are returned for all records and are displayed below. Notice, the [Last Name] field had to be included inside of brackets.

NOTE: The rightmost 3 characters of the [Last Name] field have been retrieved; they are now in the column called *Last*. The original data has not been modified, and since this is a select query, no tables have been changed.

ID field	Last	First Name
1	oth	Katherine
2	man	Mike
3	man	Shirley
4	nne	Tom
5	nce	Anderson
6	nce	Motherbee
7	nce	Fatherbee
8	nce	Sisterbee
9	yer	Tony

Here the query done again and the length is changed to 6.

Field:	ID field	Last: Right([Last Name],6)	First Name
Table:	LIVE-TEST		LIVE-TEST
Sort:			
Show:	✓	✓	✓
Criteria:			
or:			

Here is the output.

ID field	Last	First Name
1	deroth	Katherine
2	eaoman	Mike
3	eaoman	Shirley
4	Dionne	Tom
5	wrence	Anderson
6	wrence	Motherbee
7	wrence	Fatherbee
8	wrence	Sisterbee
9	enoyer	Tony

The maximum number of characters returned will be 6. If the field does not contain that many characters then all characters will be returned.

Try this function with different values for length until you feel comfortable. This function will be used again when we do Update queries and Append queries. These two types of queries (Update and Append) can change the values of the data in the original source table.

Functioning with Access – 2013
Chapter 2 – Text functions – Select queries

Authors guide (This material is from Access help).

Right Function

Returns a **Variant** (**String**) containing a specified number of characters from the left side of a string.

Syntax

Right(*string*, *length*)

The **Right** function syntax has these named arguments:

Part	Description
string	Required. String expression from which the rightmost characters are returned. If *string* contains Null, **Null** is returned.
length	Required; **Variant** (**Long**). Numeric expression indicating how many characters to return. If 0, a zero-length string ("") is returned. If greater than or equal to the number of characters in *string*, the entire string is returned.

Right Function Example

This example uses the **Right** function to return a specified number of characters from the right side of a string.

```
Dim AnyString, MyStr
AnyString = "Hello World"    ' Define string.
MyStr = Right(AnyString, 1)     ' Returns "d".
MyStr = Right(AnyString, 6)     ' Returns " World".
MyStr = Right(AnyString, 20)    ' Returns "Hello World".
```

A string of characters called 'AnyString' is given a value of "Hello World"
The Right function retrieves a number of characters (1, 7 or 20)

Access 2013 will take you to the Developer Network screen when you look up the Right function. Click on the Blue Right function to proceed.

The MID function explained.

The 1st step is to create a new Select query (or modify the query used for the Left function). Go to the Query part of Access, create a new query, insert the LIVE-TEST table, select the [ID field], [Last Name] and [First Name] fields. Change the text in the [Last Name column. Type in **Last: Mid(fieldname, start position, length)** (fieldname is *Last Name, start position is 5* and the *length* is 3) as shown below.

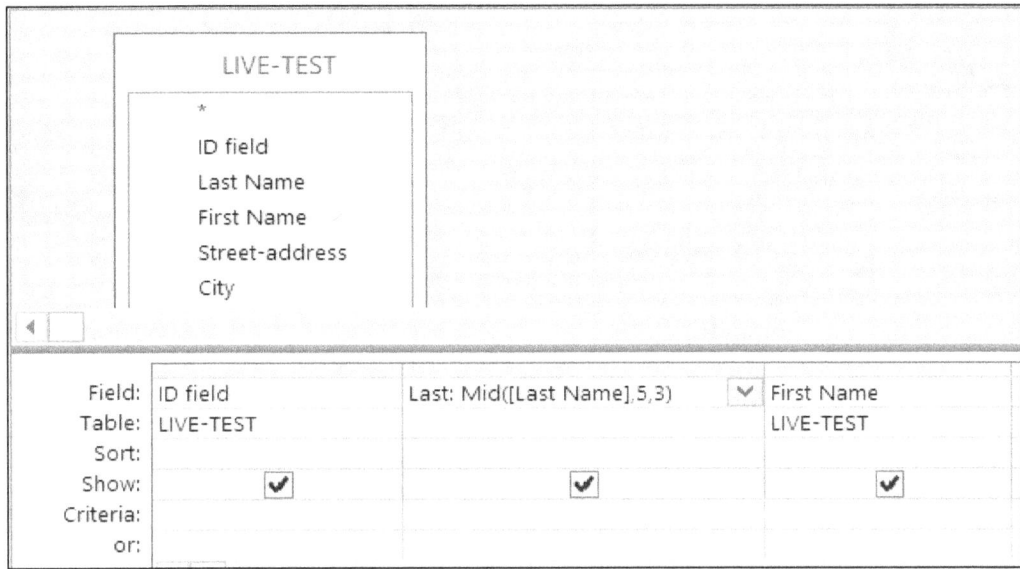

The above query will return to the screen the [ID field], 3 characters of the [Last Name] field (renamed as Last) starting from the 5th character position, and the [First Name] field. These values are returned for all records and are displayed below. Notice, the [Last Name] field had to be included inside of brackets.

NOTE: The 3 characters of the [Last Name] field have been retrieved; they are now in the column called *Last*. The original data has not been modified, and since this is a select query, no tables have been changed.

ID field	Last	First Name
1	rot	Katherine
2	man	Mike
3	man	Shirley
4	ne	Tom
5	enc	Anderson
6	enc	Motherbee
7	enc	Fatherbee
8	enc	Sisterbee
9	oye	Tony

Here the query done again, the start position is changed to 2,
and the length is changed to 6.

Field:	ID field	Last: Mid([Last Name],2,6)	First Name
Table:	LIVE-TEST		LIVE-TEST
Sort:			
Show:	✔	✔	✔
Criteria:			
or:			

Here is the output.

ID field	Last	First Name
1	ederot	Katherine
2	eaoman	Mike
3	eaoman	Shirley
4	ionne	Tom
5	awrenc	Anderson
6	awrenc	Motherbee
7	awrenc	Fatherbee
8	awrenc	Sisterbee
9	eenoye	Tony

The maximum number of characters returned will be 6, if the field does not contain that many characters after position 2, then all characters available will be returned. This is why record 4 only has 5 characters.

Try this function with different values for length until you feel comfortable. This function will be used again when we do Update queries and Append queries. These two types of queries (Update and Append) can change the values of the data.

Authors guide (This material is from Access help).
Mid Function

Returns a **Variant** (**String**) containing a specified number of characters from a string.

Syntax

Mid(*string*, *start*[, *length*])

The **Mid** function syntax has these named arguments:

Part	Description
string	Required. String expression from which characters are returned. If *string* contains Null, **Null** is returned.
start	Required; Long. Character position in *string* at which the part to be taken begins. If *start* is greater than the number of characters in *string*, **Mid** returns a zero-length string ("").
length	Optional; **Variant** (**Long**). Number of characters to return. If omitted or if there are fewer than *length* characters in the text (including the character at *start*), all characters from the *start* position to the end of the string are returned.

Mid Function Example

The first example uses the **Mid** function to return a specified number of characters from a string.

```
Dim MyString, FirstWord, LastWord, MidWords
MyString = "Mid Function Demo"    ' Create text string.
FirstWord = Mid(MyString, 1, 3)   ' Returns "Mid".
LastWord = Mid(MyString, 14, 4)   ' Returns "Demo".
MidWords = Mid(MyString, 5)       ' Returns "Function Demo".
```

A string of characters called 'MyString' is given a value of "Mid Function Name"
The Mid function can retrieve a variable number of characters (3, 4 or 13)

This function may never have any practical usage in your workings with this software.
Having the ability to remove or pull back a character string out of a larger character string may be useful if the data that you are working with is part of a large data string. This will enable you to retrieve the data without having to retype the data.

Joining text field values together (Concatenation).

To join together text, the ampersand is used. To insert spaces between the fields, you must include some separator or filler like ", ". Below is an example of combining [Last Name] and [First Name] together. This is the code to bring back the joined data:
Total Name: [Last Name] & ", " & [First Name].

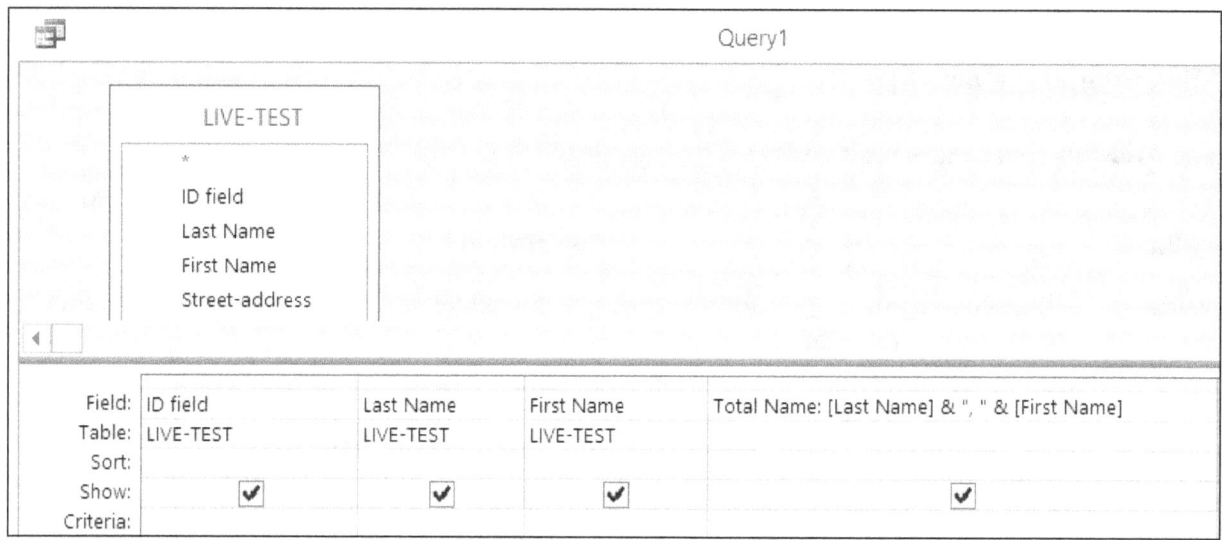

Here is the output from this query; the names have been joined in the column called 'Total Name". The Last Name will be followed by a comma and a space, then the First name.

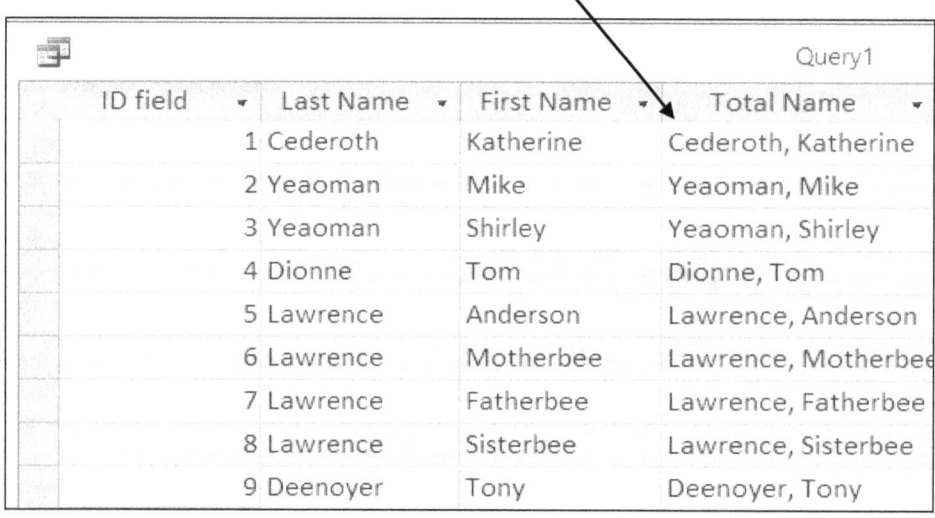

Notice, in the query, the field names are surrounded by brackets because the field names contain a space in each. The new field 'Total Name" was created to hold the data. Since this a Select query, no values in the original table are changed.

Now, the next query will incorporate the use of multiple functions in one column. Using the Left and the Right functions to combine data from two fields into another field called [Code Name]. Notice that the two fields have spaces in the name, brackets must be used to define the field. If you do not use brackets, the error message, which follows, will appear (using the LIVE-TEST table)

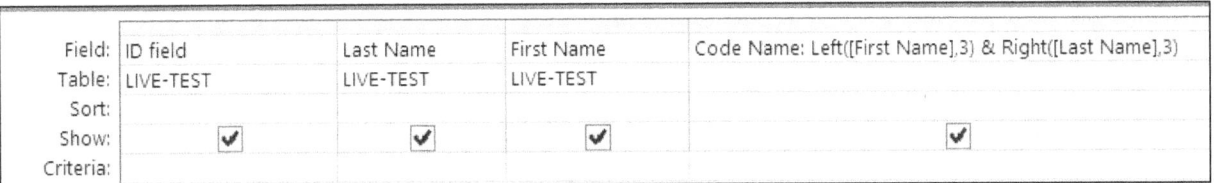

Here is the formula: **Code Name: Left([First Name],3) & Right([Last Name],3)**.
(NOTE: remember not to include the period in the above formula. This period just ends the sentence).

This is the output from the above query.

ID field	Last Name	First Name	Code Name
1	Cederoth	Katherine	Katoth
2	Yeaoman	Mike	Mikman
3	Yeaoman	Shirley	Shiman
4	Dionne	Tom	Tomnne
5	Lawrence	Anderson	Andnce
6	Lawrence	Motherbee	Motnce
7	Lawrence	Fatherbee	Fatnce
8	Lawrence	Sisterbee	Sisnce
9	Deenoyer	Tony	Tonyer

ERROR INFORMATION: Here is the error message caused by not properly placing brackets around a Field name that has spaces. This was done by removing the brackets from around the [First Name] field as follows:
Code Name: Left(First Name,3) & Right([Last Name],3).

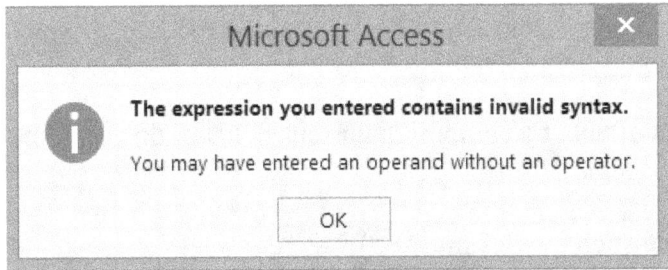

The message is not very informative; however the software does try to indicate where the problem is by highlighting the error.

Field:	ID field	Last Name	First Name	Code Name: Left(First Name,3) & Right([Last Name],3)
Table:	LIVE-TEST	LIVE-TEST	LIVE-TEST	
Sort:				
Show:	✓	✓	✓	✓

Now, something that is harder to show you have mastered this technique.
Use the Left, Mid and Right functions along with spacing and a comma between the fields.

Field:	ID field	Last Name	First Name	Code Name: Left([First Name],3) & ", " & Mid([Last Name],2,3) & ", " & Right([Last Name],3)
Table:	LIVE-TEST	LIVE-TEST	LIVE-TEST	
Sort:				
Show:	✓	✓	✓	✓
Criteria:				

The formula is:
Code Name: Left([First Name],3) & ", " & Mid([Last Name],2,3) & ", " & Right([Last Name],3).

The way to read this is: Retrieve the left 3 characters from the [First Name] field, place a comma and a space after this text. Add from the [Last Name] field 3 characters starting with the 2nd character, place a comma and space after that. Then add the 3 rightmost characters (the last 3) from the [Last Name] field. Once this makes sense to you, the mystery of string manipulation, using functions, becomes less of a mystery.

This is the output of this Select query.

ID field	Last Name	First Name	Code Name
1	Cederoth	Katherine	Kat, ede, oth
2	Yeaoman	Mike	Mik, eao, man
3	Yeaoman	Shirley	Shi, eao, man
4	Dionne	Tom	Tom, ion, nne
5	Lawrence	Anderson	And, awr, nce
6	Lawrence	Motherbee	Mot, awr, nce
7	Lawrence	Fatherbee	Fat, awr, nce
8	Lawrence	Sisterbee	Sis, awr, nce
9	Deenoyer	Tony	Ton, een, yer

This illustrates the ability to create new fields of data by combining current fields or through the addition of formatting (adding a comma or spaces).

To thoroughly use Access, the ability to create such queries must be mastered.

Try these for practice; always using the LIVE-TEST table and not modifying the data (**create Select queries**).

The Len function explained.

If you are creating a report, how many characters is the data in a field? Some of the field sizes in this database are 50 characters. The maximum number of characters a text field will hold is over 250 characters, but a particular field may not contain that many characters of data. [Street-address] is such a field. Each record DOES NOT have a 50 character long street address.

If you want to size the fields on a report, you need to know how many characters are in a field. The following query will show you how to find this information.

The formula is: **Address length: Len([Street-address])**. Here is the query.

Field:	ID field	Last Name	First Name	Street-address	Address length: Len([Street-address])
Table:	LIVE-TEST	LIVE-TEST	LIVE-TEST	LIVE-TEST	
Sort:					
Show:	✔	✔	✔	✔	✔
Criteria:					

Here is the output.

ID field	Last Name	First Name	Street-address	Address length
1	Cederoth	Katherine	141 Grant	9
2	Yeaoman	Mike	322 Sheffield	13
3	Yeaoman	Shirley	1112 Canada	11
4	Dionne	Tom	Route 4, 277 W(	17
5	Lawrence	Anderson	PO box 12A79, s	20
6	Lawrence	Motherbee	PO box 12A79, s	20
7	Lawrence	Fatherbee	PO box 12A79, s	20
8	Lawrence	Sisterbee	PO box 12A79, s	21
9	Deenoyer	Tony	1456 Bad Ax	11

Authors guide (This material is from Access help).

Len Function Returns a Long containing the number of characters in a string or the number of bytes required to store a variable.

Syntax Len(*string* | *varname*)

The **Len** function syntax has these parts:

Part	Description
string	Any valid string expression. If *string* contains Null, Null is returned.
Varname	Any valid variable name. If *varname* contains **Null**, **Null** is returned. If *varname* is a Variant, **Len** treats it the same as a **String** and always returns the number of characters it contains.

The InStr function explained.

The position of a character inside of a longer character is often needed. If you are working with data that has a common character in it (like a comma or a space or a dash), you can find out what position the character is occupying. This has been useful in working with names when the [Last Name] is followed by a comma and a space, then the [First Name]. The eventual goal is to return all of the characters that occur before the comma,

Use the **InStr** function to find out the position of the comma in the [Street-address] field.

Field:	ID field	Last Name	First Name	Street-address	Comma location: InStr([Street-address],",")
Table:	LIVE-TEST	LIVE-TEST	LIVE-TEST	LIVE-TEST	
Sort:					
Show:	✓	✓	✓	✓	✓
Criteria:					

The formula is as follows: **Comma location: InStr([Street-address],",")** and this is what returns when ran. A value of 0 will be returned is a comma is not found (records 1, 2, 3 & 9).

ID field	Last Name	First Name	Street-address	Comma location
1	Cederoth	Katherine	141 Grant	0
2	Yeaoman	Mike	322 Sheffield	0
3	Yeaoman	Shirley	1112 Canada	0
4	Dionne	Tom	Route 4, 277 West	8
5	Lawrence	Anderson	PO box 12A79, slot 7	13
6	Lawrence	Motherbee	PO box 12A79, slot 8	13
7	Lawrence	Fatherbee	PO box 12A79, slot 9	13
8	Lawrence	Sisterbee	PO box 12A79, slot 10	13
9	Deenoyer	Tony	1456 Bad Ax	0

There are many ways to use this function incorrectly. The information returned can be combined with other functions. Below, take the number found when searching for the position of the comma and subtract 1 from it. This only works for the records that have a comma in the [Street-address] field. This will be done in multiple steps. I now introduce the use of the Criteria row when doing a Select Query.

First, this is how to select records that have a comma. In the Criteria row place this formula: **InStr([Street-address],",")>0.**

Field:	ID field	Last Name	First Name	Street-address	Comma location: InStr([Street-address],",")
Table:	LIVE-TEST	LIVE-TEST	LIVE-TEST	LIVE-TEST	
Sort:					
Show:	✓	✓	✓	✓	✓
Criteria:					InStr([Street-address],",")>0

This returns only the records where the comma position is greater than 0. This means a comma is in the record and only those records with a comma will be returned.

Functioning with Access – 2013
Chapter 2 – Text functions – Select queries

When ran, the following is returned:

ID field	Last Name	First Name	Street-address	Comma location
4	Dionne	Tom	Route 4, 277 West	8
5	Lawrence	Anderson	PO box 12A79, slot 7	13
6	Lawrence	Motherbee	PO box 12A79, slot 8	13
7	Lawrence	Fatherbee	PO box 12A79, slot 9	13
8	Lawrence	Sisterbee	PO box 12A79, slot 10	13

Now subtract 1 from the Comma location; we want to know how many characters are BEFORE the comma (this will give the # of characters in the Street address and not include the comma). The formula is:

Comma location: InStr([Street-address],",") - 1.

Field:	ID field	Last Name	First Name	Street-address	Comma location: InStr([Street-address],",")-1
Table:	LIVE-TEST	LIVE-TEST	LIVE-TEST	LIVE-TEST	
Sort:					
Show:	✓	✓	✓	✓	✓
Criteria:					InStr([Street-address],",")>0

Now, rerun the query. The field name 'Comma location' is not accurate, so it will be called Pre-Comma characters.

ID field	Last Name	First Name	Street-address	Comma location
4	Dionne	Tom	Route 4, 277 West	7
5	Lawrence	Anderson	PO box 12A79, slot 7	12
6	Lawrence	Motherbee	PO box 12A79, slot 8	12
7	Lawrence	Fatherbee	PO box 12A79, slot 9	12
8	Lawrence	Sisterbee	PO box 12A79, slot 10	12

The formula to calculate the position before the comma location is now joined with the Left function. This will allow only the characters to the Left of the comma to be retrieved.

The formula is
Pre-Comma characters: Left([Street-address],InStr([Street-address],",") - 1).

Field:	ID field	Last Name	First Name	Street-address	Pre-Comma characters: Left([Street-address],InStr([Street-address],",")-1)
Table:	LIVE-TEST	LIVE-TEST	LIVE-TEST	LIVE-TEST	
Sort:					
Show:	✓	✓	✓	✓	✓
Criteria:					InStr([Street-address],",")>0

The output of this is:

ID field	Last Name	First Name	Street-address	Pre-Comma characters
4	Dionne	Tom	Route 4, 277 West	Route 4
5	Lawrence	Anderson	PO box 12A79, slot 7	PO box 12A79
6	Lawrence	Motherbee	PO box 12A79, slot 8	PO box 12A79
7	Lawrence	Fatherbee	PO box 12A79, slot 9	PO box 12A79
8	Lawrence	Sisterbee	PO box 12A79, slot 10	PO box 12A79

To bring back the characters to the right of the comma requires you to know the length of the field and the position of the comma. Add one to the position of the comma, subtract this total from the length and you will get the number of characters that are to the right of the comma.

The formula for After-Comma characters:
Right([Street-address],Len([Street-address])-InStr([Street-address],",") - 1).

Field:	ID field	Last Name	First Name	Street-address	After-Comma characters: Right([Street-address],Len([Street-address])-InStr([Street-address],",")-1)
Table:	LIVE-TEST	LIVE-TEST	LIVE-TEST	LIVE-TEST	
Sort:					
Show:	✓	✓	✓	✓	✓
Criteria:					InStr([Street-address],",")>0

Now, rerun the query:

ID field	Last Name	First Name	Street-address	After-Comma characters
4	Dionne	Tom	Route 4, 277 West	277 West
5	Lawrence	Anderson	PO box 12A79, slot 7	slot 7
6	Lawrence	Motherbee	PO box 12A79, slot 8	slot 8
7	Lawrence	Fatherbee	PO box 12A79, slot 9	slot 9
8	Lawrence	Sisterbee	PO box 12A79, slot 10	slot 10

For the 1st record: Len([Street-address] = 17,
   InStr([Street-address],",") = 8
   Right([Street-address], ((17) – (8) – (1)) = Right([Street-address], 8).

So the formula works out to **Right([Street-address], 8)** which returns **277 West.**

This technique can be used to retrieve data and modify the presented values. Once again because we are working with Select queries no data in the system will be changed.

Authors guide (This material is from Access help).

InStr Function Returns a number specifying the position of the first occurrence of one string within another (Note: it does not show the position of multiple occurrences).

Syntax   InStr([start,]string1, string2[, compare])   (string1 and string2 are required).

The InStr function syntax has these arguments:

Part	Description
Start	Optional. Numeric expression that sets the starting position for each search. If omitted, search begins at the first character position. If *start* contains Null, an error occurs. The *start* argument is required if *compare* is specified.
string1	Required. String expression being searched.
string2	Required. String expression sought.
Compare	Optional. Specifies the type of string comparison. If *compare* is Null, an error occurs. If *compare* is omitted, the Option Compare setting determines the type of comparison. Specify a valid LCID (LocaleID) to use locale-specific rules in the comparison.

Return Values

If	InStr returns
string1 is zero-length	0
string1 is Null	Null
string2 is zero-length	*start*
string2 is Null	Null
string2 is not found	0
string2* is found within *string1	**Position at which match is found**
start > *string2*	0

LTrim, RTrim, and Trim Functions explained.

LTrim is used to remove leading spaces in a field. I have modified the [Last Name] and [First Name] fields to have leading and ending spaces. Access removes the ending space but leaves the leading spaces on [Last Name] and [First Name] fields as shown below.

ID field	Last Name	First Name
1	Cederoth	Katherine
2	Yeaoman	Mike
3	Yeaoman	Shirley
4	Dionne	Tom
5	Lawrence	Anderson
6	Lawrence	Motherbee
7	Lawrence	Fatherbee
8	Lawrence	Sisterbee
9	Deenoyer	Tony

Now we will make a query to join the two fields together into a field called [Total Name]. The formula is:
Total Name: [First Name] & " " & [Last Name].

Field:	ID field	Last Name	First Name	Total Name: [First Name] & " " & [Last Name]
Table:	LIVE-TEST	LIVE-TEST	LIVE-TEST	
Sort:				
Show:	✔	✔	✔	✔

The output will include the leading spaces.

This formula should only place 2 spaces between the First Name and Last Name. The data has leading spaces which must be removed as seen in the output which follows.

ID field	Last Name	First Name	Total Name
1	Cederoth	Katherine	Katherine Cederoth
2	Yeaoman	Mike	Mike Yeaoman
3	Yeaoman	Shirley	Shirley Yeaoman
4	Dionne	Tom	Tom Dionne
5	Lawrence	Anderson	Anderson Lawrence
6	Lawrence	Motherbee	Motherbee Lawrence
7	Lawrence	Fatherbee	Fatherbee Lawrence
8	Lawrence	Sisterbee	Sisterbee Lawrence
9	Deenoyer	Tony	Tony Deenoyer

A query will be made using all three functions in different columns.

Functioning with Access – 2013
Chapter 2 – Text functions – Select queries

Field:	ID field	Last Name	First Name	Total Name-LTrim: LTrim([First Name	Total Name-Trim: Trim([First	Total Name-RTrim: RTrim([First
Table:	LIVE-TEST	LIVE-TEST	LIVE-TEST			
Sort:						
Show:	✓	✓	✓	✓	✓	✓
Criteria:						

The formulas are:
    Total Name-LTrim: LTrim([First Name]) & " " & LTrim([Last Name])
    Total Name-Trim: Trim([First Name]) & " " & Trim([Last Name])
    Total Name-RTrim: RTrim([First Name]) & " " & RTrim([Last Name])

This is what returns when the query is ran.

ID field	Last Name	First Name	Total Name-LTrim	Total Name-Trim	Total Name-RTrim
1	Cederoth	Katherine	Katherine Cederoth	Katherine Cederoth	Katherine Cederoth
2	Yeaoman	Mike	Mike Yeaoman	Mike Yeaoman	Mike Yeaoman
3	Yeaoman	Shirley	Shirley Yeaoman	Shirley Yeaoman	Shirley Yeaoman
4	Dionne	Tom	Tom Dionne	Tom Dionne	Tom Dionne
5	Lawrence	Anderson	Anderson Lawrence	Anderson Lawrence	Anderson Lawrence
6	Lawrence	Motherbee	Motherbee Lawrence	Motherbee Lawrence	Motherbee Lawrence
7	Lawrence	Fatherbee	Fatherbee Lawrence	Fatherbee Lawrence	Fatherbee Lawrence
8	Lawrence	Sisterbee	Sisterbee Lawrence	Sisterbee Lawrence	Sisterbee Lawrence
9	Deenoyer	Tony	Tony Deenoyer	Tony Deenoyer	Tony Deenoyer

The LTrim and the Trim function removed the spaces, the RTrim did not.
So both the Ltrim and Trim function will remove leading spaces.

Now the formulas are changed to use these same 3 functions in an incorrect way.

Field:	ID field	Last Name	First Name	Total Name-LTrim: LTrim([First N	Total Name-Trim: Trim([F	Total Name-RTrim: RTrim([First
Table:	LIVE-TEST	LIVE-TEST	LIVE-TEST			
Sort:						
Show:	✓	✓	✓	✓	✓	✓
Criteria:						
or:						

There is no trimming on the [Last Name] field, this results in all leading spaces on the [Last Name] field still appearing.

The formulas are:
    Total Name-LTrim: LTrim([First Name] & " " & [Last Name])
    Total Name-Trim: Trim([First Name] & " " & [Last Name])
    Total Name-RTrim: RTrim([First Name] & " " & [Last Name])

The fields are concatenated together, then spaces are removed. The output is shown below.

ID field	Last Name	First Name	Total Name-LTrim	Total Name-Trim	Total Name-RTrim
1	Cederoth	Katherine	Katherine Cederoth	Katherine Cederoth	Katherine Cederoth
2	Yeaoman	Mike	Mike Yeaoman	Mike Yeaoman	Mike Yeaoman
3	Yeaoman	Shirley	Shirley Yeaoman	Shirley Yeaoman	Shirley Yeaoman
4	Dionne	Tom	Tom Dionne	Tom Dionne	Tom Dionne
5	Lawrence	Anderson	Anderson Lawrence	Anderson Lawrence	Anderson Lawrence
6	Lawrence	Motherbee	Motherbee Lawrence	Motherbee Lawrence	Motherbee Lawrence
7	Lawrence	Fatherbee	Fatherbee Lawrence	Fatherbee Lawrence	Fatherbee Lawrence
8	Lawrence	Sisterbee	Sisterbee Lawrence	Sisterbee Lawrence	Sisterbee Lawrence
9	Deenoyer	Tony	Tony Deenoyer	Tony Deenoyer	Tony Deenoyer

The spaces on the Last Name field have to be removed before the fields are joined.

NOTE: If you have spaces inside of a text string and need to remove them, the Replace Function can often do the work that you need.

Authors guide (This material is from Access help).
LTrim, RTrim, and Trim Functions

Returns a **Variant (String)** containing a copy of a specified string without leading spaces (**LTrim**), trailing spaces (**RTrim**), or both leading and trailing spaces (**Trim**).

Syntax   LTrim(*string*)   RTrim(*string*)   Trim(*string*)

New functions to change the case of a text string.
LCase Function   Returns a String that has been converted to lowercase.
Syntax LCase(*string*)
The required *string* argument is any valid string expression. If *string* contains Null, Null is returned.

Remarks
Only uppercase letters are converted to lowercase; all lowercase letters and nonletter characters remain unchanged.

UCase Function   Returns a **Variant (String)** containing the specified string, converted to uppercase.
SyntaxUCase(*string*)
The required *string* argument is any valid string expression. If *string* contains Null, **Null** is returned.

Remarks
Only lowercase letters are converted to uppercase; all uppercase letters and nonletter characters remain unchanged.

Functioning with Access – 2013
Chapter 2 – Text functions – Select queries

The Replace function explained.

The data in the [Info] field has 2 spaces in various locations. You could get focus on each, press F2 and edit each one. This would not take long for this small database. If there were thousands of records, this could be a very long process. So, use the Replace function to change every instance of 2 spaces (records 5, 6, 7 & 8) with 1 space and remove the occurrences of 2 spaces and a period with just a period (records 3 & 4).

Field:	ID field	Last Name	First Name	Info
Table:	LIVE-TEST	LIVE-TEST	LIVE-TEST	LIVE-TEST
Sort:				
Show:	✓	✓	✓	✓
Criteria:				
or:				

Here is the data:

ID fie	Last Name	First Nan	Info
1	Cederoth	Katherine	Moved away due to ballteam losses.
2	Yeaoman	Mike	Married early in life.
3	Yeaoman	Shirley	Dropped out of high school, became a pilot .
4	Dionne	Tom	Works on a farm and has hopes of being a doctor .
5	Lawrence	Anderson	Young child with many toys.
6	Lawrence	Motherbee	Mother of a young child.
7	Lawrence	Fatherbee	Father of a young child.
8	Lawrence	Sisterbee	Sister of a young child.
9	Deenoyer	Tony	Leap day baby, has bad attitude.

Here is the formula used to Replace the 2 spaces with a single space:
Good info: Replace([Info]," "," "). This places the data into the Good info field.

Field:	ID field	Last Name	First Name	Info	Good info: Replace([Info]," "," ")
Table:	LIVE-TEST	LIVE-TEST	LIVE-TEST	LIVE-TEST	
Sort:					
Show:	✓	✓	✓	✓	✓
Criteria:					
or:					

Functioning with Access – 2013
Chapter 2 – Text functions – Select queries

Here is the output.

ID fie	Last Name	First Nan	Info	Good info
1	Cederoth	Katherine	Moved away due to ballteam losses.	Moved away due to ballteam losses.
2	Yeaoman	Mike	Married early in life.	Married early in life.
3	Yeaoman	Shirley	Dropped out of high school, became a pilot .	Dropped out of high school, became a pilot .
4	Dionne	Tom	Works on a farm and has hopes of being a doctor .	Works on a farm and has hopes of being a doctor .
5	Lawrence	Anderson	Young child with many toys.	Young child with many toys.
6	Lawrence	Motherbee	Mother of a young child.	Mother of a young child.
7	Lawrence	Fatherbee	Father of a young child.	Father of a young child.
8	Lawrence	Sisterbee	Sister of a young child.	Sister of a young child.
9	Deenoyer	Tony	Leap day baby, has bad attitude.	Leap day baby, has bad attitude.

This did the work; however, there are a couple records where the decimal has two spaces before it. These need to be removed and not have the 2 spaces replaced by 1.

The initial formula to Replace 2 spaces and a period with just a period is:
Good info2: Replace([Info]," .",".")

Field:	ID field	Last Name	First Name	Info	Good info: Replace([Info]," ","")	Good info2: Replace([Info]," .",".")
Table:	LIVE-TEST	LIVE-TEST	LIVE-TEST	LIVE-TEST		
Sort:						
Show:	✓	✓	✓	✓	✓	✓
Criteria:						
or:						

Here is the output:

ID fie	Last Name	First Nan	Good info	Good info2
1	Cederoth	Katherine	Moved away due to ballteam losses.	Moved away due to ballteam losses.
2	Yeaoman	Mike	Married early in life.	Married early in life.
3	Yeaoman	Shirley	Dropped out of high school, became a pilot .	Dropped out of high school, became a pilot.
4	Dionne	Tom	Works on a farm and has hopes of being a doctor .	Works on a farm and has hopes of being a doctor.
5	Lawrence	Anderson	Young child with many toys.	Young child with many toys.
6	Lawrence	Motherbee	Mother of a young child.	Mother of a young child.
7	Lawrence	Fatherbee	Father of a young child.	Father of a young child.
8	Lawrence	Sisterbee	Sister of a young child.	Sister of a young child.
9	Deenoyer	Tony	Leap day baby, has bad attitude.	Leap day baby, has bad attitude.

The spaces are removed from before the period, but the 2 spaces still in the output. Now we will combine these commands together.

Here is the query. Here is the formula:
Good info: Replace(Replace([Info],"   "," ")," .",".").

Field:	ID field	Last Name	First Name	Info	Good info: Replace(Replace([Info]," "," ")," .",".")
Table:	LIVE-TEST	LIVE-TEST	LIVE-TEST	LIVE-TEST	
Sort:					
Show:	✓	✓	✓	✓	✓
Criteria:					
or:					

This replaces a character in a text string which already has had characters replaced.

ID	Last Name	First Name	Info	Good info
1	Cederoth	Katherine	Moved away due to ballteam losses.	Moved away due to ballteam losses.
2	Yeaoman	Mike	Married early in life.	Married early in life.
3	Yeaoman	Shirley	Dropped out of high school, became a pilot .	Dropped out of high school, became a pilot.
4	Dionne	Tom	Works on a farm and has hopes of being a doctor .	Works on a farm and has hopes of being a doctor.
5	Lawrence	Anderson	Young child with many toys.	Young child with many toys.
6	Lawrence	Motherbee	Mother of a young child.	Mother of a young child.
7	Lawrence	Fatherbee	Father of a young child.	Father of a young child.
8	Lawrence	Sisterbee	Sister of a young child.	Sister of a young child.
9	Deenoyer	Tony	Leap day baby, has bad attitude.	Leap day baby, has bad attitude.

So the Replace function removed the 2 spaces followed by a period with just a period and replaced the 2 spaces with just one space next. While this can be done with 2 queries, it can be also done with one if you have enough time to practice (It did the outside one first).

Authors guide (This material is from Access help).
Replace Function

Description
Returns a string in which a specified substring has been replaced with another substring a specified number of times.

Syntax
Replace(*expression*, *find*, *replace*[, *start*[, *count*[, *compare*]]])
The Replace function syntax has these named arguments:

Part	Description
expression	Required. **String expression containing substring to replace.**
find	**Required. Substring being searched for.**
replace	**Required. Replacement substring.**
start	Optional. Position within expression where substring search is to begin. If omitted, 1 is assumed. (Not required)
count	Optional. Number of substring substitutions to perform. If omitted, the default value is –1, which means make all possible substitutions. (Not required)
compare	Optional. Numeric value indicating the kind of comparison to use when evaluating substrings. (Not required)

Explore your SQL

As you do your queries, you are creating SQL behind the scenes. To see this SQL create a query and select View, Design View is highlighted.

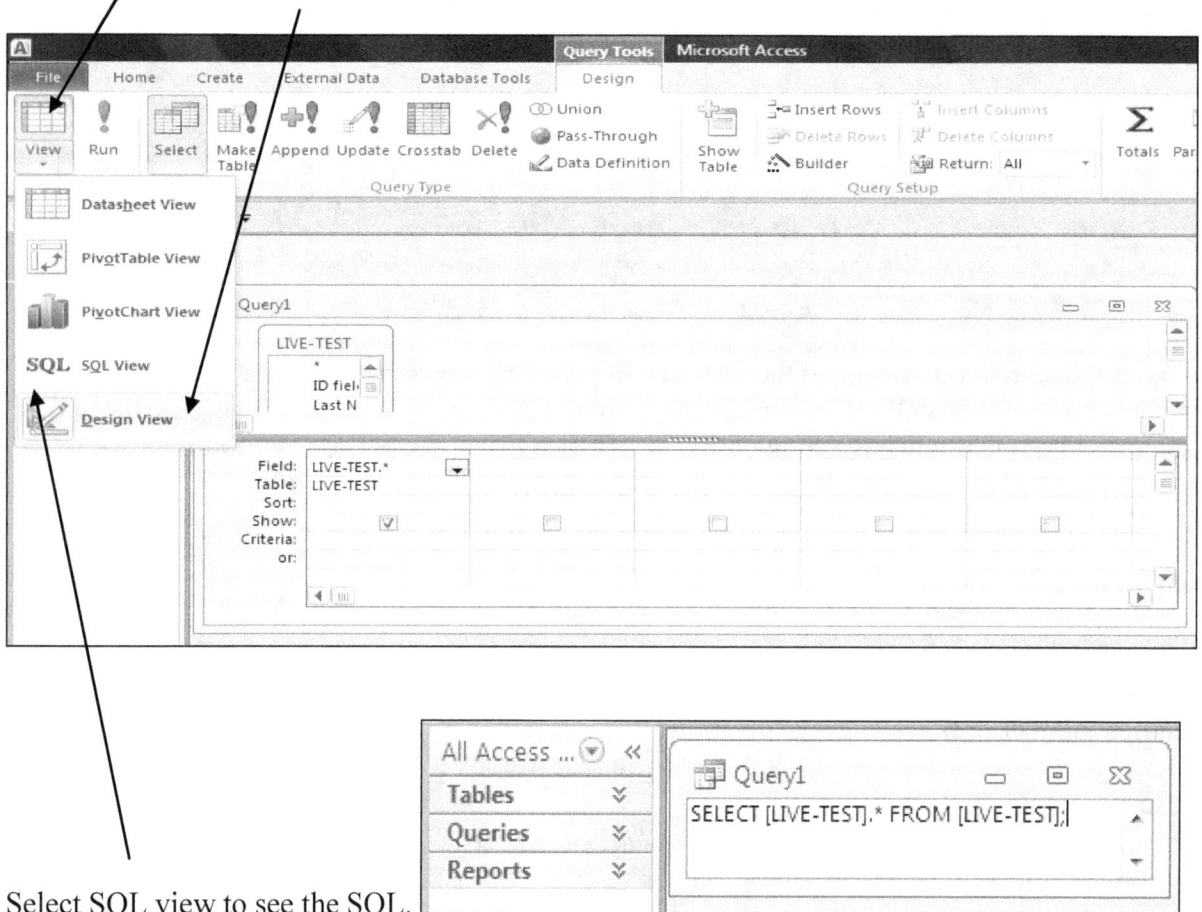

Select SQL view to see the SQL.

Now here is a more complicated one.

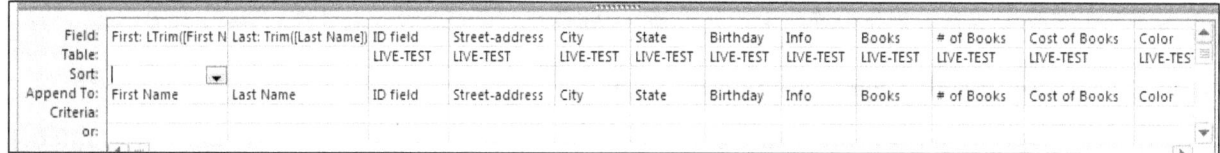

And here is the SQL for an Append Query that inserts values into a table

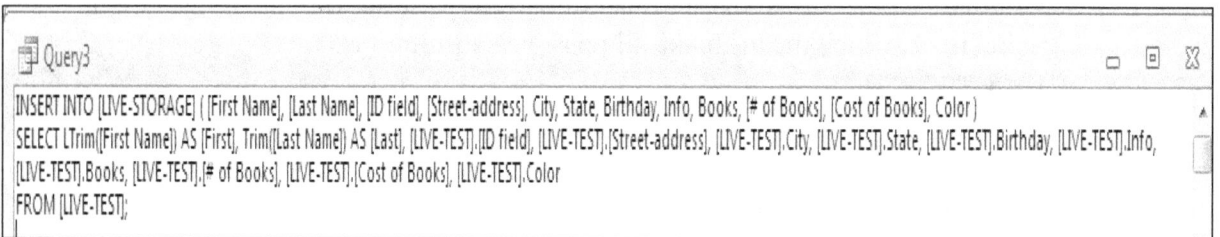

So as you create queries, go look at the SQL. You can modify the SQL to suite your needs. Some advanced Access users start here to expand their capabilities.

Chapter 3 - Math functions – Select queries.

To get value out of Access, you have to be able to use the Functions that are supplied with the software. The ability to create Databases, Tables, Reports and Forms is basic and essential, but it will be the Functions in Access that are needed to fully comprehend and utilize the power of Access.

One way to see the functions available in the software is to go through a query.
Open any query, then press the Builder button.

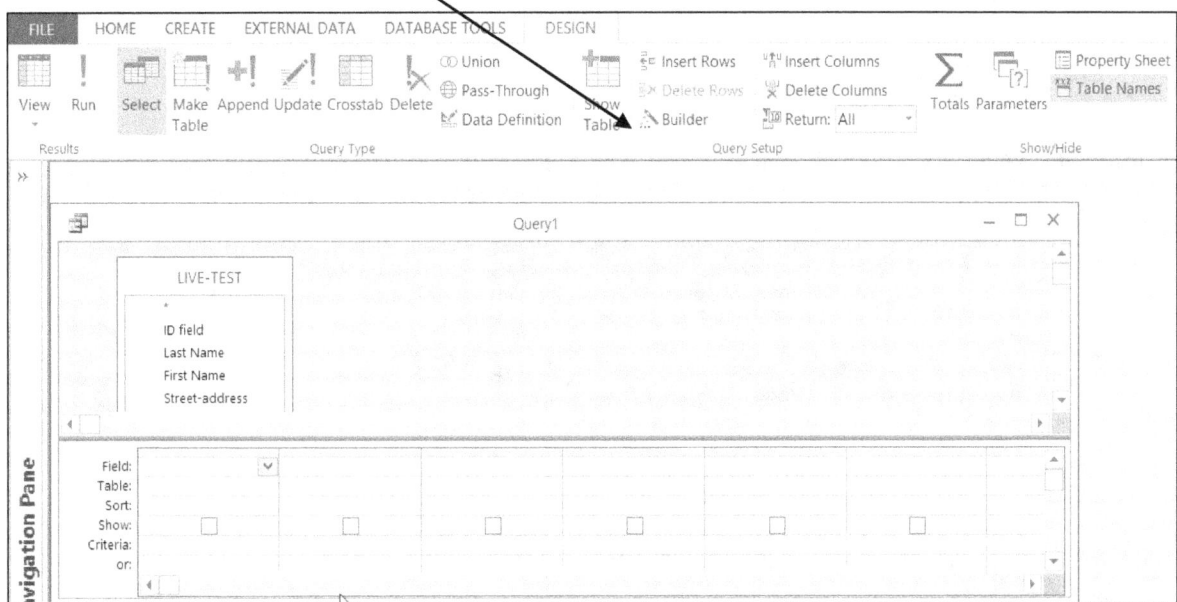

Select the Functions, then Built-In Functions. You will see a window as shown below.

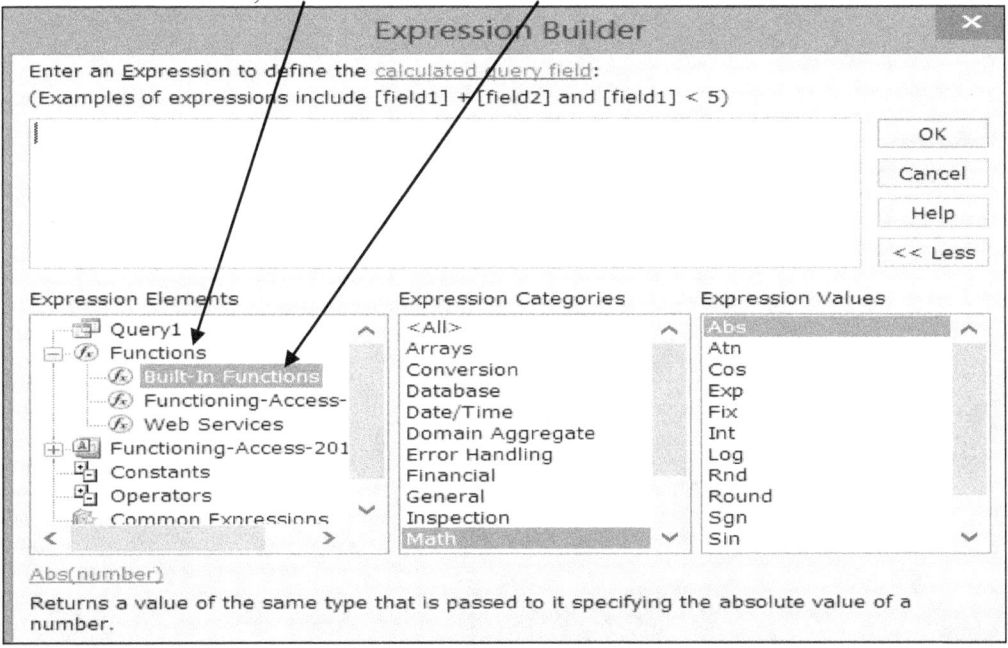

Functioning with Access – 2013
Chapter 3 – Math functions – Select queries

The second section shows a list of all Categories of functions. The third section shows the functions available for the Category that is selected in the second column.

Select Math from the Expressions Category. Now the available Math functions (in the Expression Values column) are shown.

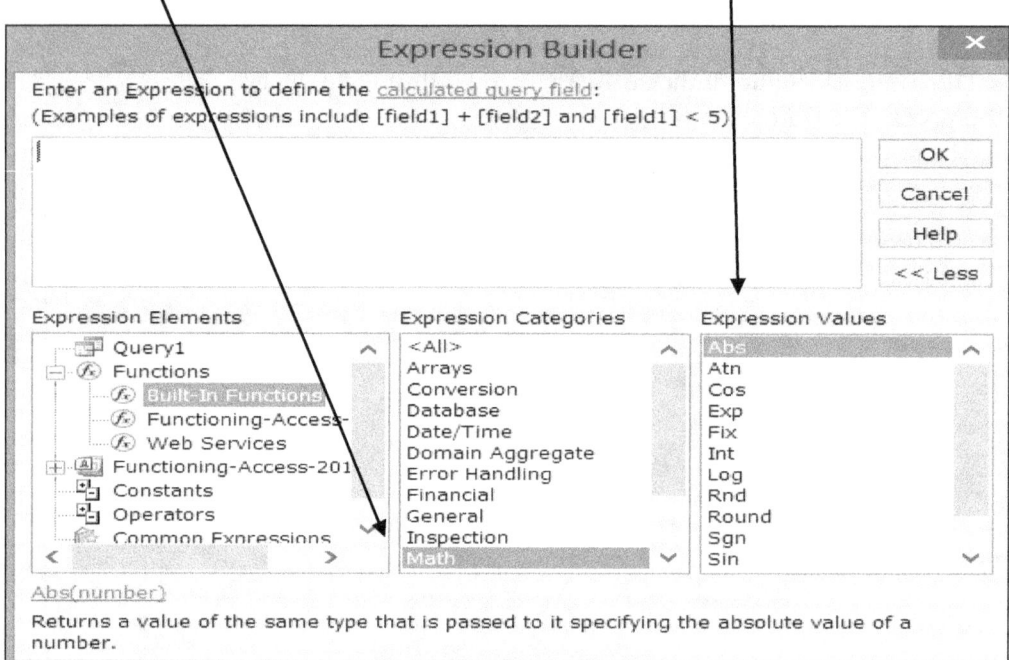

On the following pages are useful Math functions used in Select queries.

Average function explained.

Create a new query as shown below; include the LIVE-TEST table.

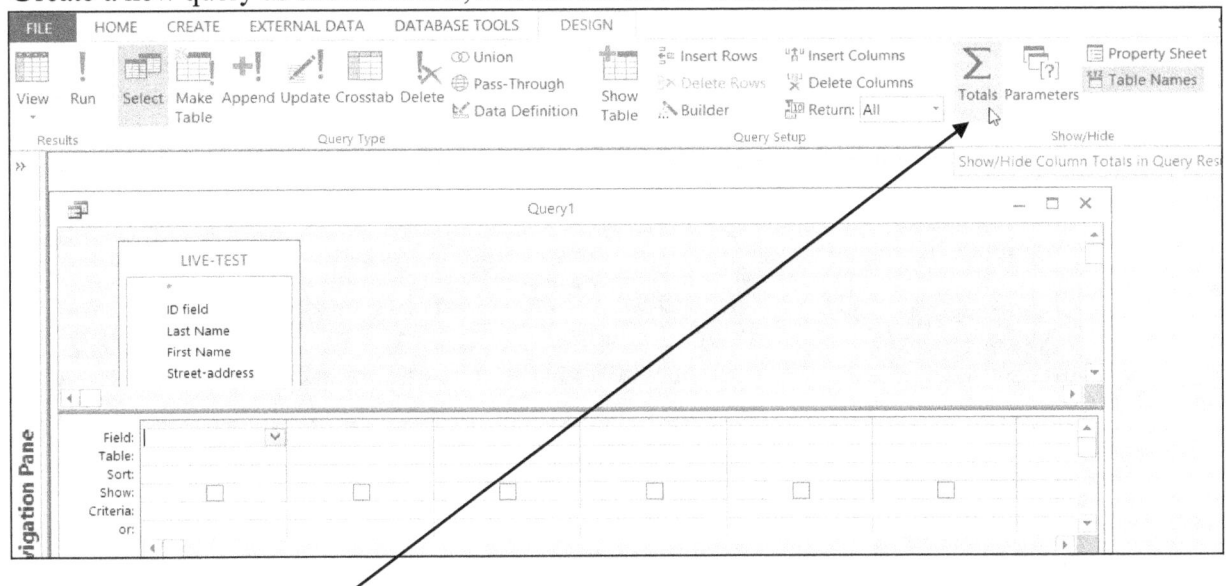

Select the Totals button Σ, the appearance of the query will change to the following.

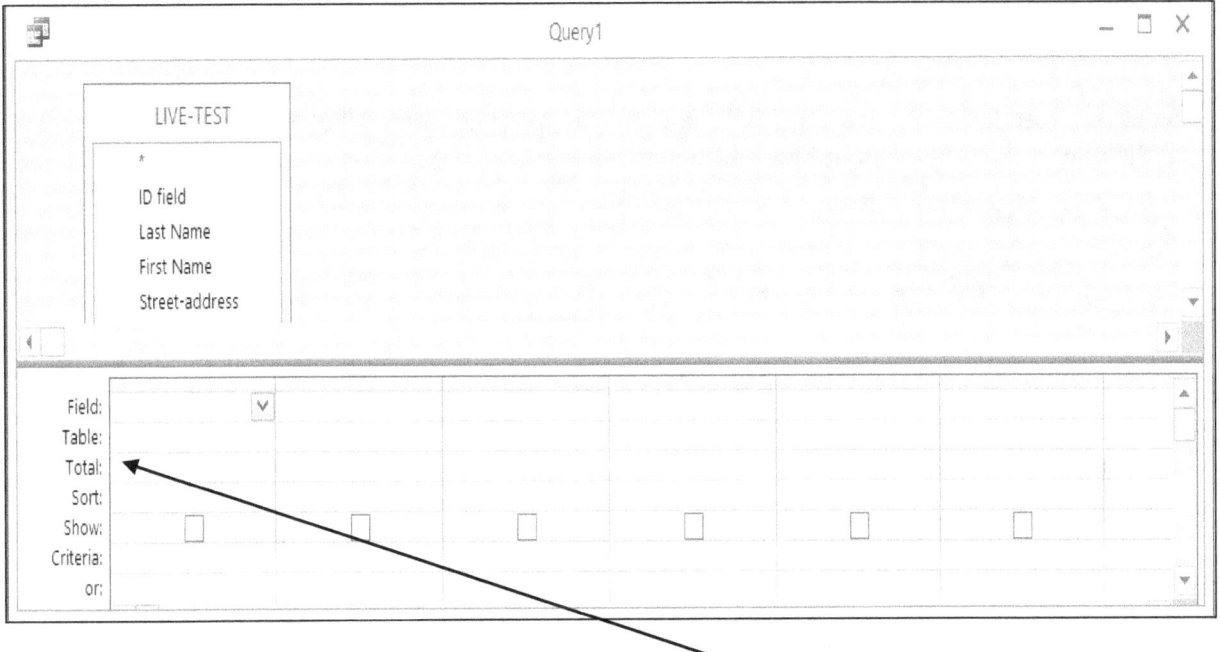

A new line will be shown in the query; this line will be called 'Total'.

Select the field [# of Books], then click on the dropdown available in the 'Total' row as shown below.

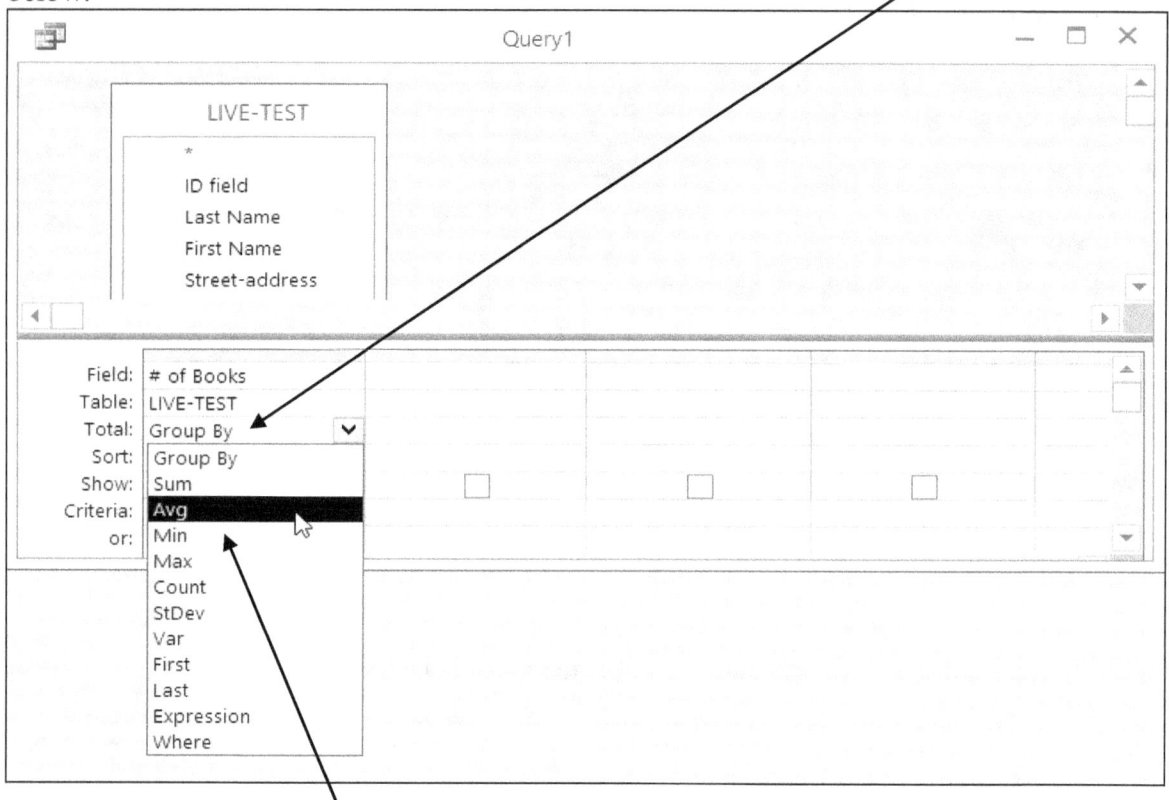

Select Avg from the dropdown, this will calculate an average of the [# of Books].
Run the query, the output should look like the following.

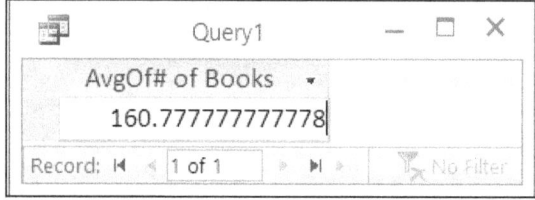

This brings back the average, however it also formats it to have many decimal places.

A 2nd way to do this is to create a new query, remove the Total row and type this formula:
Average of Books: Avg([# of Books]).

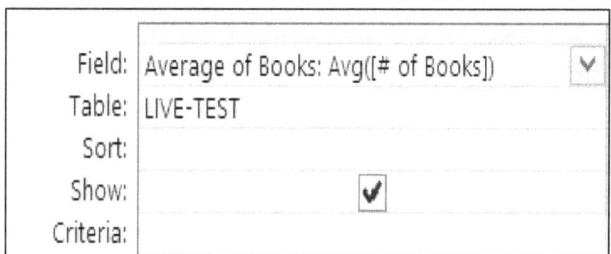

This will return a field called [Average of Books] as shown below.

Both methods create an answer, which has many decimal places; this will be fixed on the next page. The second method gives you more control over the new field name. The remaining examples will use this method.

Round function.

Adding a Round function to this formula will allow the query to bring back a limited number of decimal places

The formula for this is: **Average of Books: Round(Avg([# of Books]),2)**.

Running the query again will return the following.

The format of the Round function is **Round(field, #-of-decimals)**.

This function when placed around the Avg functions will allow you to create queries which have set number of decimal places.

Int & Fix functions.

If you do not want decimal places, use the Fix or Int functions. These two functions return only the Integer portion (values to the left of the decimal.

The formula for Int() is: **Average of Books: Int(Avg([# of Books]))**.
The formula for Fix() is: **Average of Books: Fix(Avg([# of Books]))**.

These formulas will return the following value which has no decimals.

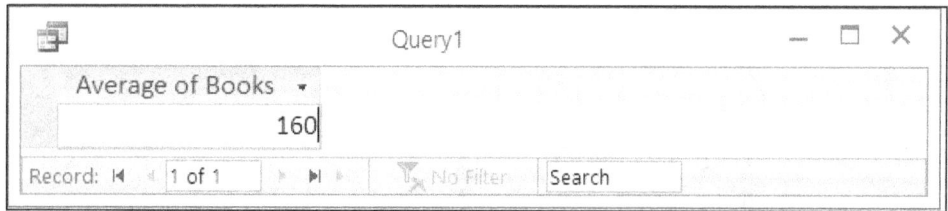

Authors guide (This material is from Access help).

Average function

Description: Returns the average (arithmetic mean) of its arguments, which can be numbers, names, or references that contain numbers.
Syntax: AVERAGE(number1,number2,...)
Number1   Number1, Number2, ..are 1 to 30 numeric arguments for which you want the average.

Round function

Description: Returns a number rounded to a specified number of decimal places.
Syntax: Round(expression [,numdecimalplaces])

Int, Fix Functions

Description: Returns the integer portion of a number.
Syntax **Int**(*number*), **Fix**(*number*)

The required *number* argument is a Double or any valid numeric expression. If *number* contains Null, **Null** is returned.

Remarks

Both **Int** and **Fix** remove the fractional part of *number* and return the resulting integer value.

The difference between **Int** and **Fix** is that if *number* is negative, **Int** returns the first negative integer less than or equal to *number*, whereas **Fix** returns the first negative integer greater than or equal to *number*. For example, **Int** converts -8.4 to -9, and **Fix** converts -8.4 to -8.

Count function explained.

Another function that can be used is the **Count** function. The query will count the number of records in a field ([ID field]). I used a field that has unique values to get my count. Some software will provide a count of unique values, not the total number of records.

This will return the number of records in the table.

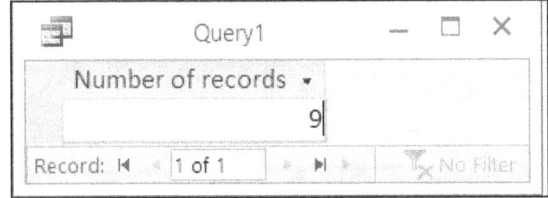

The formula is: **Number of records: Count([ID field])**.

Authors guide (This material is from Access help).
Count function

Description
Counts how many numbers and cells that contain numbers are in the list of arguments.

Syntax
COUNT(value1,value2,...)
Value1   Value1, Value2, ... are 1 to 30 arguments that can contain or refer to a variety of different types of data, but only numbers are counted.

Max function explained.

The Max functions will return the largest value (Maximum) in a column (field).

The query is as shown below: The data is being presented in a field called [Largest Value].

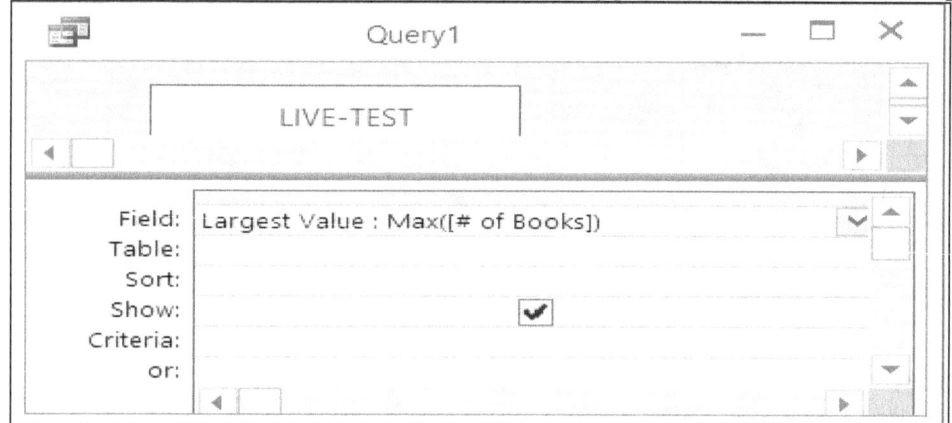

The formula is: **Largest Value : Max([# of Books]).**

Authors guide (This material is from Access help).

MAX
Returns the largest value in a set of values. Ignores logical values and text.

Syntax
MAX(number1,number2,...)

Min function explained.

The Min functions will return the smallest value (Minimum)

The query is as shown below: The data is being presented in a field called [Smallest Value].

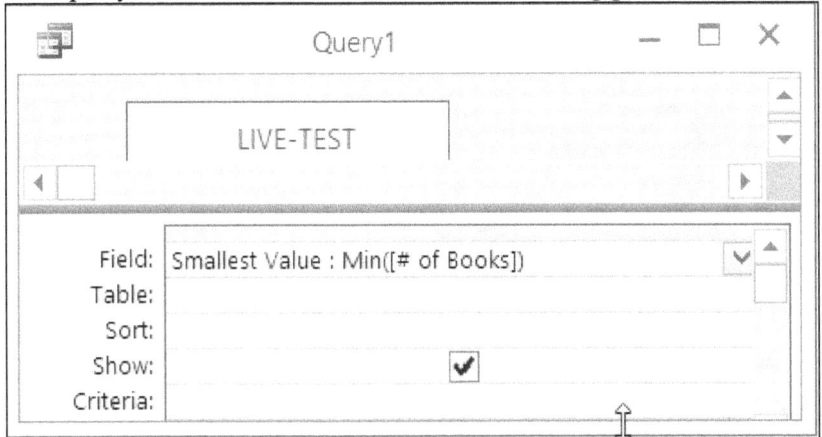

The formula is: **Smallest Value : Min([# of Books]).**

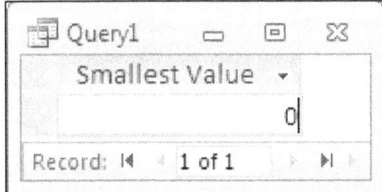

Authors guide (This material is from Access help).

MIN
Returns the smallest number in a set of values. Ignores logical values and text.

Syntax
MIN(number1,number2,...)

Sum function explained.

The Sum functions will add up the values provided in a numeric field.

The query is as shown below: The data is being presented in the Sum of the values in the [# of Books] field.

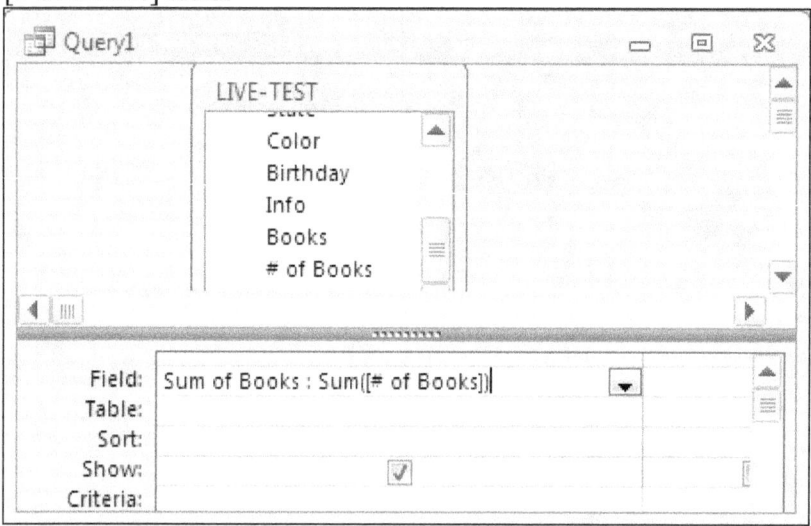

The formula is: **Sum of Books: Sum([# of Books])**.

Authors guide (This material is from Access help).

SUM
Adds all the numbers in a range of cells.

Syntax
SUM(number1,number2,...)

Functioning with Access – 2013
Chapter 3 – Math functions – Select queries

To examine the functions, go to Help by pressing the '?' in the upper right, the software will take you out to the web-based help. The software is making you part of an online community. As a developer, this was useful, but the responses were not immediate and often were confusing.

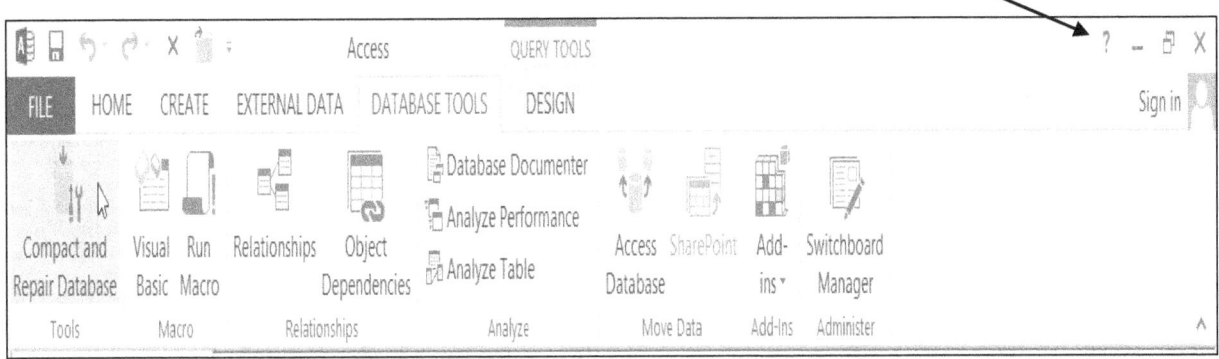

By pressing the '?', you are taken to this form which wants to search online.

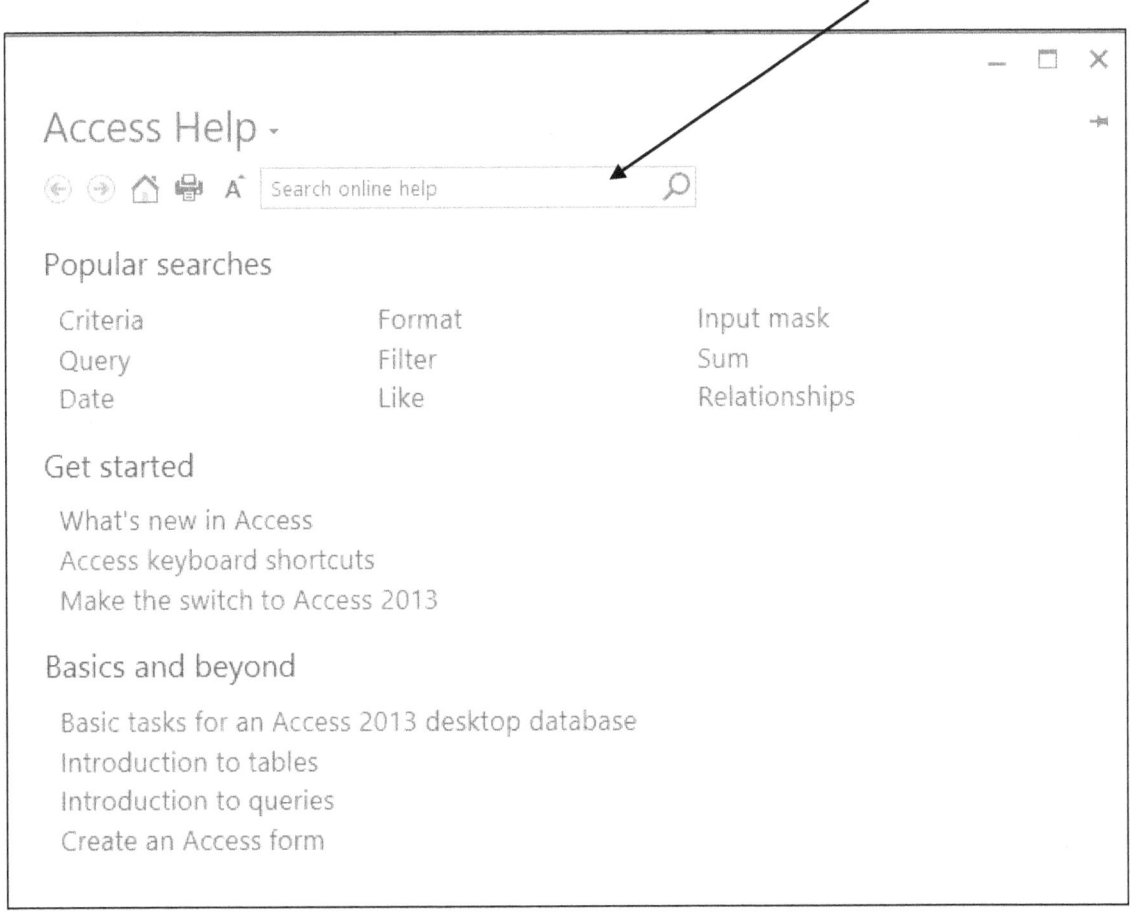

Functioning with Access – 2013
Chapter 3 – Math functions – Select queries

NOTE: You can also serach your computer by selecting the down arrow to the right of the words Access Help. On my pc this provided no real help looking for functions. This is shown below.

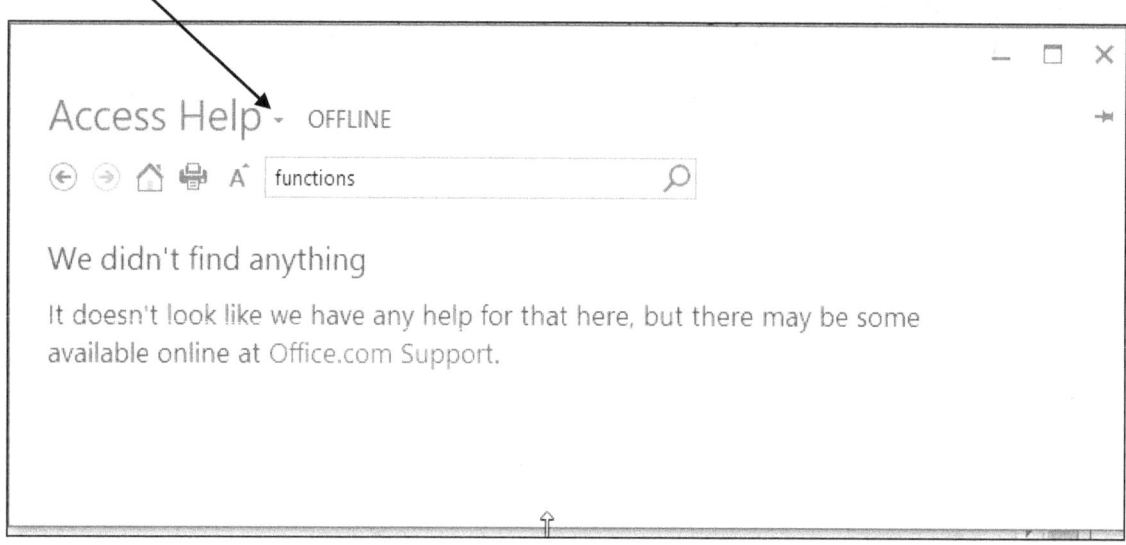

Type in Functions, and then press the magnifying glass.

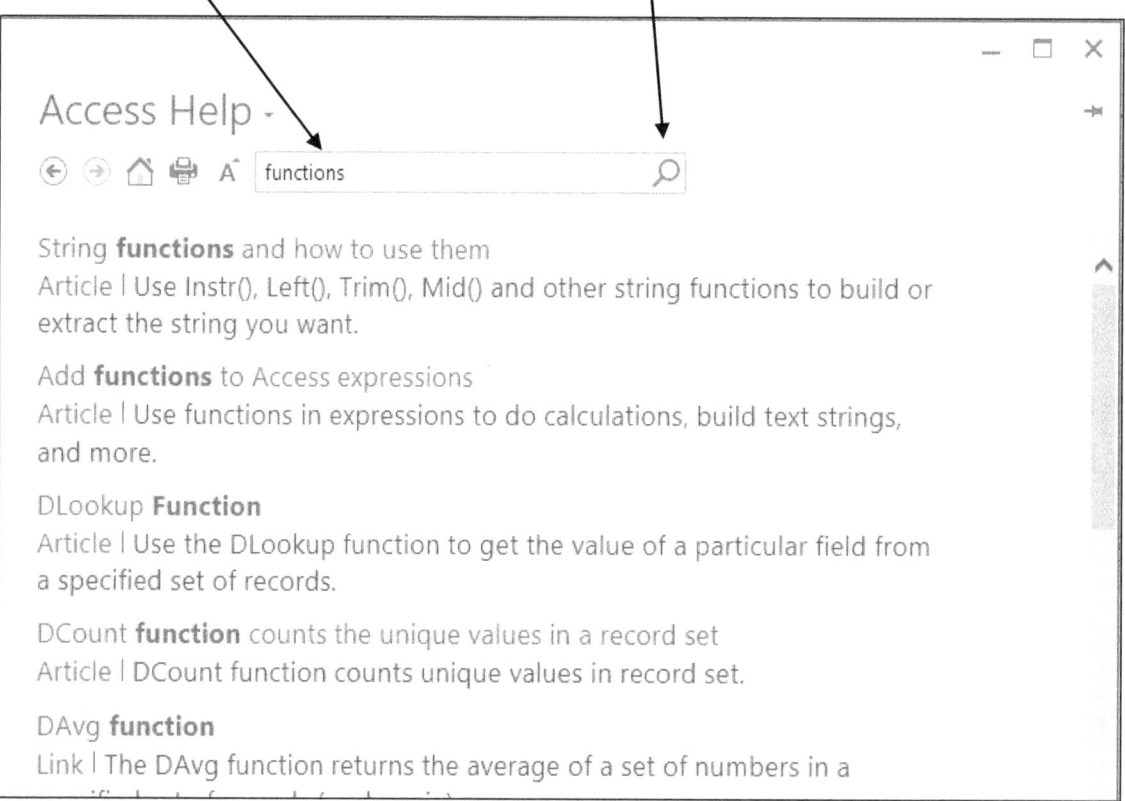

What will be returned are 'Articles' and 'Links' which may be very useful. Feel free to use this method to learn moreabout Access functions. This book uses a different approch.

Functioning with Access – 2013
Chapter 3 – Math functions – Select queries

If you type in 'Expression Builder', Access does provide Links and Articles that may be useful.

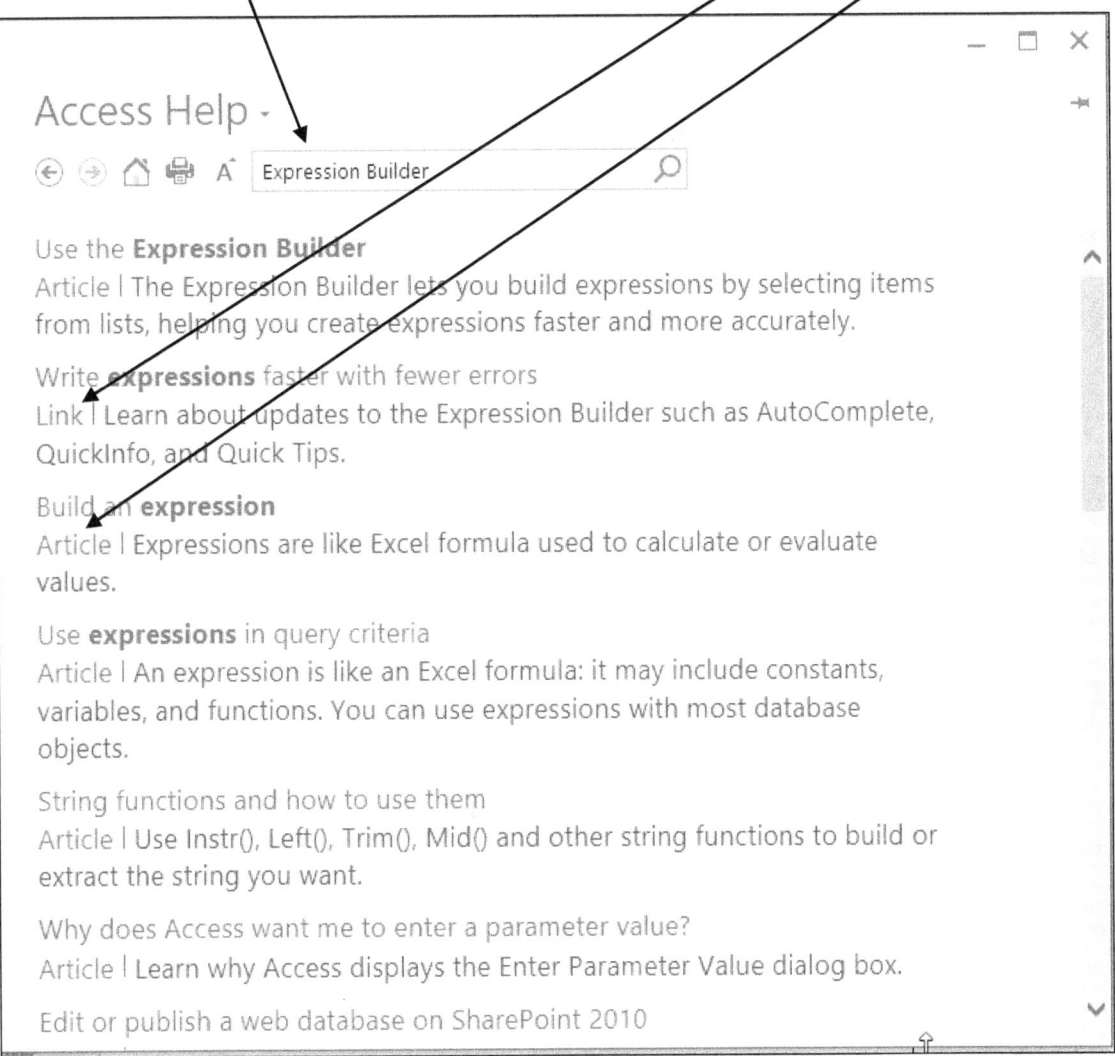

Functioning with Access – 2013
Chapter 3 – Math functions – Select queries

Creating a query and using the Builder is the easiest way to explore functions, as shown below.

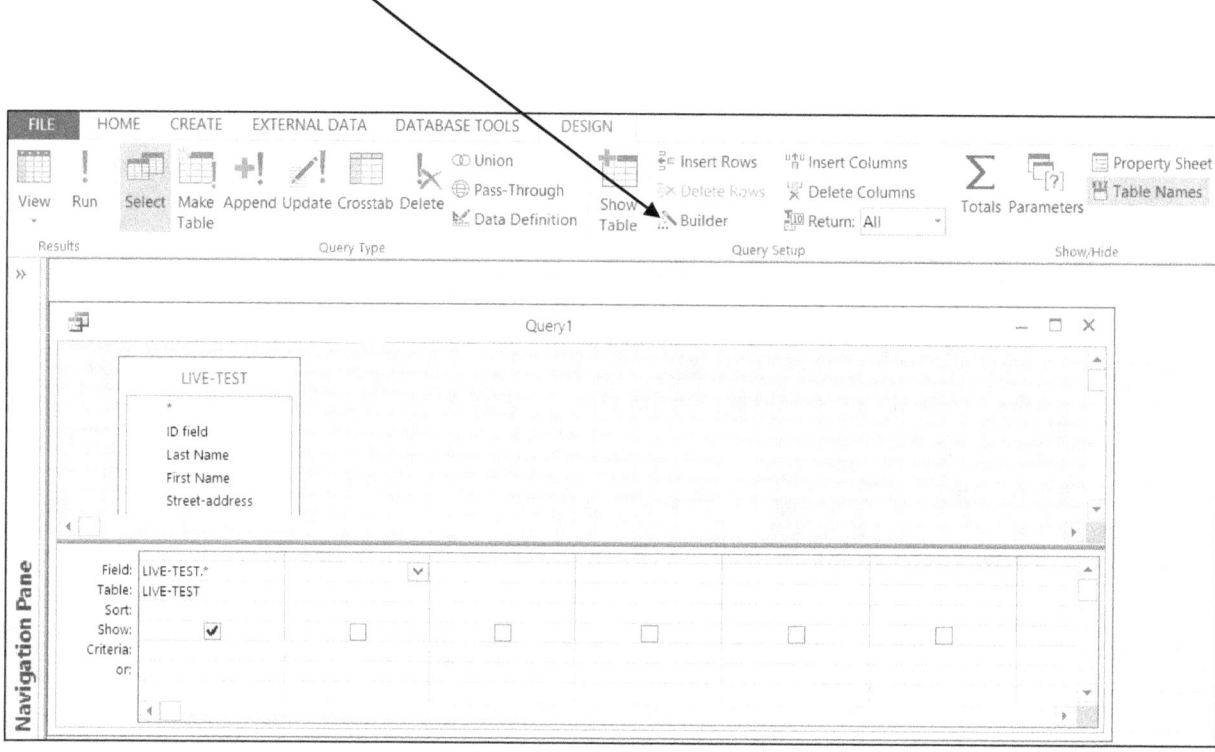

As shown earlier in the book, this provides you with a working area to explore the functions and to read the help specific to each function.

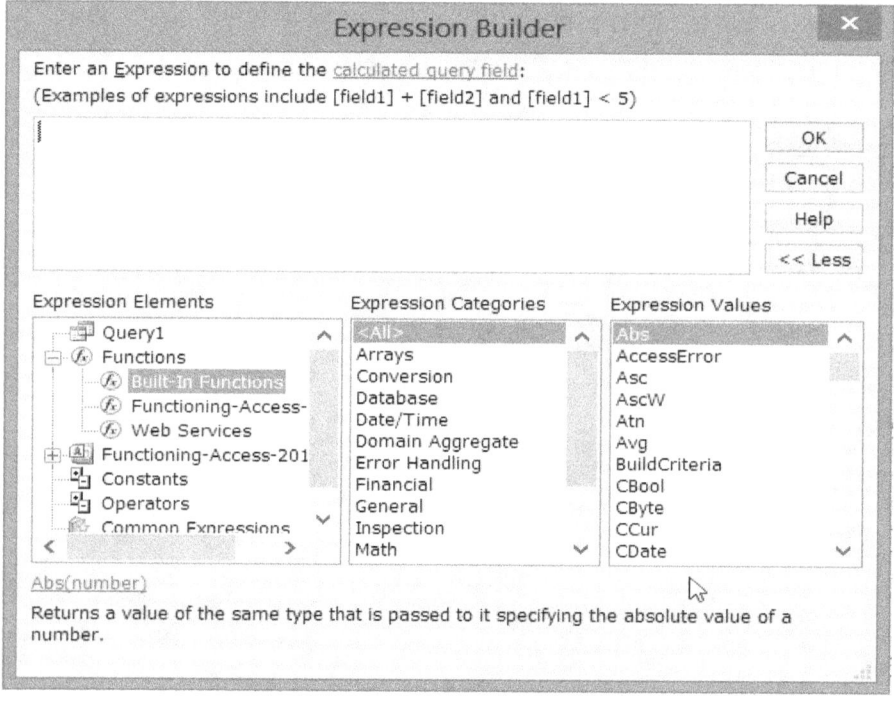

Chapter 4 - Date functions – Select queries.

To get value out of Access, you have to be able to use the Functions that are supplied with the software. The ability to create Databases, Tables, Reports and Forms is basic and essential, but it will be the Functions in Access that are needed to fully comprehend and utilize the power of Access. **(Note: in presentations of returned data, all records may not be shown).**

One way to see the functions available in the software is to go through a query.
Open any query, then press the Expression Builder button.

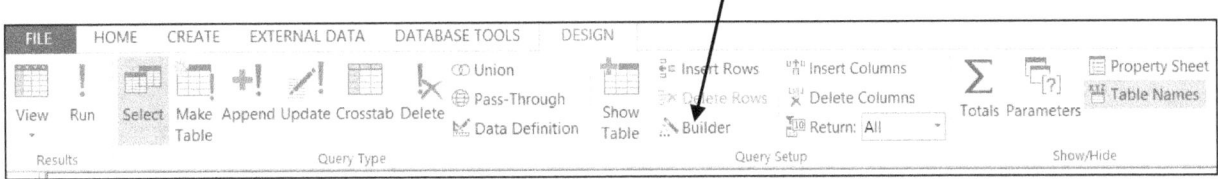

Select the Functions, then Built-In functions, then select Date/Time in the middle column.

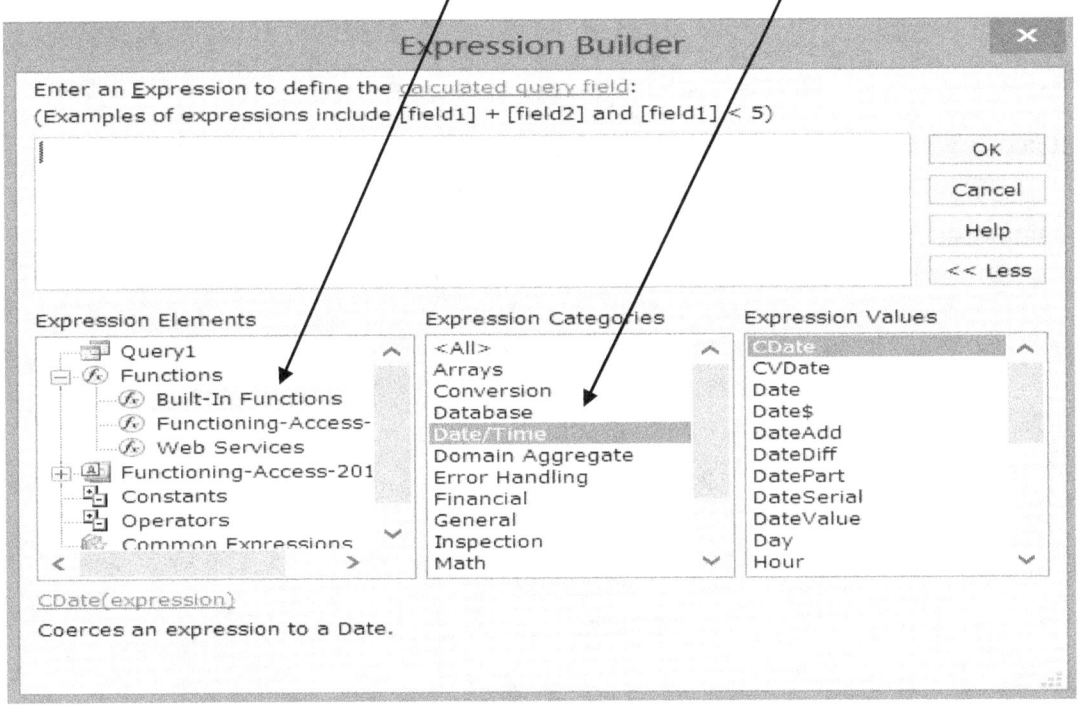

Once selected, you will see the screen above. This presents all of the Date/Time functions

On the following pages are examples of Date/Time functions.

DateDiff function explained.

To see how this function works, another date field is required. Access has a variable called Now() which returns today's Data/Time. Create a new query, as shown below, that includes the LIVE-TEST table. Select the Birthday field and type in the Now() function in another column. The field is named [Today].

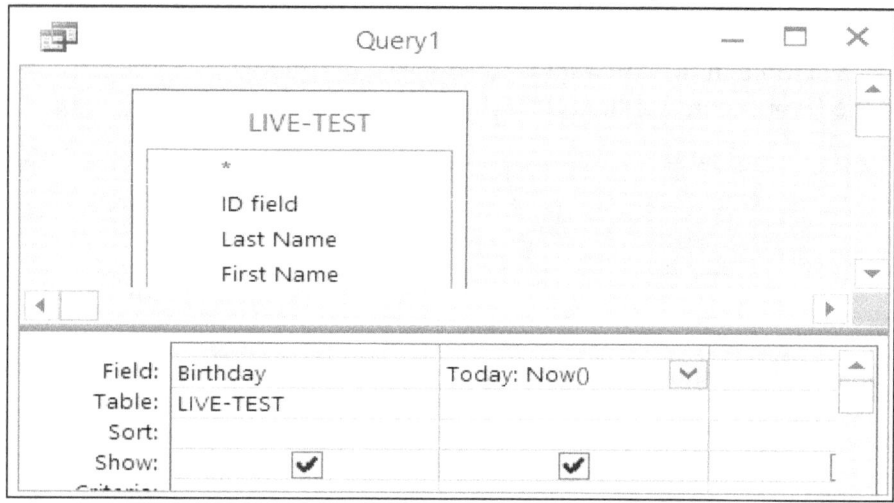

The Now() function will return its default value, which include the date and time and will be same value for every record. The complete formula is: **Today: Now()**.

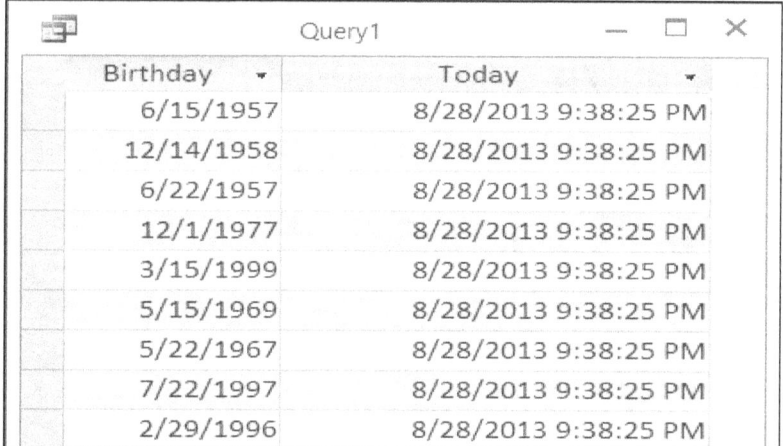

The Today field needs to be formatted to remove the Time. This can be done in a query by using formatting commands. The Format commands from Access are explained in a few pages. To return only the years of the Date/Time field the command will be Format(Now(), "yyyyy"). This command is used to provide today's year value in a field called [Formatted Year]. This is shown in the next query **(NOTE the use of double quotes as opposed to single quotes, I find that both will work in some instances. In this book I will be using double quotes).**

Below is a query to show formatting of the Now() function to show only the year.
The formula is: **Formatted Year: Format(Now(), "yyyy").**

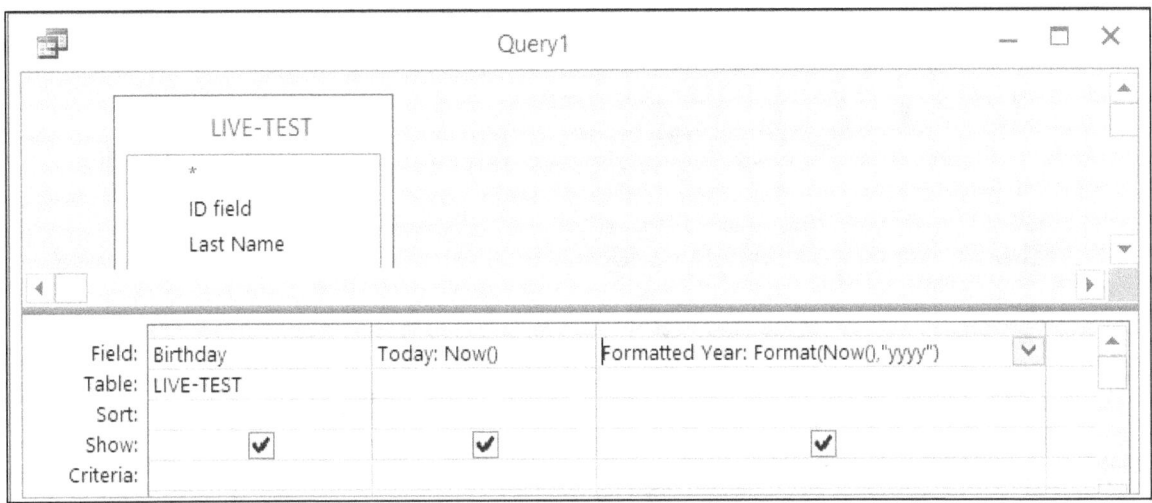

This is the output.

Birthday	Today	Formatted Year
6/15/1957	8/28/2013 9:53:06 PM	2013
12/14/1958	8/28/2013 9:53:06 PM	2013
6/22/1957	8/28/2013 9:53:06 PM	2013
12/1/1977	8/28/2013 9:53:06 PM	2013
3/15/1999	8/28/2013 9:53:06 PM	2013
5/15/1969	8/28/2013 9:53:06 PM	2013
5/22/1967	8/28/2013 9:53:06 PM	2013
7/22/1997	8/28/2013 9:53:06 PM	2013

Now the DateDiff() function can be tested.
The formula is: **Date Difference: DateDiff("yyyy",[Birthday],Now()).**

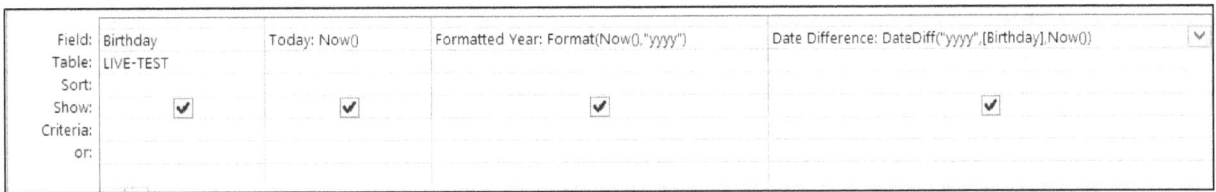

The values from this formula follow in the field [Date Difference]. This field is showing the number of year's difference between the [Birthday] field and the date for Today (which was 08/28/2013).

Birthday	Today	Formatted Year	Date Difference
6/15/1957	8/28/2013 10:01:15 PM	2013	56
12/14/1958	8/28/2013 10:01:15 PM	2013	55
6/22/1957	8/28/2013 10:01:15 PM	2013	56
12/1/1977	8/28/2013 10:01:15 PM	2013	36
3/15/1999	8/28/2013 10:01:15 PM	2013	14
5/15/1969	8/28/2013 10:01:15 PM	2013	44
5/22/1967	8/28/2013 10:01:15 PM	2013	46
7/22/1997	8/28/2013 10:01:15 PM	2013	16
2/29/1996	8/28/2013 10:01:15 PM	2013	17

By placing "yyyy" in the formula returns the number of years between two dates.

Format Function explained.

This example shows various uses of the **Format** function to format values using both named formats and user-defined formats. For the date separator (/), time separator (:), and AM/ PM literal, the actual formatted output displayed by your system depends on the locale settings on which the code is running. When times and dates are displayed in the development environment, the short time format and short date format of the code locale are used. When displayed by running code, the short time format and short date format of the system locale are used, which may differ from the code locale. For this example, English/U.S. is assumed. MyStr is the output field to show output of the formula.

Authors guide (This material is from Access help).
Returns current system time in the system-defined long time format.
MyStr = **Format**(Time, "Long Time")

Returns current system date in the system-defined long date format.
MyStr = **Format**(Date, "Long Date")

MyStr = **Format**(MyTime, "h:m:s")   ' Returns "17:4:23".
MyStr = **Format**(MyTime, "hh:mm:ss AMPM")   ' Returns "05:04:23 PM".
MyStr = **Format**(MyDate, "dddd, mmm d yyyy") ' Returns "Wednesday, ' Jan 27 1993".

User-defined formats.
MyStr = **Format**(5459.4, "##,##0.00")   ' Returns "5,459.40".
MyStr = **Format**(334.9, "###0.00")   ' Returns "334.90".
MyStr = **Format**(5, "0.00%")   ' Returns "500.00%".
MyStr = **Format**("HELLO", "<") ' Returns "hello" ("<" causes the text to be lower case).
MyStr = **Format**("This is it", ">") ' Returns "THIS IS IT" (">" causes the text to be upper case).

Authors guide (This material is from Access help).

DateDiff Function

Description

Returns a Variant (Long) specifying the number of time intervals between two specified dates.

Syntax

DateDiff(*interval, date1, date2*[, *firstdayofweek*[, *firstweekofyear*]])

The **DateDiff** function syntax has these named arguments:

Part	Description
interval	Required. String expression that is the interval of time you use to calculate the difference between *date1* and *date2*.
date1, date2	Required; **Variant (Date)**. Two dates you want to use in the calculation.
firstdayofweek	Optional. A constant that specifies the first day of the week. If not specified, Sunday is assumed.
firstweekofyear	Optional. A constant that specifies the first week of the year. If not specified, the first week is assumed to be the week in which January 1 occurs.

Settings

The *interval* argument has these settings:

Setting	Description	Setting	Description
yyyy	Year	w	Weekday
q	Quarter	ww	Week
m	Month	h	Hour
y	Day of year	n	Minute
d	Day	s	Second

Remarks

You can use the **DateDiff** function to determine how many specified time intervals exist between two dates. For example, you might use **DateDiff** to calculate the number of days between two dates, or the number of weeks between today and the end of the year.

To calculate the number of days between *date1* and *date2*, you can use either Day of year ("y") or Day ("d"). When *interval* is Weekday ("w"), **DateDiff** returns the number of weeks between the two dates. If *date1* falls on a Monday, **DateDiff** counts the number of Mondays until *date2*. It counts *date2* but not *date1*. If *interval* is Week ("ww"), however, the **DateDiff** function returns the number of calendar weeks between the two dates. It counts the number of Sundays between *date1* and *date2*. **DateDiff** counts *date2* if it falls on a Sunday; but it doesn't count *date1*, even if it does fall on a Sunday.

If *date1* refers to a later point in time than *date2*, the **DateDiff** function returns a negative number.

The *firstdayofweek* argument affects calculations that use the "w" and "ww" interval symbols.

If *date1* or *date2* is a date literal, the specified year becomes a permanent part of that date. However, if *date1* or *date2* is enclosed in double quotation marks (" "), and you omit the year, the current year is inserted in your code each time the *date1* or *date2* expression is evaluated. This makes it possible to write code that can be used in different years.

When comparing December 31 to January 1 of the immediately succeeding year, **DateDiff** for Year ("yyyy") returns 1 even though only a day has elapsed.

Note: For *date1* and *date2*, if the **Calendar** property setting is Gregorian, the supplied date must be Gregorian. If the calendar is Hijri, the supplied date must be Hijri.

Authors guide (This material is from Access help).

Now Function

Description
Returns a Variant (Date) specifying the current date and time according your computer's system date and time. This function requires no other formatting and is as simple as it appears.

Syntax
Now()

DateAdd Function explained.

To add to a date field, many options are available. Here is the [Birthday] field and [Birthday + 7], which adds 7 days to [Birthday]. The formula is: **Birthday + 7: [Birthday]+7.**

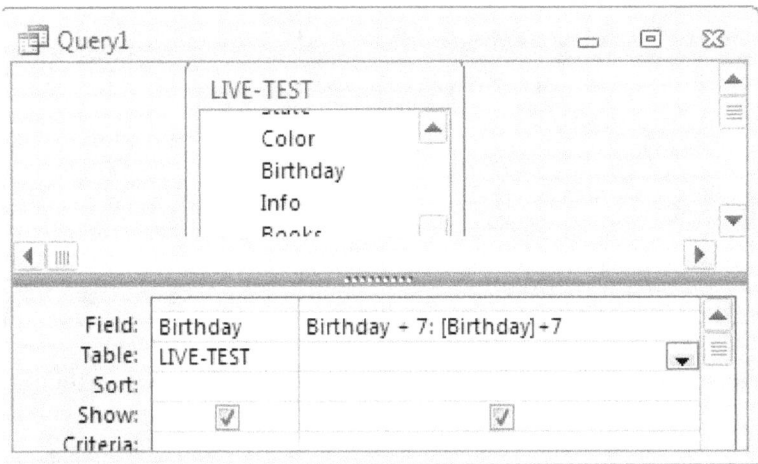

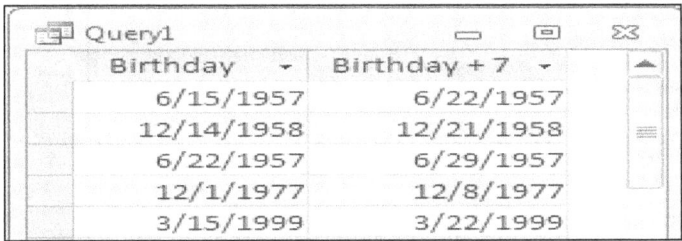

The DateAdd function allows you to determine how you are adding to a Date, whether it is a Month, Year, Week or a Day.

To add two months to birthdate the functions would look like this:
DateAdd('m', 2, Birthday).

In the query below, I have added 60 days to [Birthday] and in another field, added 2 months using the DateAdd function.

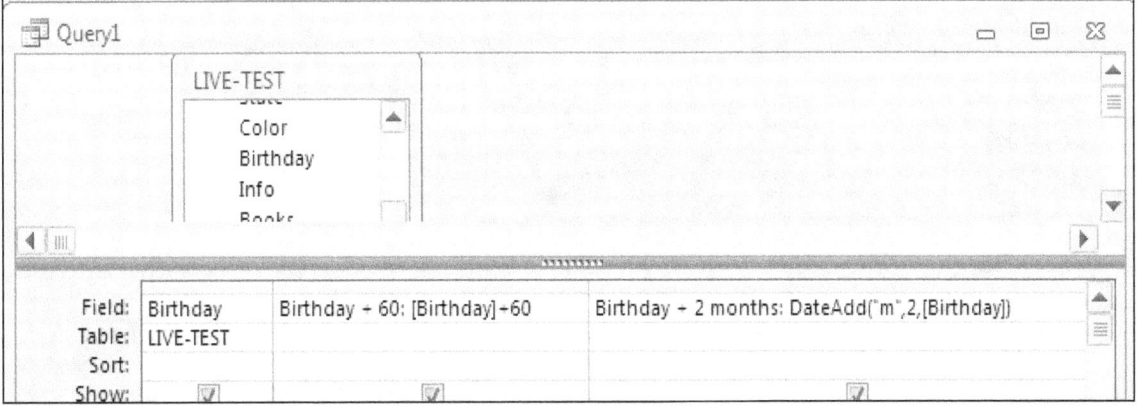

The output form this query illustrates that adding 60 days to a date is not the same as adding two months.

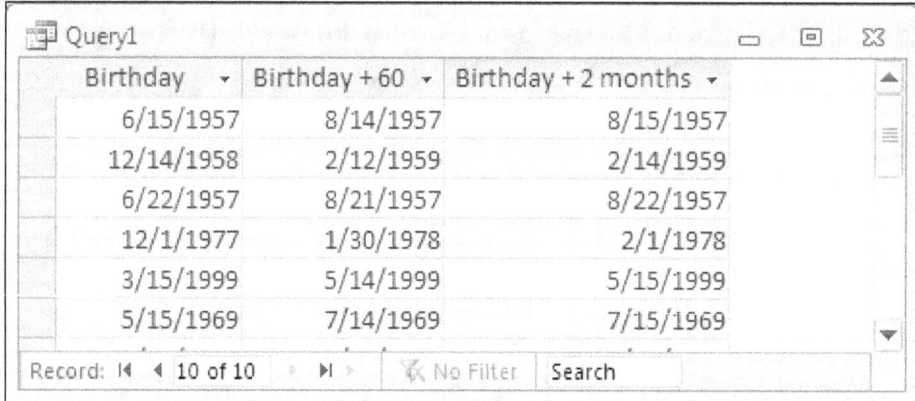

Using the DateDiff function learned earlier, the formula can show the differences between them.

The formula is:
Difference: DateDiff("d",([Birthday]+60),DateAdd("m",2,[Birthday])).

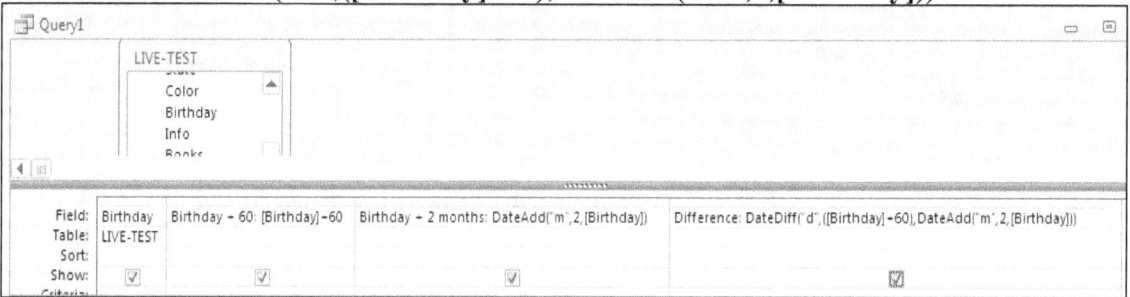

Here is the output, the difference between the two fields is displayed in the [Difference] field.

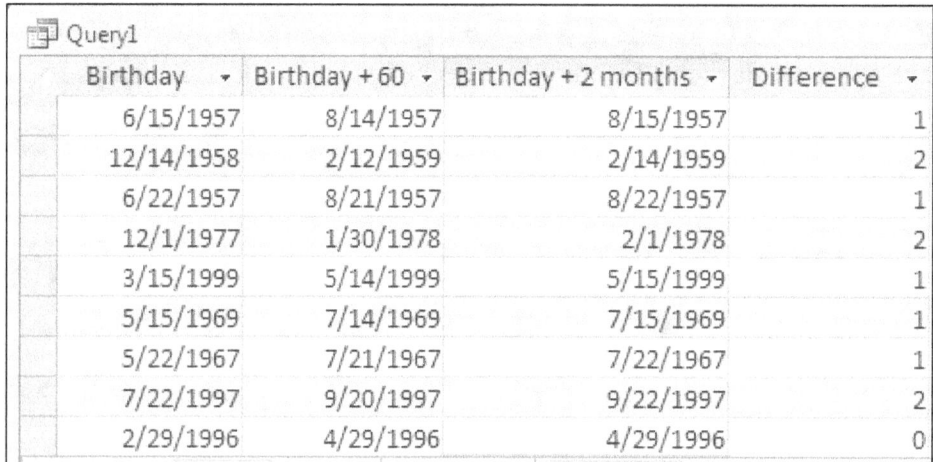

This is important to realize adding 60 days to a Date is not the same as adding 2 months.

Functioning with Access – 2013
Chapter 4 – Date functions – Select queries

Authors guide (This material is from Access help).

DateAdd Function

This example takes a date and, using the **DateAdd** function, displays a corresponding date a specified number of months in the future.

DateAdd(*interval, number, date***)**

The **DateAdd** function syntax has these named arguments:

Part	Description
interval	Required. String expression that is the interval of time you want to add.
number	Required. Numeric expression that is the number of intervals you want to add. It can be positive (to get dates in the future) or negative (to get dates in the past).
Date	Required. **Variant** (**Date**) or literal representing date to which the interval is added.

Settings

The *interval* argument has these settings:

Setting	Description	Setting	Description	Setting	Description	Setting	Description
Yyyy	Year	Ww	Week	y	Day of year	W	Weekday
Q	Quarter	H	Hour	d	Day		
M	Month	N	Minute	S	Second		

Remarks

You can use the **DateAdd** function to add or subtract a specified time interval from a date. For example, you can use **DateAdd** to calculate a date 30 days from today or a time 45 minutes from now.

To add days to *date*, you can use Day of Year ("y"), Day ("d"), or Weekday ("w").

The **DateAdd** function won't return an invalid date. The following example adds one month to January 31: DateAdd("m", 1, "31-Jan-95")

In this case, **DateAdd** returns 28-Feb-95, not 31-Feb-95. If *date* is 31-Jan-96, it returns 29-Feb-96 because 1996 is a leap year. If the calculated date proceeds the year 100 (that is, you subtract more years than are in *date*), an error occurs. If *number* isn't a Long value, it is rounded to the nearest whole number before being evaluated.

DatePart Function explained.

DatePart function will return the value specified from a date. Below the month 'm' was specified. The formula is: **Month of Birthday: DatePart("m", [Birthday]).**

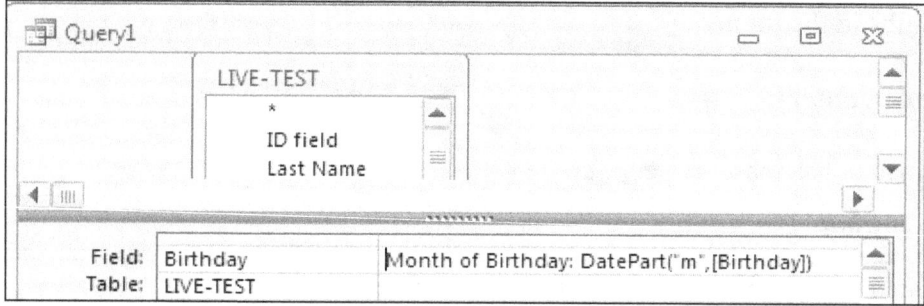

Below the number of the month is returned.

Birthday	Month of Birthday
6/15/1957	6
12/14/1958	12
6/22/1957	6
12/1/1977	12
3/15/1999	3
5/15/1969	5
5/22/1967	5

Below are three more examples: Week of the year of the [Birthday] (1-52), Day of the year of the [Birthday] (1-365(356 for Leap year)). Day of the month of the [Birthday] (1-31) and Day of the week of the [Birthday] (1-7).

The formulas are: **Week of Birthday: DatePart("ww",[Birthday])**
Day of year for Birthday: DatePart("y",[Birthday])
Day of month for Birthday: DatePart("d",[Birthday])
Day of week for Birthday: DatePart("w",[Birthday]).

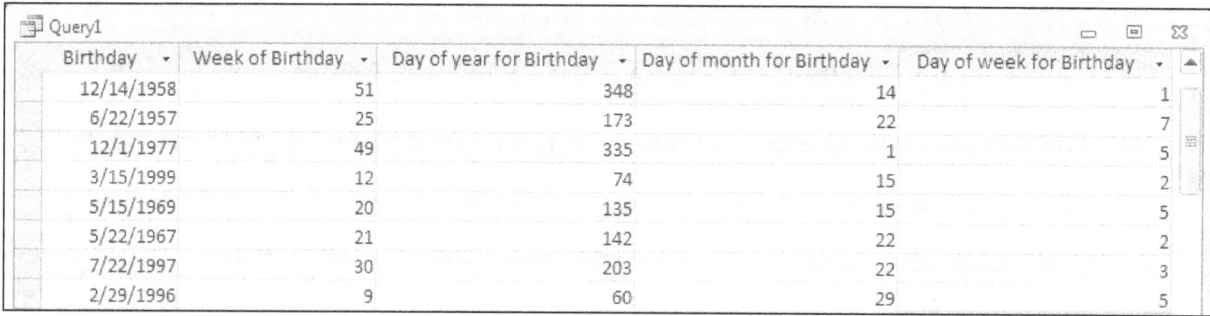

Functioning with Access – 2013
Chapter 4 – Date functions – Select queries

Authors guide (This material is from Access help).

DatePart Function

Returns a **Variant** (**Integer**) containing the specified part of a given date.

Syntax
DatePart(*interval, date*[*,firstdayofweek*[*, firstweekofyear*]])

The **DatePart** function syntax has these named arguments:

Part	Description
interval	Required. String expression that is the interval of time you want to return.
date	Required. **Variant** (**Date**) value that you want to evaluate.
firstdayofweek	Optional. A constant that specifies the first day of the week. If not specified, Sunday is assumed.
firstweekofyear	Optional. A constant that specifies the first week of the year. If not specified, the first week is assumed to be the week in which January 1 occurs.

You can use the **DatePart** function to evaluate a date and return a specific interval of time. For example, you might use **DatePart** to calculate the day of the week or the current hour.

The *firstdayofweek* argument affects calculations that use the "w" and "ww" interval symbols.

If *date* is a date literal, the specified year becomes a permanent part of that date. However, if *date* is enclosed in double quotation marks (" "), and you omit the year, the current year is inserted in your code each time the *date* expression is evaluated. This makes it possible to write code that can be used in different years.

Functioning with Access – 2013
Chapter 4 – Date functions – Select queries

Second function explained.

The Second function will return from a Date/Time field the current second.
The coding to do this is: **The current second : Second(Now()).**

Here is an example of the query, it returns the current Date & Time to the [Today] field, also it returns the second from this field in the [The current second] field.

Field:	Birthday	Today: Now()	The current second : Second(Now())
Table:	LIVE-TEST		
Sort:			
Show:	✓	✓	✓
Criteria:			

Here is the output from the query (not all records shown).

Birthday	Today	The current second
6/15/1957	8/28/2013 10:19:04 PM	4
12/14/1958	8/28/2013 10:19:04 PM	4
6/22/1957	8/28/2013 10:19:04 PM	4
12/1/1977	8/28/2013 10:19:04 PM	4
3/15/1999	8/28/2013 10:19:04 PM	4
5/15/1969	8/28/2013 10:19:04 PM	4

Authors guide (This material is from Access help).

Second Function

Returns a **Variant** (**Integer**) specifying a whole number between 0 and 59, inclusive, representing the second of the minute.

Syntax: Second(*time*)

The required *time* argument is any Variant, numeric expression, string expression, or any combination, that can represent a time. If *time* contains Null, **Null** is returned.

Minute function explained.

The Minute function will return from a Date/Time field the current minute.
The coding to do this is: **The current minute : Minute(Now()).**

Here is an example of the query, it returns the current Date & time to the [Today] field, also it returns the minute from this field in the [The current minute] field.

Field:	Birthday	Today: Now()	The current minute : Minute(Now())
Table:	LIVE-TEST		
Sort:			
Show:	✓	✓	✓
Criteria:			

Here is the output from the query (not all records shown).

Birthday	Today	The current minute
6/15/1957	8/28/2013 10:21:39 PM	21
12/14/1958	8/28/2013 10:21:39 PM	21
6/22/1957	8/28/2013 10:21:39 PM	21
12/1/1977	8/28/2013 10:21:39 PM	21
3/15/1999	8/28/2013 10:21:39 PM	21
5/15/1969	8/28/2013 10:21:39 PM	21
5/22/1967	8/28/2013 10:21:39 PM	21

Authors guide (This material is from Access help).

Minute Function

Returns a Variant (Integer) specifying a whole number between 0 and 59, inclusive, representing the minute of the hour.

Syntax: Minute(*time*) The required time argument is any Variant, numeric expression, string expression, or any combination, that can represent a time. If time contains Null, Null is returned.

Hour function explained.

The Hour function will return from a Date/Time field the current hour.
The coding to do this is: **The current hour: Hour(Now()).**

Here is an example of the query, it returns the current Date & time to the [Today] field, also it returns the hour from this field in the [The current hour] field.

Field:	Birthday	Today: Now()	The current hour: Hour(Now())
Table:	LIVE-TEST		
Sort:			
Show:	✓	✓	✓

Here is the output from the query (not all records are shown – please realize that 10PM is 22 hours).

Birthday	Today	The current hour
6/15/1957	8/28/2013 10:23:25 PM	22
12/14/1958	8/28/2013 10:23:25 PM	22
6/22/1957	8/28/2013 10:23:25 PM	22
12/1/1977	8/28/2013 10:23:25 PM	22
3/15/1999	8/28/2013 10:23:25 PM	22
5/15/1969	8/28/2013 10:23:25 PM	22
5/22/1967	8/28/2013 10:23:25 PM	22
7/22/1997	8/28/2013 10:23:25 PM	22

Authors guide (This material is from Access help).

Hour Function

Returns a Variant (Integer) specifying a whole number between 0 and 23, inclusive, representing the hour of the day.

Syntax: Hour(*time*)   The required time argument is any Variant, numeric expression, string expression, or any combination, that can represent a time. If time contains Null, Null is returned.

Day function explained.

The Day function will return from a Date/Time field the number of the day.
The coding to do this is: **The birthday: Day([Birthday]).**

Here is an example of the query, it returns the current Date & time to the [Today] field, also it returns the day from the [Birthday] field in the [The birthday] field.

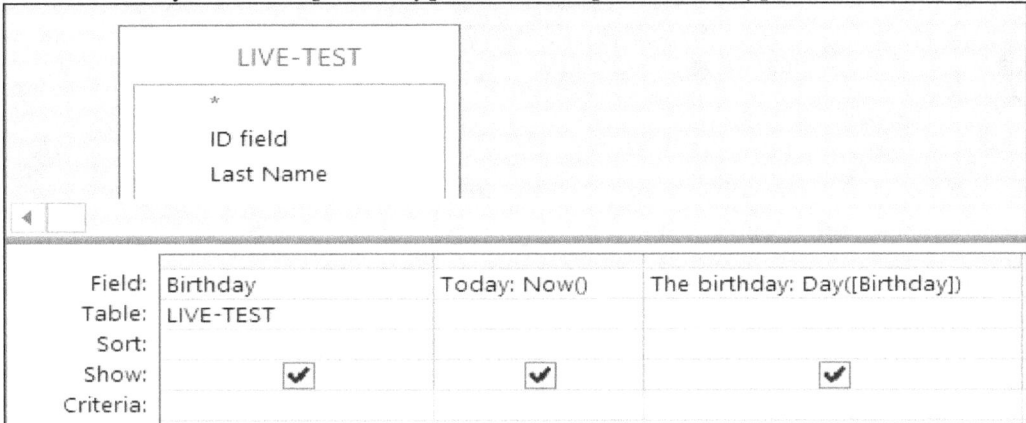

Here is the output from the query.

Birthday	Today	The birthday
6/15/1957	8/28/2013 10:26:18 PM	15
12/14/1958	8/28/2013 10:26:18 PM	14
6/22/1957	8/28/2013 10:26:18 PM	22
12/1/1977	8/28/2013 10:26:18 PM	1
3/15/1999	8/28/2013 10:26:18 PM	15
5/15/1969	8/28/2013 10:26:18 PM	15
5/22/1967	8/28/2013 10:26:18 PM	22
7/22/1997	8/28/2013 10:26:18 PM	22

Authors guide (This material is from Access help).

Day Function

Returns a Variant (Integer) specifying a whole number between 1 and 31, inclusive, representing the day of the month.

Syntax: Day(*date*) The required date argument is any Variant, numeric expression, string expression, or any combination, that can represent a date. If date contains Null, Null is returned.

WeekDay function explained.

The WeekDay function will return from a Date/Time field the day of the week.
The coding to do this is: **Day of week for birthday: WeekDay([Birthday]).**

Here is an example of the query, it returns the current Date & time to the [Today] field, also it returns the day of the week from the birthday field in the [Day of the week for birthday] field.

Field:	Birthday	Today: Now()	Day of week for birthday: Weekday([Birthday])
Table:	LIVE-TEST		
Sort:			
Show:	✔	✔	✔
Criteria:			

Here is the output from the query.

Birthday	Today	Day of week for birthday
6/15/1957	8/28/2013 10:28:13 PM	7
12/14/1958	8/28/2013 10:28:13 PM	1
6/22/1957	8/28/2013 10:28:13 PM	7
12/1/1977	8/28/2013 10:28:13 PM	5
3/15/1999	8/28/2013 10:28:13 PM	2
5/15/1969	8/28/2013 10:28:13 PM	5
5/22/1967	8/28/2013 10:28:13 PM	2
7/22/1997	8/28/2013 10:28:13 PM	3
2/29/1996	8/28/2013 10:28:13 PM	5

WeekDay function explained (continued).

This function has an optional part to it, by adding a number between 1 and 7, you can determine the beginning day of the week. The value 1 indicates Sunday, so 2 is Monday, 3 is Tuesday and 7 is Saturday. The above function has 2 days added to it, thus indicating that the week starts on Tuesday. The query is run again with a new field: [Day of week for birthday shifted]. This is using Tuesday as the start of the week, so each value returned for the day of the week is decreased by 2.

The formula is: **Day of week for birthday shifted: Weekday([Birthday],3).**

Field:	Birthday	Day of week for birthday: Weekday([Birthday])	Day of week for birthday shifted: Weekday([Birthday],3)
Table:	LIVE-TEST		
Sort:			
Show:	✓	✓	✓
Criteria:			

Here is the output; the last column is 2 less than the second column.

Birthday	Day of week for birthday	Day of week for birthday shifted
6/15/1957	7	5
12/14/1958	1	6
6/22/1957	7	5
12/1/1977	5	3
3/15/1999	2	7
5/15/1969	5	3
5/22/1967	2	7
7/22/1997	3	1
2/29/1996	5	3

Authors guide (This material is from Access help).

WeekDay Function

Returns a **Variant** (**Integer**) containing a whole number representing the day of the week.

Syntax: Weekday(*date*, [*firstdayofweek*])

The **Weekday** function syntax has these named arguments:

Part	Description
Date	Required. Variant, numeric expression, string expression, or any combination, that can represent a date. If *date* contains Null, **Null** is returned.
firstdayofweek	Optional. A constant that specifies the first day of the week. If not specified, **vbSunday** is assumed.

Settings

The *firstdayofweek* argument has these settings:

Constant	Value	Description
vbUseSystem	0	Use the NLS API setting.
vbSunday	1	Sunday (default)
vbMonday	2	Monday
vbTuesday	3	Tuesday
vbWednesday	4	Wednesday
vbThursday	5	Thursday
vbFriday	6	Friday
vbSaturday	7	Saturday

WeekDayName function explained.

The WeekDay function will return from a Date/Time field the name of the day.
The coding to do this is:
   Name of day for birthday: WeekDayName(WeekDay([Birthday])).

Here is an example of the query, it returns the Birthday to the [Birthday] field, also it returns the name of the day birthday field in the [Name of day for birthday] field.

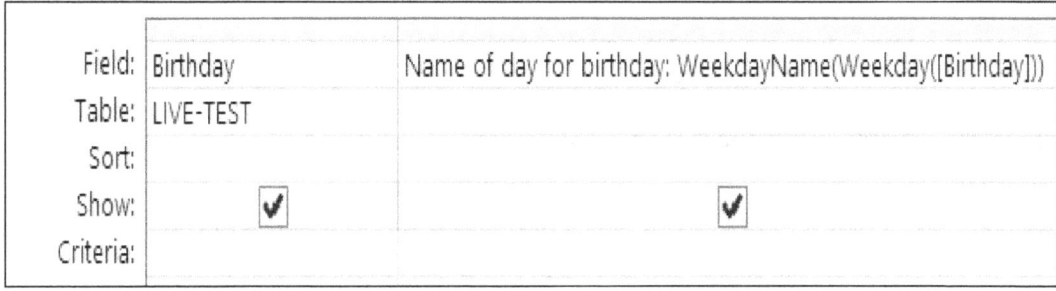

Here is the output.

Birthday	Name of day for birthday
6/15/1957	Saturday
12/14/1958	Sunday
6/22/1957	Saturday
12/1/1977	Thursday
3/15/1999	Monday
5/15/1969	Thursday
5/22/1967	Monday
7/22/1997	Tuesday
2/29/1996	Thursday

WeekDayName function explained (continued).

This function has an optional part to it; by adding 1 you can abbreviate the name.

The formula is:
Abbreviated name of day for birthday: WeekDayName(Weekday([Birthday]),1).

Field:	Birthday	Abbreviated name of day for birthday: WeekdayName(Weekday([Birthday]),1)
Table:	LIVE-TEST	
Sort:		
Show:	✓	✓

Here is the output; the last column is the system abbreviation of the name of the day.

Birthday	Abbreviated name of day for birthday
6/15/1957	Sat
12/14/1958	Sun
6/22/1957	Sat
12/1/1977	Thu
3/15/1999	Mon

Authors guide (This material is from Access help).

WeekdayName Function

Description: Returns a string indicating the specified day of the week.

Syntax: WeekdayName(weekday, abbreviate, firstdayofweek)

The **WeekdayName** function syntax has these parts:

Part	Description
weekday	Required. The numeric designation for the day of the week. Numeric value of each day depends on setting of the *firstdayofweek* setting.
abbreviate	Optional. **Boolean** value that indicates if the weekday name is to be abbreviated. If omitted, the default is **False**, which means that the weekday name is not abbreviated.
firstdayofweek	Optional. Numeric value indicating the first day of the week. See Settings section for values.

Month function explained.

The Month function will return from a Date/Time field the number of the month (1-12).

The coding to do this is:
Number of month for birthday: Month ([Birthday]).

Here is an example of the query; it returns the month number to the [Number of month for Birthday] field.

Field:	Birthday	Number of month for birthday: Month([Birthday])
Table:	LIVE-TEST	
Sort:		
Show:	✓	✓
Criteria:		

Here is the output.

Birthday	Number of month for birthday
6/15/1957	6
12/14/1958	12
6/22/1957	6
12/1/1977	12
3/15/1999	3
5/15/1969	5
5/22/1967	5
7/22/1997	7
2/29/1996	2

Authors guide (This material is from Access help).

Month Function

Returns a **Variant** (**Integer**) specifying a whole number between 1 and 12, inclusive, representing the month of the year.

Syntax: Month(*date*)

Year function explained.

The Year function will return from a Date/Time field the year.

The coding to do this is:
  Year of birth: Year ([Birthday]).

Here is an example of the query, it returns the year to the [Year born] field.

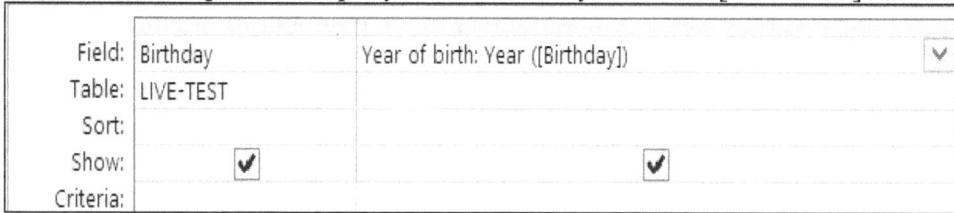

Here is the output.

Birthday	Year of birth
6/15/1957	1957
12/14/1958	1958
6/22/1957	1957
12/1/1977	1977
3/15/1999	1999
5/15/1969	1969

Authors guide (This material is from Access help).

Year Function Returns a Variant (Integer) containing a whole number representing the year.

Syntax: Year(date)

Timer function explained.

The Timer function will return from a Date/Time field the number of seconds since midnight. Each hour has 3,600 seconds; one day has 24 * 3,600 seconds (86,400).

The coding to do this is:
Timer value: Timer().

Here is an example of the query, it returns the value of the Now() function to the [Current Date and Time] field and Timer value to the [Timer Value] field.

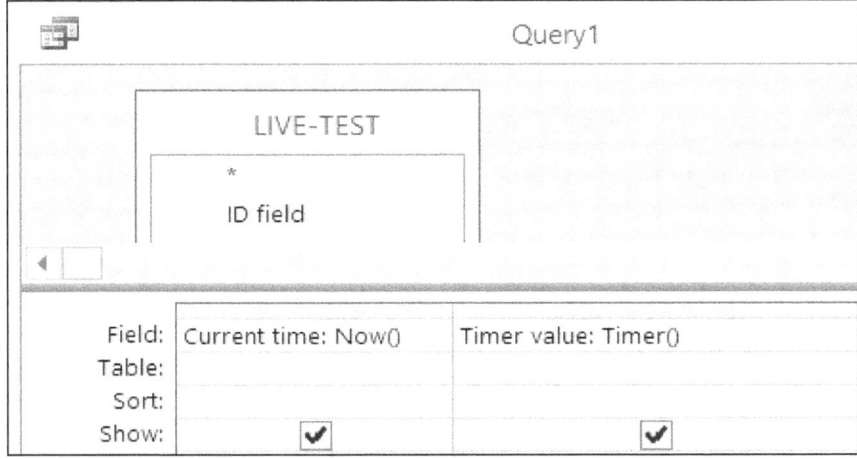

Here is the output.
11 hours (11 am) = 39,600 seconds since midnight
14 minutes   =   840 seconds
49 seconds   =   49 seconds
     Total   = 40,489 seconds

The decimals are shown because no formatting was added. The Timer () function shows the time to the 7th decimal value.

Timer function explained (continued).

To remove the decimal, the Int() function will be added.

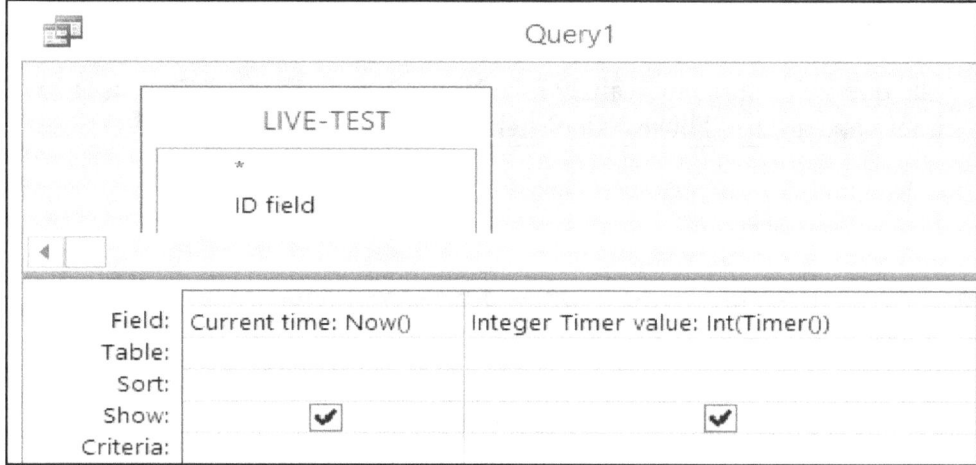

Here is the output rounded to the nearest second (note, this query was ran again so a different time is displayed).

Here is the output.
11 hours (11 am) = 39,600 seconds since midnight
24 minutes   = 1,200 seconds
59 seconds   =   59 seconds
      Total   = 41,099 seconds

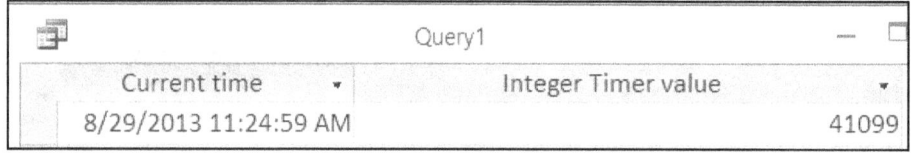

Authors guide (This material is from Access help).

Timer Function

Returns a **Single** representing the number of seconds elapsed since midnight.

Syntax Timer

Remarks In Microsoft Windows the **Timer** function returns fractional portions of a second. On the Macintosh, timer resolution is one second.

Visual Basic for Access (VBA) code.

Authors guide (This material is from Access help).

Second Function Example

This example uses the **Second** function to obtain the second of the minute from a specified time. In the development environment, the time literal is displayed in short time format using the locale settings of your code.

```
Dim MyTime, MySecond
MyTime = #4:35:17 PM#    ' Assign a time.
MySecond = Second(MyTime)    ' MySecond contains 17.
```

Minute Function Example

This example uses the **Minute** function to obtain the minute of the hour from a specified time. In the development environment, the time literal is displayed in short time format using the locale settings of your code.

```
Dim MyTime, MyMinute
MyTime = #4:35:17 PM#    ' Assign a time.
MyMinute = Minute(MyTime)    ' MyMinute contains 35.
```

Hour Function Example

This example uses the **Hour** function to obtain the hour from a specified time. In the development environment, the time literal is displayed in short time format using the locale settings of your code.

```
Dim MyTime, MyHour
MyTime = #4:35:17 PM#    ' Assign a time.
MyHour = Hour(MyTime)    ' MyHour contains 16.
```

Day Function Example

This example uses the Day function to obtain the day of the month from a specified date. In the development environment, the date literal is displayed in short format using the locale settings of your code.

```
Dim MyDate, MyDay
MyDate = #February 12, 1969#    ' Assign a date.
MyDay = Day(MyDate)    ' MyDay contains 12.
```

Visual Basic for Access (VBA) code (continued).
Authors guide (This material is from Access help).

Weekday Function Example
This example uses the **Weekday** function to obtain the day of the week from a specified date.
```
Dim MyDate, MyWeekDay
MyDate = #February 12, 1969#    ' Assign a date.
MyWeekDay = Weekday(MyDate)    ' MyWeekDay contains 4 because
    ' MyDate represents a Wednesday. (Sunday is 1, Monday is 2, ….. Saturday is 7)
```

Month Function Example
This example uses the **Month** function to obtain the month from a specified date. In the development environment, the date literal is displayed in short date format using the locale settings of your code.

```
Dim MyDate, MyMonth
MyDate = #February 12, 1969#    ' Assign a date.
MyMonth = Month(MyDate)    ' MyMonth contains 2.  (January is 1, February is 2…..December is 12)
```

Year Function Example
This example uses the Year function to obtain the year from a specified date. In the development environment, the date literal is displayed in short date format using the locale settings of your code.
```
Dim MyDate, MyYear
MyDate = #February 12, 1969#    ' Assign a date.
MyYear = Year(MyDate)    ' MyYear contains 1969.
```

Timer Function Example
This example uses the Timer function to pause the application. The example also uses DoEvents to yield to other processes during the pause. This is programing and you may never use this (but you could).

```
Dim PauseTime, Start, Finish, TotalTime
If (MsgBox("Press Yes to pause for 5 seconds", 4)) = vbYes Then
    PauseTime = 5    ' Set duration.
    Start = Timer    ' Set start time.
    Do While Timer < Start + PauseTime
        DoEvents    ' Yield to other processes.
    Loop
    Finish = Timer    ' Set end time.
    TotalTime = Finish - Start    ' Calculate total time.
    MsgBox "Paused for " & TotalTime & " seconds"
Else
    End
End If
```

Chapter 5 - Text functions – Update queries.

Text (Character) functions that Update values are explained in this chapter. These functions are very powerful in changing the text associated with database fields. These same functions can be used on Forms and Reports as well as with the queries, which are being used to illustrate their functionality. Use the explanation in chapter 2 related to how to get to the Expression Builder for Text functions. These functions are explained in chapter 2, and again in 8.

Function Name	Function format	Function use – why use it?
Left (with Like)	Left(field, length)	To retrieve a set number of characters from the left side of a field.
Right (with Like)	Right(field, length)	To retrieve a set number of characters from the right side of a field.
Mid (see Replace)	Mid(field, start position, length)	To retrieve a set number of characters starting from a position in a field.
Len	Len(field)	Used to determine how long a field is.
InStr	InStr(field, ",")	Used to determine where a character string is located in a field or character string.
LTrim	LTrim(field)	Removes leading spaces from a field.
RTrim	RTrim(field)	Removes ending spaces from a field.
Trim	Trim(field)	Removes leading or ending spaces from a field.
LCase	LCase(field)	Changes all uppercase characters to lowercase. Does not affect any none letters.
UCase	UCase(field)	Changes all lowercase characters to uppercase. Does not affect any none letters.
Replace	Replace(field, "7","8")	Replaces one character string with another character string. In this example it replaces 7 with 8 in the field called field.

Functioning with Access – 2013
Chapter 5 – Text functions – Update queries

The Left function explained.

The 1st step is to create a new Update query. Go to the Query part of Access, create a new query, and insert the LIVE-TEST table. Below is the current data for the [Last Name], [First Name] and [Street-Address] fields. We desire to change the [Street-address] of anyone who has the Left 3 characters of their last name equal to 'Law' (the Lawrence family moved in this example).

The original data in the LIVE-TEST table

Last Name	First Name	Street-address
Cederoth	Katherine	141 Grant
Yeaoman	Mike	322 Sheffield
Yeaoman	Shirley	1112 Canada
Dionne	Tom	Route 4, 277 West
Lawrence	Anderson	PO box 12A79, slot 7
Lawrence	Motherbee	PO box 12A79, slot 8
Lawrence	Fatherbee	PO box 12A79, slot 9
Lawrence	Sisterbee	PO box 12A79, slot 10
Deenoyer	Tony	1456 Bad Ax

Once you create a new query, select the *Update* for Query type

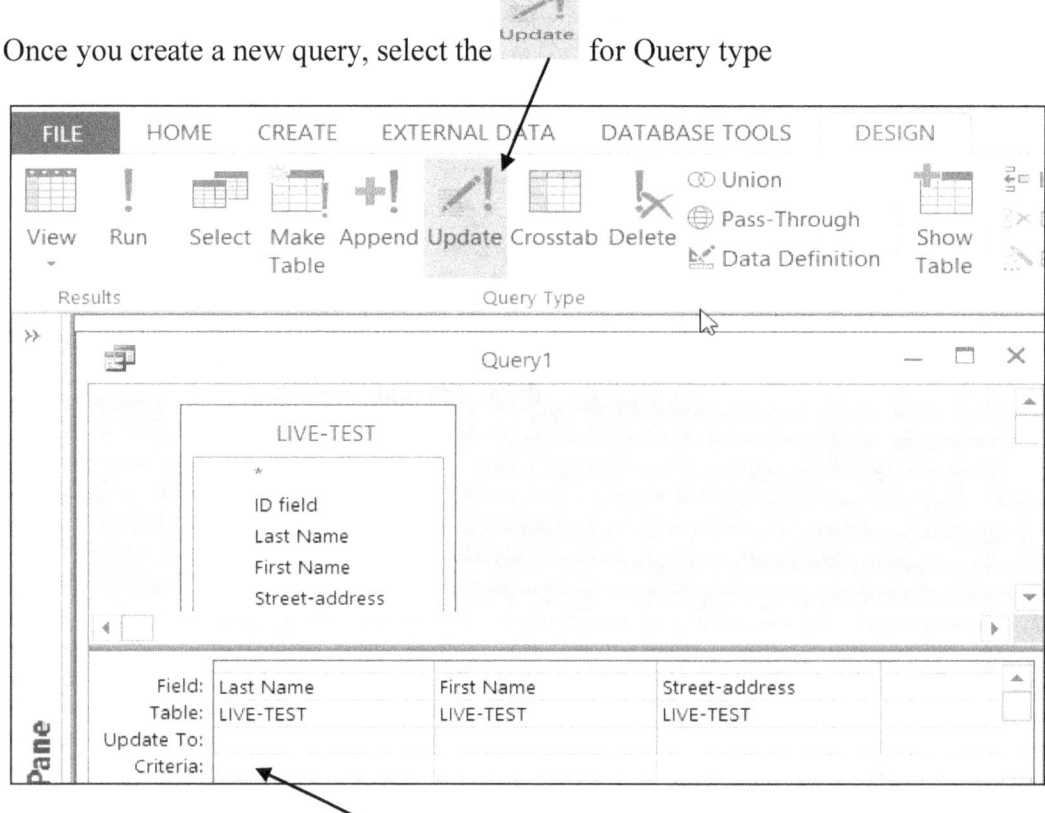

This will provide you with a new Criteria row in your query.

Functioning with Access – 2013
Chapter 5 – Text functions – Update queries

Using the following Criteria:
Like (Left([Enter first 3 characters of Last Name to change Street-address],3)) & "*"
A prompt will ask the user for the first 3 characters of the [Last Name].
You need to include 'Like' in the criteria along with an asterisk (*).

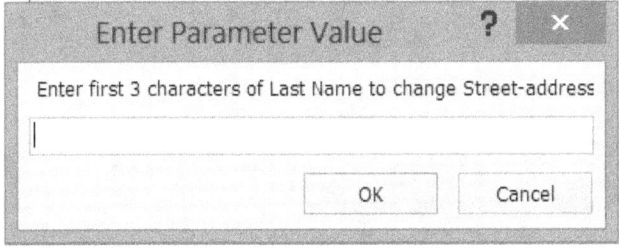

Notice a new **Update To** row; this is where we enter the new values for our selected records. In the Update To row, a value '1234 Peachgrove' has been inserted.

This prompt is called a **Parameter Query** – the user is entering a value (query parameter).

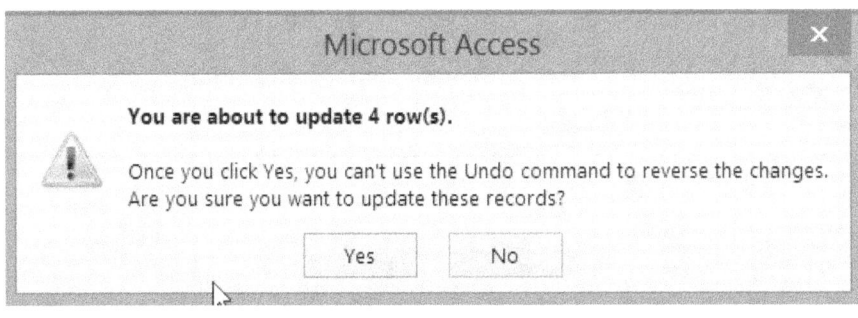

Type in **Law**, and press the OK button.

This message appears to insure you want to change the records. It found 4 that met the criteria.

Press the [Yes] button.

- 89 -

Here is the output; the four records for the Lawrence family have been changed.

ID field	Last Name	First Name	Street-address
1	Cederoth	Katherine	141 Grant
2	Yeaoman	Mike	322 Sheffield
3	Yeaoman	Shirley	1112 Canada
4	Dionne	Tom	Route 4, 277 West
5	Lawrence	Anderson	1234 Peachgrove
6	Lawrence	Motherbee	1234 Peachgrove
7	Lawrence	Fatherbee	1234 Peachgrove
8	Lawrence	Sisterbee	1234 Peachgrove
9	Deenoyer	Tony	1456 Bad Ax

Try this function with different values for length until you feel comfortable.
To refresh the LIVE-TEST table, run the **qry-Make-LIVE-TEST** query and answer the prompts to delete the table and make the new table. This is shown below and on the following page (this was also covered in Chapter 1).

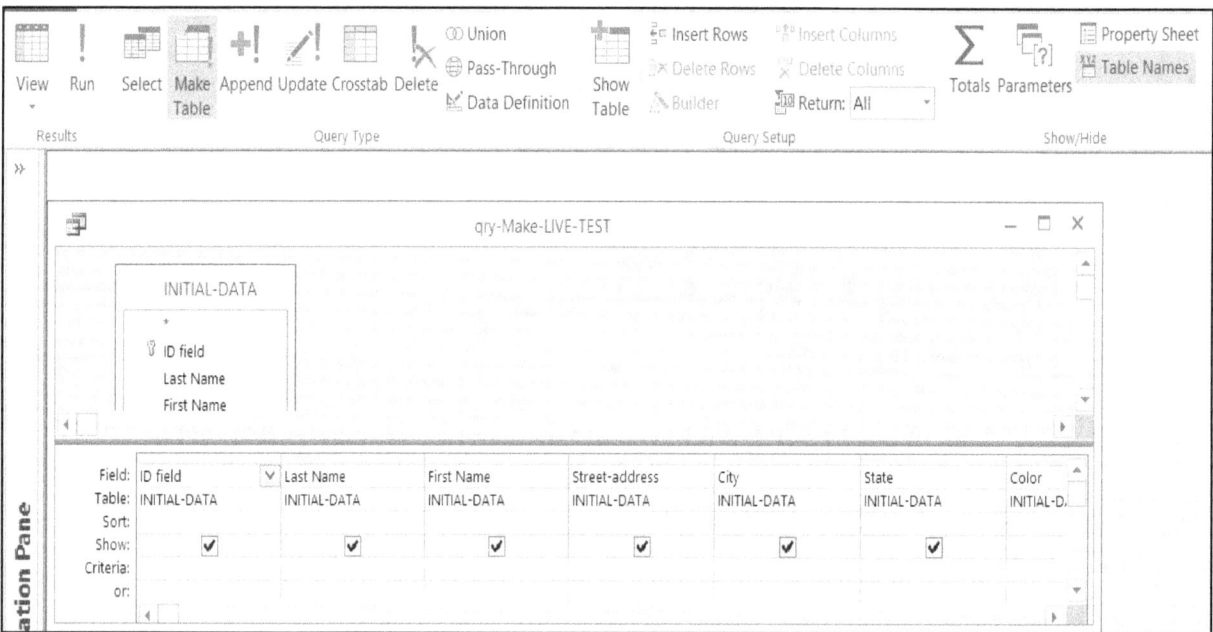

This message appears when you run the query.

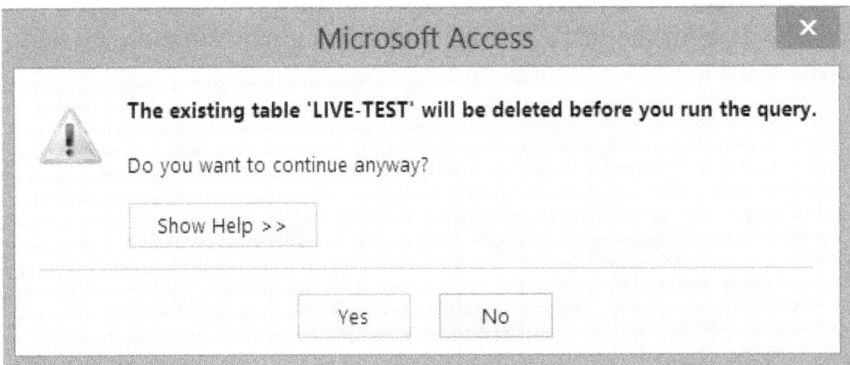

The Make table query is used to remove the previous table where the values are changed.

This will make a new table with the same name with the original data.

Press the [Yes] button above to delete the table

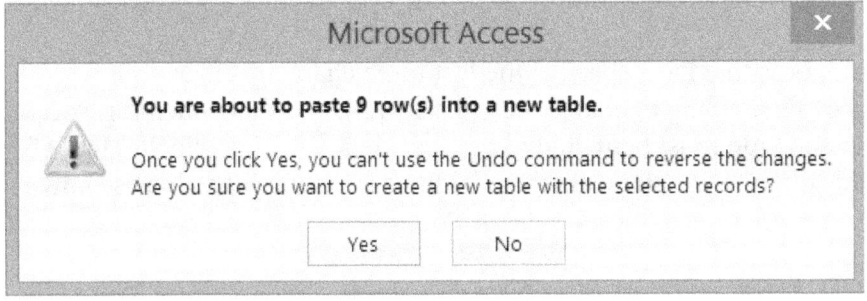

The LIVE-TEST table is a workspace table. We make changes to it, delete it, and recreate it and do more testing on its data.

Click the [Yes] button above to complete the process.

Remember as you do this query, go look at the SQL while you are in design mode. Looking at the SQL may give you another perspective of how to use Access queries.

The Right function explained.

The 1st step is to create a new Update query (or modify the query used for the Left function). In this query, the individuals who have 'bee' as the last 3 characters of their First Name are going to have it changed to 'buzz'.

Here is the original data.

ID field	Last Name	First Name
1	Cederoth	Katherine
2	Yeaoman	Mike
3	Yeaoman	Shirley
4	Dionne	Tom
5	Lawrence	Anderson
6	Lawrence	Motherbee
7	Lawrence	Fatherbee
8	Lawrence	Sisterbee
9	Deenoyer	Tony

Three records will be changed (#6, 7, 8).

The criteria to select only the records that have 'bee' as the last three characters is as follows: Right([Enter last 3 characters of First Name to change bee to buzz],3), and then when ran you must type in 'bee'. The 'Like' function must be included because there are characters to the left of the 'bee'. Practice doing this query and update another field to some practice value as shown below.

Like ("*" & Right([Enter last 3 characters of First Name to change bee to buzz],3))

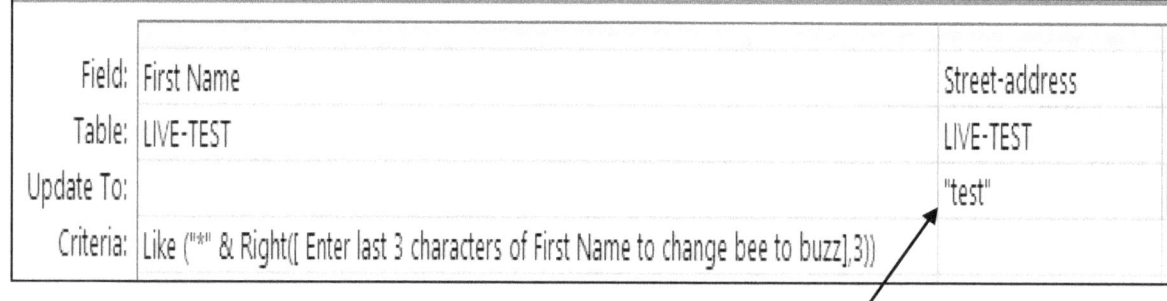

A practice value of 'test' is being inserted into the [Street-address] field when the query is satisfied.

Once the correct records are being updated, run the query (**qry-Make-LIVE-TEST**) to repopulate the data. This repopulating of data will remove all experimental data.

Functioning with Access – 2013
Chapter 5 – Text functions – Update queries

Now make the formula to update just the records that are needed to be changed. Every record that is being updated has different names, so the formula to update the name becomes complicated.

The formula is as follows: **Left([First Name],(Len([First Name])-3)) & "buzz"**.

Field:	First Name
Table:	LIVE-TEST
Update To:	Left([First Name],(Len([First Name])-3)) & "buzz"
Criteria:	Like ("*" & Right([Enter last 3 characters of First Name to change bee to buzz],3))
or:	

To understand this formula, start from the middle and work out.

From the length of the First Name field **(Len([First Name])**, subtract 3. This removed the rightmost 3 characters. This value (call it LL) will be the number of characters of the First Name excluding 'bee'. This value (LL) is sent to the Left function.

Left([First Name], LL) returns the number of characters from [First Name] (after removing 3 characters). To this part of the [First Name] we add the text 'buzz'.

Run the query, it will prompt you (this is again a Parameter query).

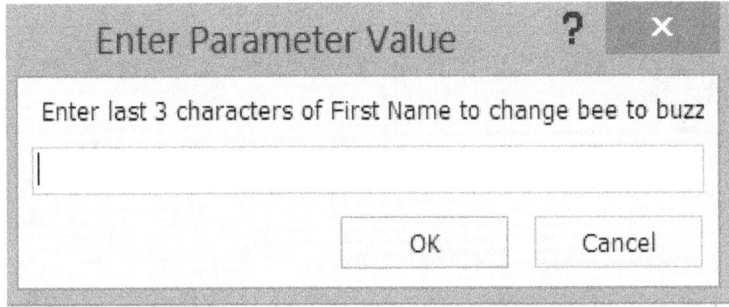

As you are prompted for input; type in 'bee'.

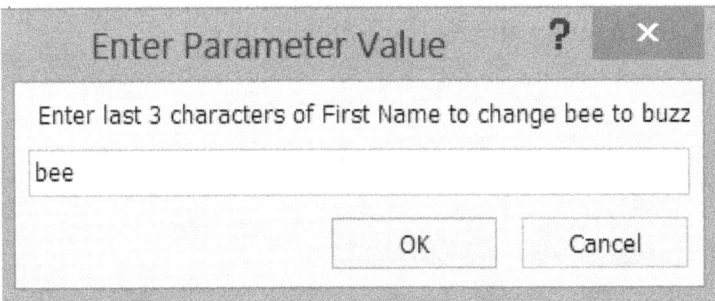

You will be prompted to confirm these changed to the records. Select the 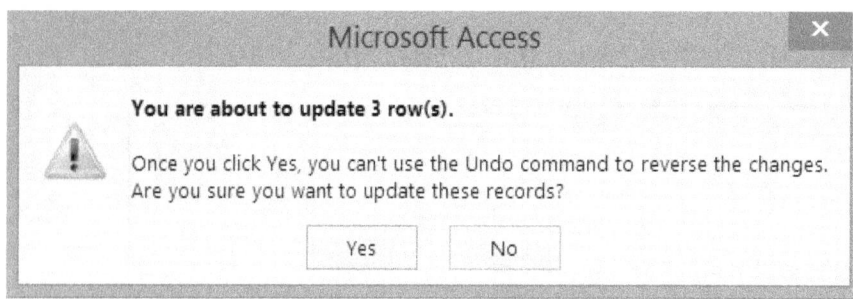 button.

Below is the updated information in the table. No more 'bee', all are changed to 'buzz'.

ID field	Last Name	First Name
1	Cederoth	Katherine
2	Yeaoman	Mike
3	Yeaoman	Shirley
4	Dionne	Tom
5	Lawrence	Anderson
6	Lawrence	Motherbuzz
7	Lawrence	Fatherbuzz
8	Lawrence	Sisterbuzz
9	Deenoyer	Tony

Records #6, 7 and 8 are changed.

Nothing about this query is easy, but working it step-by-step will enable you to experiment with many functions. Having the **qry-Make-LIVE-TEST** query allows you to 'UNDO' changes you have made to your data.

Try this function with different values for length until you feel comfortable.

The MID function explained (with errors in logic).

The MID function was used earlier in the book. It brings back a substring of text from a larger string of text. This should be easily incorporated with a prompt to allow a user to find instances of a text string (in criteria) and replace them.

In the below table, the PO box value will be changed for a few individuals. Here is the original data and in the Street Address field, four records have a PO box of '12A79'. This value needs to be changed to '12B79'.

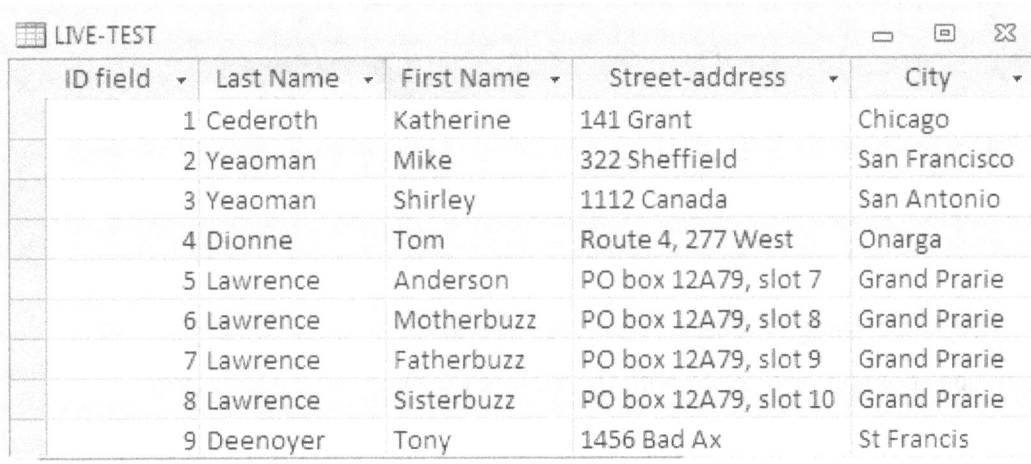

The Mid function needs to have the start position and the length. The start position is 8 and the length is 5.

Create a Select query to test selecting unique records that have '12A79'.
Here is the formula: **Mid([Enter the bad PO Box value - 5 characters],8,5).**

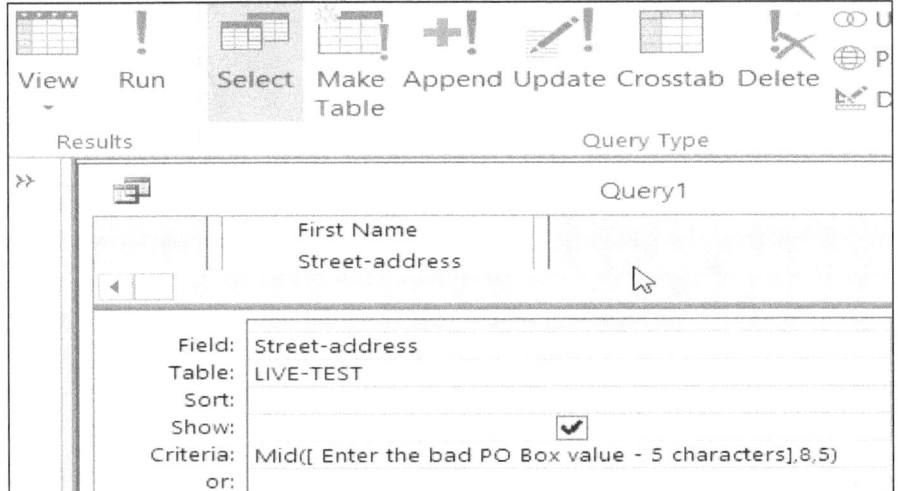

Following is the prompt to enter the characters to fulfill the search criteria.

Functioning with Access – 2013
Chapter 5 – Text functions – Update queries

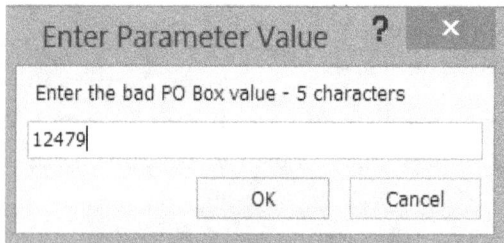

This does not work because there are leading characters and following characters; changes to the formula are made below.

Like ("*" & (Mid([Enter the bad PO Box value - 5 characters],8,5) & "*").

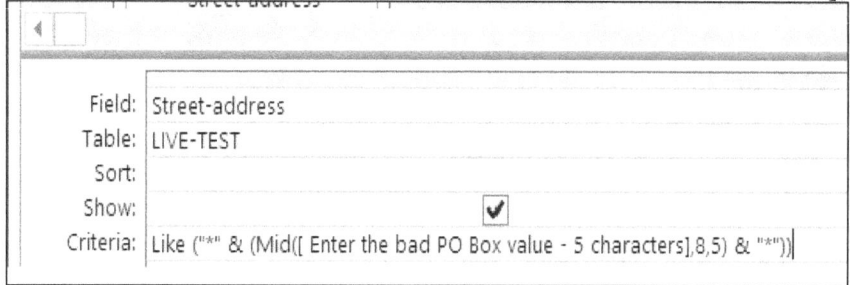

Why this does not work. Access has 2 wildcards '*' in the query, so all text is returned. The Mid function does not appear to work with the same logic that I have used before.

Reading the information from Access Help, it seems logical that the MID function should find and return the records that have '12A79' in positions 8 to 12. However, it does not.

A different function will have to be used to find and replace a character string inside of a larger character string. The Mid function does not seem to work with prompts for values.

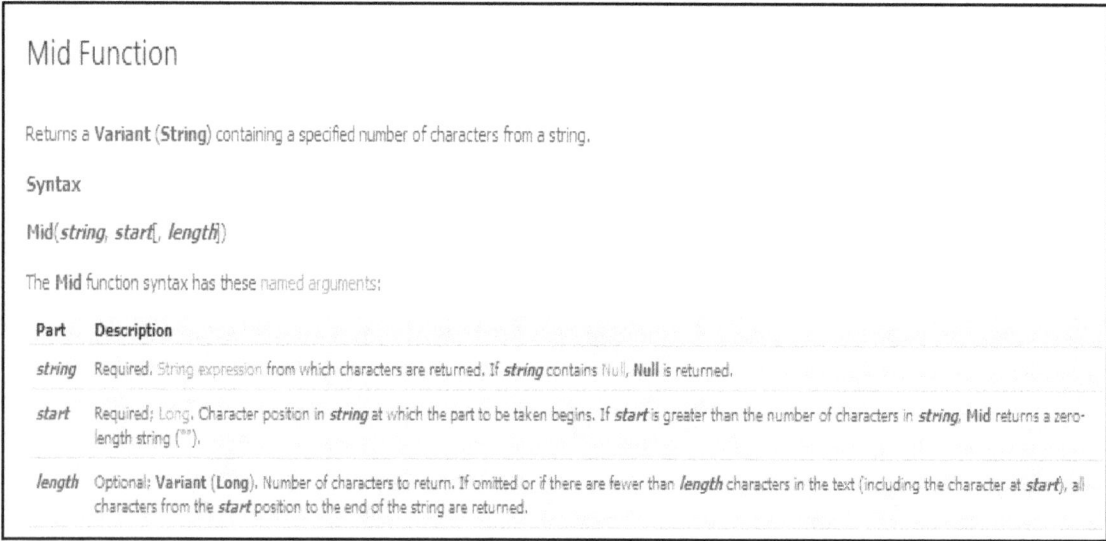

- 96 -

A formula that will find the specific records is this: **Like ("*" & "12A79" & "*")**.

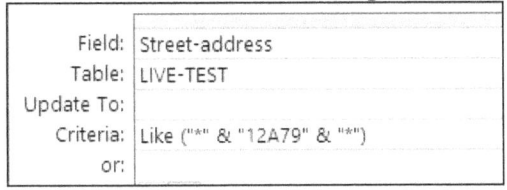

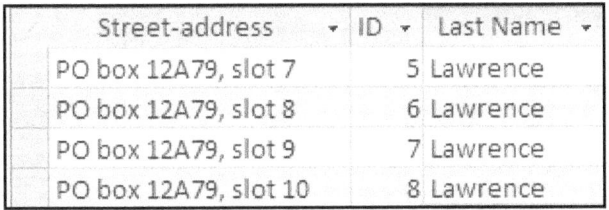

The four records are found. So Access does not return the 5 characters from the prompt as expected. Now that the a formula is found to retrieve the specific records, use the Replace function to update the records.

The Replace function explained.

The Replace function is used, the formula is as follows:
Update To: **Replace([Street-address],"12A79","12B79")**.
The Criteria is: **Like ("*" & "12A79" & "*")**.

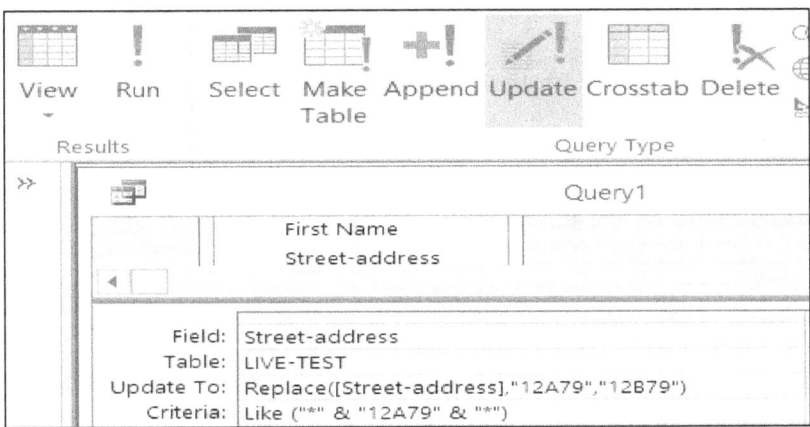

Here is the prompt

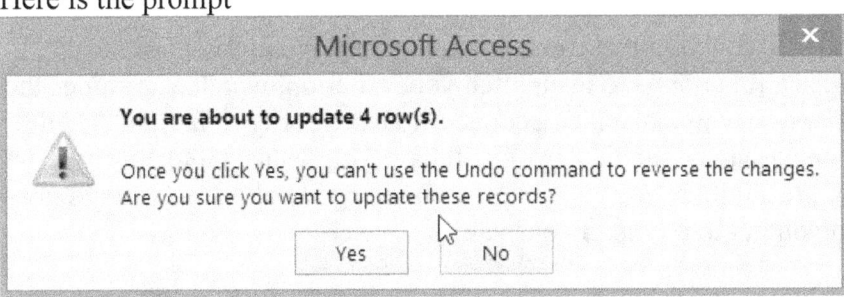

Select the [Yes] button and the four records are changed.

ID field	Last Name	First Name	Street-address	City
1	Cederoth	Katherine	141 Grant	Chicago
2	Yeaoman	Mike	322 Sheffield	San Francisco
3	Yeaoman	Shirley	1112 Canada	San Antonio
4	Dionne	Tom	Route 4, 27 West	Onarga
5	Lawrence	Anderson	PO box 12B79, slot 7	Grand Prarie
6	Lawrence	Motherbuzz	PO box 12B79, slot 8	Grand Prarie
7	Lawrence	Fatherbuzz	PO box 12B79, slot 9	Grand Prarie
8	Lawrence	Sisterbuzz	PO box 12B79, slot 10	Grand Prarie
9	Deenoyer	Tony	1456 Bad Ax	St Francis

Authors guide (This material is from Access help).

The Replace Function (also shown in Chapter 2).

Description Returns a string in which a specified substring has been replaced with another substring a specified number of times.

Syntax Replace(*expression*, *find*, *replace*[, *start*[, *count*[, *compare*]]])
The Replace function syntax has these named arguments:

Part	Description
expression	Required. String expression containing substring to replace.
find	Required. Substring being searched for.
replace	Required. Replacement substring.
start	Optional. Position within *expression* where substring search is to begin. If omitted, 1 is assumed.
count	Optional. Number of substring substitutions to perform. If omitted, the default value is –1, which means make all possible substitutions.
compare	Optional. Numeric value indicating the kind of comparison to use when evaluating substrings. See Settings section for values.

The Replace function is a wonderful function that can be used in many situations. The most important part of using the Replace function is to insure that your criterion, which determines the records changed, is correct. Always try to make a Select query to test your criteria first. Then make an Update query to implement your change. If you still have your Make table query then even if you do not follow these precautions, you can restore your original values. If you did not make a Make table query, then you get to retype in your values.

The Len function explained.

How many characters is the data in a field? The task is to determine if the number of characters in one field is a value, and then update some field. In the example below, if the [First Name] is over 8 characters, then the [Street-address] will be changed to 'Apartment'.

The formula is: **Len([First Name])>"8"**.

Here is the query

Field:	Street-address
Table:	LIVE-TEST
Update To:	"Apartment"
Criteria:	Len([First Name]) > "8"

Here is the prompt:

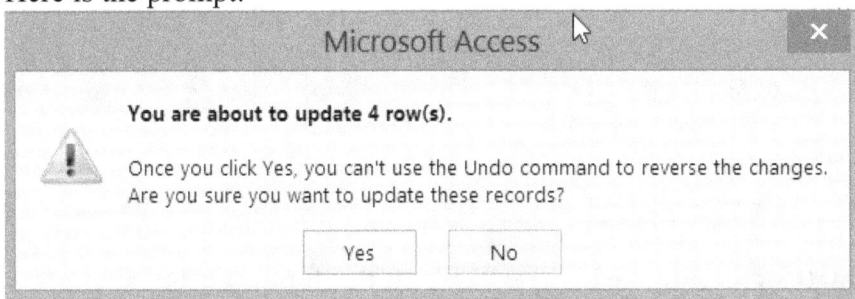

Here is the output.

ID field	Last Name	First Name	Street-address
1	Cederoth	Katherine	Apartment
2	Yeaoman	Mike	322 Sheffield
3	Yeaoman	Shirley	1112 Canada
4	Dionne	Tom	Route 4, 277 West
5	Lawrence	Anderson	PO box 12A79, slot 7
6	Lawrence	Motherbee	Apartment
7	Lawrence	Fatherbee	Apartment
8	Lawrence	Sisterbee	Apartment
9	Deenoyer	Tony	1456 Bad Ax

The four records where the [First Name] is over 8 characters now have a [Street-address] of 'Apartment'.

The InStr function explained.

The position of a character inside of a longer character is often needed. If you are working with data that has a common character in it (like a comma or a space or a dash), you can find out what position the character is occupying. This has been useful in working with names when the [Last Name] is followed by a comma and a space, then the [First Name].

Use the **InStr** function to find out the position of the comma in the [Street-address] field. If the position is a certain value (13 in example below), then the [Street-address] value changes to 'Lives at home'. Here is the initial data:

ID field	Last Name	First Name	Street-address
1	Cederoth	Katherine	141 Grant
2	Yeaoman	Mike	322 Sheffield
3	Yeaoman	Shirley	1112 Canada
4	Dionne	Tom	Route 4, 277 West
5	Lawrence	Anderson	PO box 12A79, slot 7
6	Lawrence	Motherbee	PO box 12A79, slot 8
7	Lawrence	Fatherbee	PO box 12A79, slot 9
8	Lawrence	Sisterbee	PO box 12A79, slot 10
9	Deenoyer	Tony	1456 Bad Ax

The formula is as follows: **InStr([Street-address],",") = "13"**. If this formula is found to be true for a record, the [Street-address] will be changed to 'Lives at home".

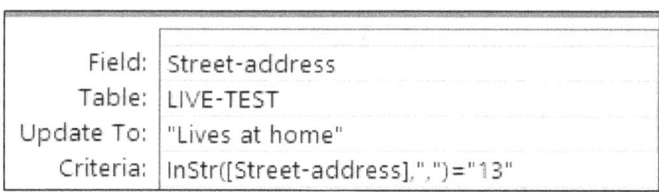

When ran, this message displays, press the Yes button.

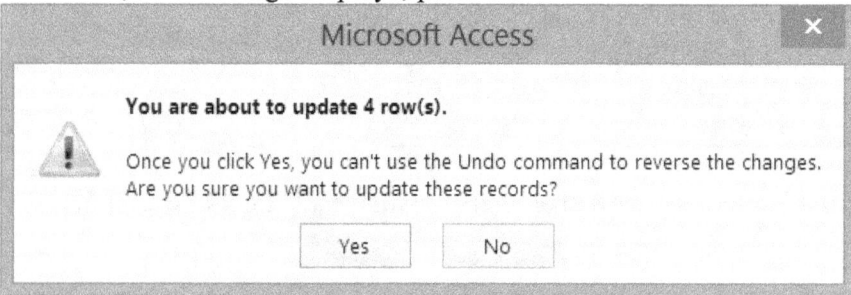

Functioning with Access – 2013
Chapter 5 – Text functions – Update queries

The new data is shown in the table as shown below.

ID field	Last Name	First Name	Street-address
1	Cederoth	Katherine	141 Grant
2	Yeaoman	Mike	322 Sheffield
3	Yeaoman	Shirley	1112 Canada
4	Dionne	Tom	Route 4, 277 West
5	Lawrence	Anderson	Lives at home
6	Lawrence	Motherbee	Lives at home
7	Lawrence	Fatherbee	Lives at home
8	Lawrence	Sisterbee	Lives at home
9	Deenoyer	Tony	1456 Bad Ax

Using the InStr function to test the value of data in a larger string can be useful if you have consistent data. If in a long character string the 25th character is a designator for a department, using InStr will help you test the value of that character. The Update query then can change values based upon the InStr functions finding correct values.

When doing Update queries, first run the query by using a Select query to insure that the records you are expecting to change are brought back with your criteria. If you run the query and it retrieves records that are not the ones you intended to change then you can rework your selection criteria until it selects the proper records.

LTrim, RTrim, and Trim Functions explained with problems.

LTrim function is used to remove leading spaces in a field. The RTrim function is used to remove ending spaces. **The [Last Name] and [First Name] fields were modified to have leading and ending spaces.** Access removes the ending space but leaves the leading spaces on [Last Name] and [First Name] fields as shown below.

Now, make a query to join the two fields together. This is a Select query.
The formula is: **Total Name: [First Name] & " " & [Last Name].**
NOTE: Joining fields together is called 'Concatenation'.

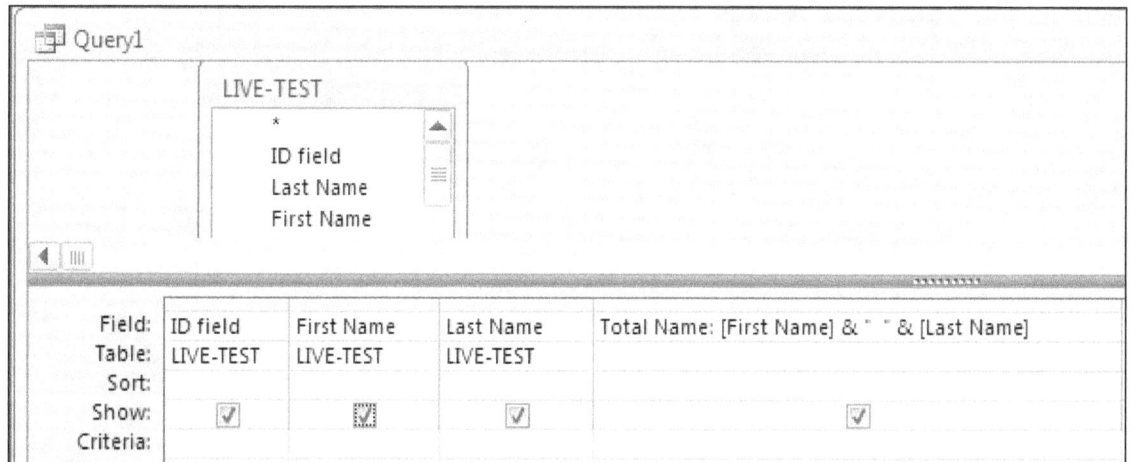

The output will include the leading spaces.

This formula should only place 2 spaces between the [First Name] and [Last Name]. The data has leading spaces, which must be removed as seen in the output that follows.

On the next page is the output of not removing the spaces BEFORE you add the fields together.

Functioning with Access – 2013
Chapter 5 – Text functions – Update queries

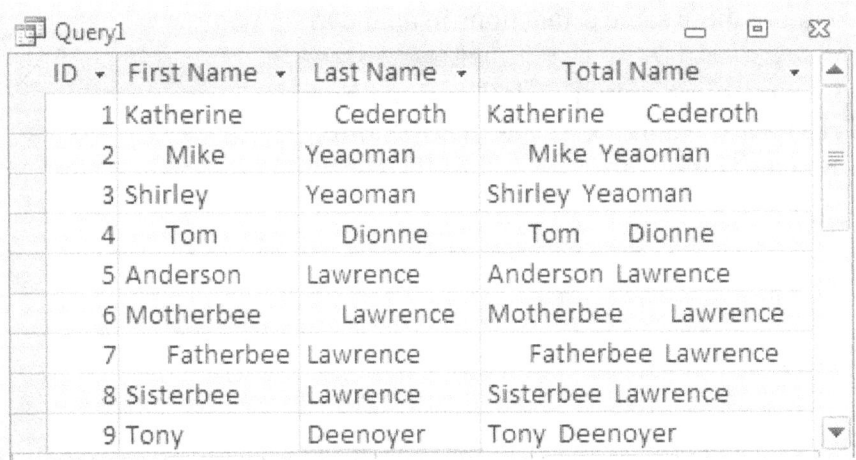

In an attempt to remove the leading spaces in the individual fields, three functions will be used: LTrim, Trim and RTrim. A query will be made using all three functions in different columns. The formulas are:

Total Name-LTrim: LTrim([First Name]) & " " & LTrim([Last Name])
Total Name-Trim: Trim([First Name]) & " " & Trim([Last Name])
Total Name-RTrim: RTrim([First Name]) & " " & RTrim([Last Name]).

Field:	ID field	First Name	Last Name	Total Name-LTrim: LTrim([First N	Total Name-Trim: Trim([First I	Total Name-RTrim: RTrim([First Name]
Table:	LIVE-TEST	LIVE-TEST	LIVE-TEST			
Sort:						
Show:	✓	✓	✓	✓	✓	✓
Criteria:						

This is what returns when the query is ran.

ID	First Name	Last Name	Total Name-LTrim	Total Name-Trim	Total Name-RTrim
1	Katherine	Cederoth	Katherine Cederoth	Katherine Cederoth	Katherine Cederoth
2	Mike	Yeaoman	Mike Yeaoman	Mike Yeaoman	Mike Yeaoman
3	Shirley	Yeaoman	Shirley Yeaoman	Shirley Yeaoman	Shirley Yeaoman
4	Tom	Dionne	Tom Dionne	Tom Dionne	Tom Dionne
5	Anderson	Lawrence	Anderson Lawrence	Anderson Lawrence	Anderson Lawrence
6	Motherbee	Lawrence	Motherbee Lawrence	Motherbee Lawrence	Motherbee Lawrence
7	Fatherbee	Lawrence	Fatherbee Lawrence	Fatherbee Lawrence	Fatherbee Lawrence
8	Sisterbee	Lawrence	Sisterbee Lawrence	Sisterbee Lawrence	Sisterbee Lawrence
9	Tony	Deenoyer	Tony Deenoyer	Tony Deenoyer	Tony Deenoyer

The LTrim and the Trim function removed the leading spaces, the RTrim did not.

The RTrim function removes spaces at the end of a field.

Now the formulas are changed to use these same 3 functions in an incorrect way. The incorrect formulas are:

Total Name-LTrim: LTrim([First Name] & " " & [Last Name])
Total Name-Trim: Trim([First Name] & " " & [Last Name])
Total Name-RTrim: RTrim([First Name] & " " & [Last Name]).

Field:	ID field	First Name	Last Name	Total Name-LTrim: LTrim([First N	Total Name-Trim: Trim([First I	Total Name-RTrim: RTrim([First Name]
Table:	LIVE-TEST	LIVE-TEST	LIVE-TEST			
Sort:						
Show:	✓	✓	✓	✓	✓	✓
Criteria:						

The fields are concatenated together, and then spaces are removed. The output is shown below.

ID	First Name	Last Name	Total Name-LTrim	Total Name-Trim	Total Name-RTrim
1	Katherine	Cederoth	Katherine Cederoth	Katherine Cederoth	Katherine Cederoth
2	Mike	Yeaoman	Mike Yeaoman	Mike Yeaoman	Mike Yeaoman
3	Shirley	Yeaoman	Shirley Yeaoman	Shirley Yeaoman	Shirley Yeaoman
4	Tom	Dionne	Tom Dionne	Tom Dionne	Tom Dionne
5	Anderson	Lawrence	Anderson Lawrence	Anderson Lawrence	Anderson Lawrence
6	Motherbee	Lawrence	Motherbee Lawrence	Motherbee Lawrence	Motherbee Lawrence
7	Fatherbee	Lawrence	Fatherbee Lawrence	Fatherbee Lawrence	Fatherbee Lawrence
8	Sisterbee	Lawrence	Sisterbee Lawrence	Sisterbee Lawrence	Sisterbee Lawrence
9	Tony	Deenoyer	Tony Deenoyer	Tony Deenoyer	Tony Deenoyer

This illustrates that spaces on the [Last Name] and [First Name] fields have to be removed before the fields are joined.

The problem with using this concatenation is the spaces are now in the middle of the field. The spaces can be removed by hand, or by fixing the data before you join the fields together. In the above example, a space is needed between the First and Last Name. Having two or three spaces is not desired and a technique to remove them follows.

Manipulation of the text in a field by using the LTrim, Trim or RTrim functions can save you time if you have large quantities of data that has leading or ending spaces.

Another function that may be easier to understand and use is the Replace function. If you have spaces inside of a text string and need to remove them, the Replace function can often do the work that you need.

For Last Name: **Replace([Last Name]," ","")** (this replace 3 spaces with 0).
For First Name: **Replace([First Name]," ","")** (this replace 3 spaces with 0).

Field:	Street-address	First Name	Last Name
Table:	LIVE-TEST	LIVE-TEST	LIVE-TEST
Update To:		Replace([First Name]," ","")	Replace([Last Name]," ","")

Functioning with Access – 2013
Chapter 5 – Text functions – Update queries

Here is the data. 3 spaces were added to the [First Name] and [Last Name] fields of 3 records (2, 4 and 9).

The Replace function is being used to replace any occurrence of three spaces "   " or with no spaces "". This can be applied to both fields in the same query. When this is run, this message appears:

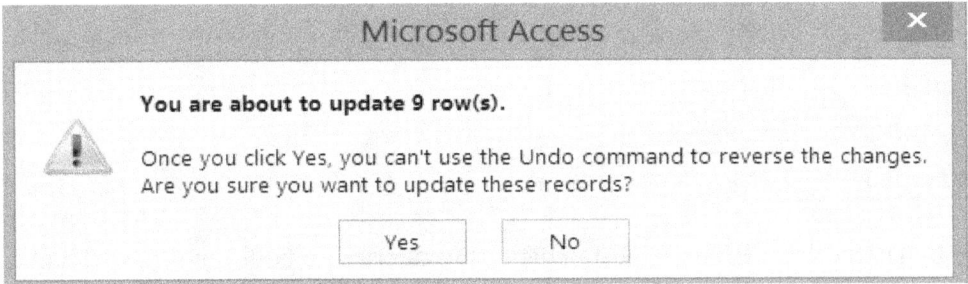

This query will examine all of the records and will only modify those that have 3 spaces "   ". This could take a long time if you have thousands of records. I did not run this query. To make this more efficient, add a limiting criterion (shown on following pages). Let's limit the records changed to those with 3 spaces. Using the InStr function can help find the records that are to be changed.

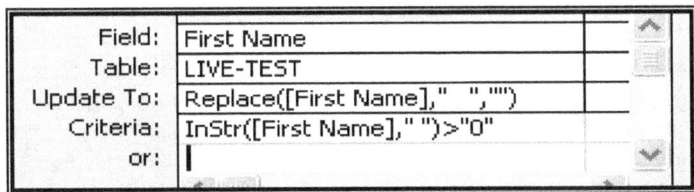

Above a criteria is used **(InStr([First Name]," ")>"0")** to test if in the [First Name] field there is a space " ". If there is a space then its position will be greater than 0.

- 105 -

Three records are found, which is what was expected.

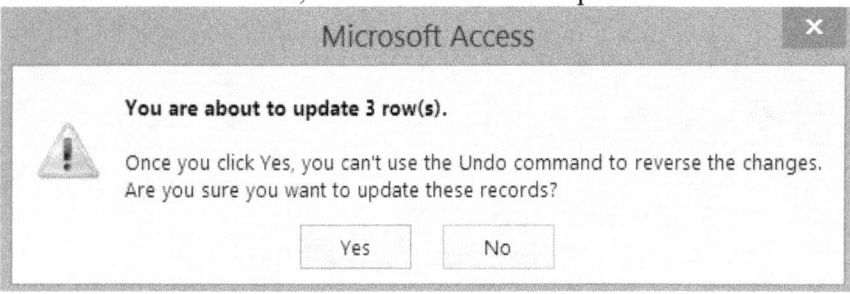

Press the [Yes] button and the selected records will be updated.

```
LIVE-STORAGE
ID field   Last Name   First Name
1          Cederoth    Katherine
2          Yeaoman     Mike
3          Yeaoman     Shirley
4          Dionne      Tom
5          Lawrence    Anderson
6          Lawrence    Motherbee
7          Lawrence    Fatherbee
8          Lawrence    Sisterbee
9          Deenoyer    Tony
```

The three records are updated (Note: When making changes to queries an additional record had a leading space added to it. This query found the leading space in the [First Name] field.

Using the InStr function to find the existence of a text string (or just a letter or letters) in a larger string can be very useful. It returns a number, greater than zero, if it finds the text string. This logic can then be placed in the criteria for the query to make changes only to the records that meet the criteria.

UCase() function.

Next, a function that changes the case of the characters in a field is illustrated. First the [Last Name] will be changed to all Uppercase, then it will be changed to all Lowercase. The code is:
UCase([Last Name]).

```
Field:       Last Name
Table:       LIVE-TEST
Update To:   UCase([Last Name])
Criteria:
```

All rows will be changed.

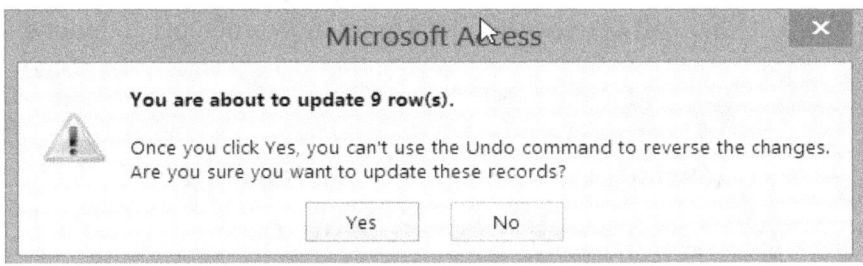

Press the Yes button. Here is the updated table.

ID field	Last Name	First Name
1	CEDEROTH	Katherine
2	YEAOMAN	Mike
3	YEAOMAN	Shirley
4	DIONNE	Tom
5	LAWRENCE	Anderson
6	LAWRENCE	Motherbee
7	LAWRENCE	Fatherbee
8	LAWRENCE	Sisterbee
9	DEENOYER	Tony

LCase() function.

Here is the query to make [Last Name] all Lowercase: **LCase([Last Name])**.

Field:	Last Name
Table:	LIVE-TEST
Update To:	LCase([Last Name])

After answering the prompt, the [Last Name] values are altered as shown below.

ID field	Last Name	First Name
1	cederoth	Katherine
2	yeaoman	Mike
3	yeaoman	Shirley
4	dionne	Tom
5	lawrence	Anderson
6	lawrence	Motherbee
7	lawrence	Fatherbee
8	lawrence	Sisterbee
9	deenoyer	Tony

Functioning with Access – 2013
Chapter 5 – Text functions – Update queries

To make the [Last Name] values have the 1st character uppercase and the remaining lowercase, functions will have to be combined. Other software have an InitUpper or WordUpper functions, Access does not.

The formula is as follows:
UCase(Left([Last Name],1)) & LCase(Right([Last Name],(Len([Last Name])-1))).

Field:	Last Name
Table:	LIVE-TEST
Update To:	UCase(Left([Last Name],1)) & LCase(Right([Last Name],(Len([Last Name])-1)))
Criteria:	

Here is the data updated after running the Update query and answering the prompt.

LIVE-TEST

ID field	Last Name	First Name
1	Cederoth	Katherine
2	Yeaoman	Mike
3	Yeaoman	Shirley
4	Dionne	Tom
5	Lawrence	Anderson
6	Lawrence	Motherbee
7	Lawrence	Fatherbee
8	Lawrence	Sisterbee
9	Deenoyer	Tony

This formula works. Here is an explanation.
UCase(Left([Last Name],1)) --- this takes the Leftmost character and makes it uppercase.
(Len([Last Name])-1)) --- this calculates the length of the [Last Name] field and subtracts 1. This value is then used by the Right function **(Right([Last Name],(Len([Last Name])-1)))** to make the remaining characters all lowercase.
This is a very hard formula, but illustrates why this book was made.

Using these Case formulas, will help you to format data that has case entry variations or enable you to control the presentation of data to others.

Chapter 6 - Math functions – Update queries.

Math functions that can update values are explained in this chapter. Mathematical operations are also shown such as multiply, divide, add or subtract. These same functions/operations can be used on Forms and Reports. These functions are explained in chapter 3, and again in 9.

Function Name	Function format	Function use – why use it?
Round	Round(field, #-of-decimals).	This function will round the field up to the next value depending upon the # of decimals you provided
Fix	Fix([field name]))	This function will return the Integer value of a field. The decimals will be removed. If you have a negative number (-8.4) this will return (-8). This is the main difference between Fix and Int.
Int	Int([field name]))	This function will return the Integer value of a field. The decimals will be removed. If you have a negative number (-8.4) this will return (-9). This is the main difference between Fix and Int.
Multiply, Divide, Add, Subtract		These are not functions, but are operations used to illustrate the software capabilities. Also, using divide will provide decimals, which I will remove by using the three functions that follow.

The following functions are covered in Chapter 9

Function Name	Function format	Function use – why use it?
Average	Avg([field name])	To place the average of a set of values into another field/table.
Count	Count([field name])	To place a Count of a set of values into another field/table.
Max	Max([field name])	To place the Maximum of a set of values into another field/table.
Min	Min([field name])	To place the Minimum of a set of values into another field/table.
Sum	Sum([field name])	To place the Sum of a set of values into another field/table.

An explanation of the Expression Builder is shown in other chapters.

Round, Fix, Int function examples.

The format of the Round function is **Round(field, #-of-decimals).**
This functions, when placed around a number field will allow you to create queries, which have set number of decimal places in the output. In the database, the costs of the books include decimals for cents. The following queries will remove the decimal part of the field.
Here is the table with limited columns shown

ID field	Last Name	First Name	# of Books	Cost of Books
1	Cederoth	Katherine	768	$56,788.22
2	Yeaoman	Mike	0	$0.00
3	Yeaoman	Shirley	500	$7,788.76
4	Dionne	Tom	35	$678.30
5	Lawrence	Anderson	4	$22.30
6	Lawrence	Motherbee	55	$5,555.55
7	Lawrence	Fatherbee	44	$4,444.44
8	Lawrence	Sisterbee	7	$77.77
9	Deenoyer	Tony	34	$456.44

This formula removes the decimals values: **(Round([Cost of Books])).**

Below the [Cost of Books] is rounded and has 0 in the cent columns. It still shows the cents.

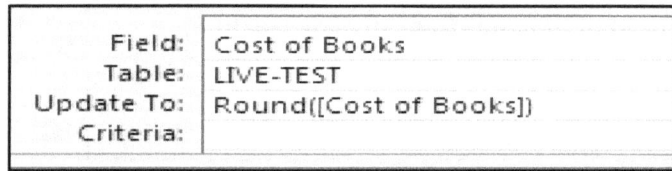

The query executes and the following prompt appears.

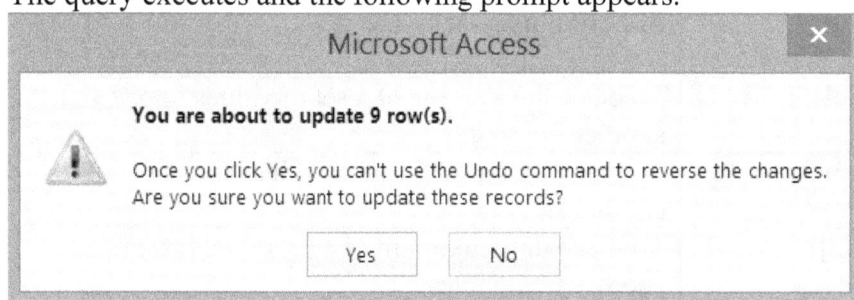

Select the [Yes] button.

Functioning with Access – 2013
Chapter 6 – Math functions – Update queries

The data is updated in the table as shown below.

ID field	Last Name	First Name	# of Books	Cost of Book
1	Cederoth	Katherine	768	$56,788.00
2	Yeaoman	Mike	0	$0.00
3	Yeaoman	Shirley	500	$7,789.00
4	Dionne	Tom	35	$678.00
5	Lawrence	Anderson	4	$22.00
6	Lawrence	Motherbee	55	$5,556.00
7	Lawrence	Fatherbee	44	$4,444.00
8	Lawrence	Sisterbee	7	$78.00
9	Deenoyer	Tony	34	$456.00

To reset the data run the qry-Make-LIVE-TEST query. The next query uses the **Int** function, **Int([Cost of Books]**. This will NOT remove the decimals.

Field:	Cost of Books
Table:	LIVE-TEST
Update To:	Int([Cost of Books])
Criteria:	

The output is the same. Lastly, the **Fix** function is used (after resetting the data).
Fix([Cost of Books]) This will NOT remove the decimals.

Field:	Cost of Books
Table:	LIVE-TEST
Update To:	Fix([Cost of Books])
Criteria:	

These three functions allow you to update the values in the records already in the table. The number of decimals presented for all three functions was 2; this is due to the field design in the LIVE-TEST table. The Initial table has this field formatted as Currency with 2 decimal places. When it is copied into LIVE-TEST this formatting is carried forward. These three functions do not alter the formatting; they only alter the values in the fields.

To alter the formatting, you will have to use the Format function outside of the 'Fix' or 'Int' functions (this is shown on the following pages).

Functioning with Access – 2013
Chapter 6 – Math functions – Update queries

Authors guide (This material is from Access help).

Different Formats for Different Numeric Values (Format Function)

A user-defined format expression for numbers can have from one to four sections separated by semicolons. If the *format* argument contains one of the named numeric formats, only one section is allowed.

If you use	The result is
One section only	The format expression applies to all values.
Two sections	The first section applies to positive values and zeros, the second to negative values.
Three sections	The first section applies to positive values, the second to negative values, and the third to zeros.
Four sections	The first section applies to positive values, the second to negative values, the third to zeros, and the fourth to Null values.

The following example has two sections: the first defines the format for positive values and zeros; the second section defines the format for negative values.

```
"$#,##0;($#,##0)"
```

The formula for this is: **Fixed Cost of Books: Format(Fix([Cost of Books]),"$#,##0")**. To show this, the query type is changed back to Select.

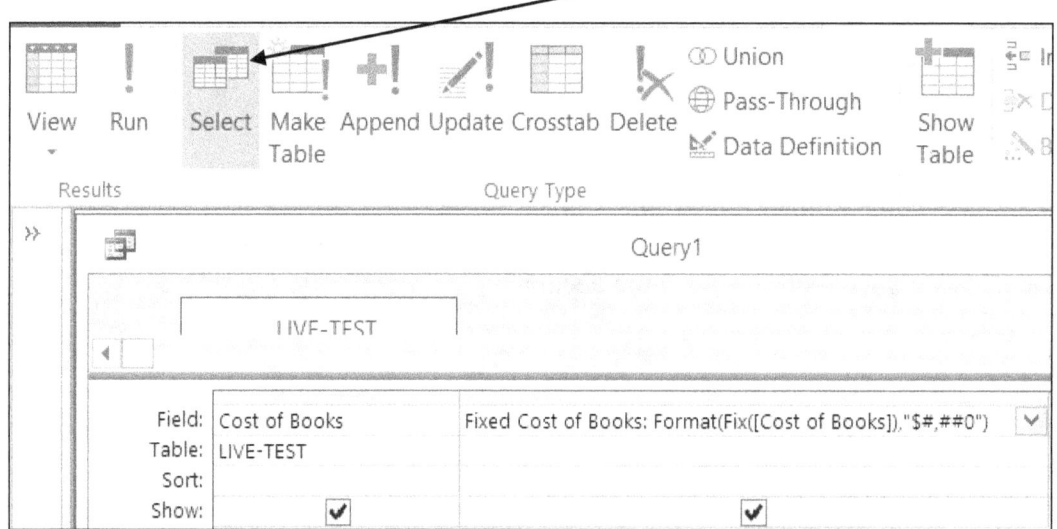

This is the output. The alignment is to the left due to formatting.

Cost of Books	Fixed Cost of Books
$56,788.22	$56,788
$0.00	$0
$7,788.76	$7,788
$678.30	$678
$22.30	$22
$5,555.55	$5,555
$4,444.44	$4,444
$77.77	$77
$456.44	$456

Functioning with Access – 2013
Chapter 6 – Math functions – Update queries

The next few pages will show how to use other math operations. Initially the table will have its values updated by adding to two fields.

Here is the initial table (some columns are hidden).

ID field	Last Name	First Name	Street-address	Books	# of Books	Cost of Book
1	Cederoth	Katherine	141 Grant	Yes	768	$56,788.22
2	Yeaoman	Mike	322 Sheffield	No	0	$0.00
3	Yeaoman	Shirley	1112 Canada	Yes	500	$7,788.76
4	Dionne	Tom	Route 4, 277 West	Yes	35	$678.30
5	Lawrence	Anderson	PO box 12A79, slot 7	Yes	4	$22.30
6	Lawrence	Motherbee	PO box 12A79, slot 8	Yes	55	$5,555.55
7	Lawrence	Fatherbee	PO box 12A79, slot 9	Yes	44	$4,444.44
8	Lawrence	Sisterbee	PO box 12A79, slot 10	Yes	7	$77.77
9	Deenoyer	Tony	1456 Bad Ax	Yes	34	$456.44

The query below will add 55 to the [# of Books] and add $3,000 to [Cost of Books].
Formulas: **[# of Books]+55** and **[Cost of Books] + 3000**. Remember to place square brackets around the field names (there are spaces in the names).

NOTE: This also works for subtraction, **[# of Books]-55** and **[Cost of Books]- 3000.**

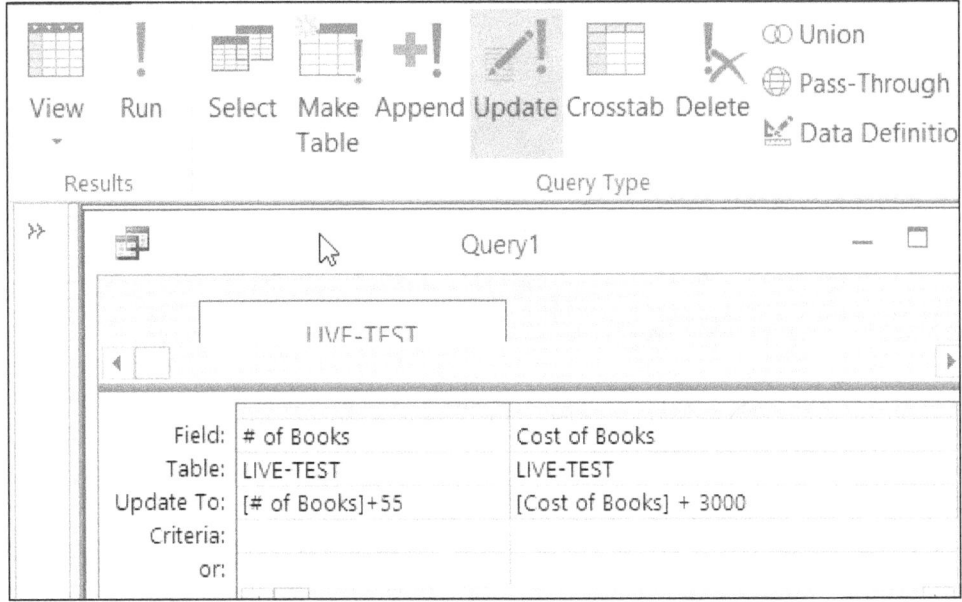

- 113 -

When this is executed, the following prompt will appear.

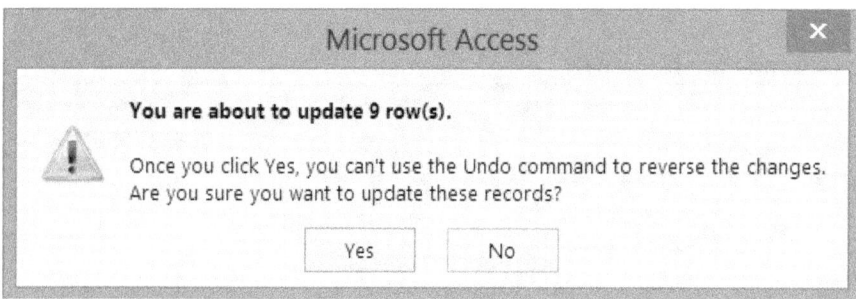

Select the [Yes] button. Below is the LIVE-TEST table after being updated.

ID field	Last Name	First Name	Street-address	Books	# of Books	Cost of Books
1	Cederoth	Katherine	141 Grant	Yes	823	$59,788.22
2	Yeaoman	Mike	322 Sheffield	No	55	$3,000.00
3	Yeaoman	Shirley	1112 Canada	Yes	555	$10,788.76
4	Dionne	Tom	Route 4, 277 West	Yes	90	$3,678.30
5	Lawrence	Anderson	PO box 12A79, slot 7	Yes	59	$3,022.30
6	Lawrence	Motherbee	PO box 12A79, slot 8	Yes	110	$8,555.55
7	Lawrence	Fatherbee	PO box 12A79, slot 9	Yes	99	$7,444.44
8	Lawrence	Sisterbee	PO box 12A79, slot 10	Yes	62	$3,077.77
9	Deenoyer	Tony	1456 Bad Ax	Yes	89	$3,456.44

The data is restored (using the qry-Make-LIVE-TEST query), now both fields are multiplied by 12.

The formulas are: [# of Books]*12 and   [Cost of Books] * 12.
Here is the query (notice it is an Update query).

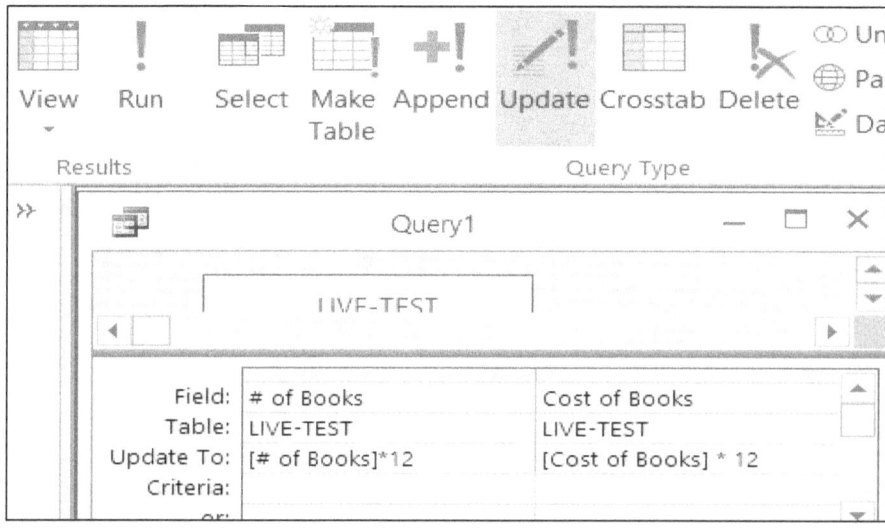

Run the query.

Functioning with Access – 2013
Chapter 6 – Math functions – Update queries

Answer the prompt by selecting the **Yes** button. Here is the table with the new data.

ID field	Last Name	First Name	Books	# of Books	Cost of Books
1	Cederoth	Katherine	Yes	9216	$681,458.64
2	Yeaoman	Mike	No	0	$0.00
3	Yeaoman	Shirley	Yes	6000	$93,465.12
4	Dionne	Tom	Yes	420	$8,139.60
5	Lawrence	Anderson	Yes	48	$267.60
6	Lawrence	Motherbee	Yes	660	$66,666.60
7	Lawrence	Fatherbee	Yes	528	$53,333.28
8	Lawrence	Sisterbee	Yes	84	$933.24
9	Deenoyer	Tony	Yes	408	$5,477.28

The data is restored, now both fields are divided by 12.

Here are the formulas: **[# of Books] / 12** and **[Cost of Books] / 12.**

Here is the query,

Field:	# of Books	Cost of Books
Table:	LIVE-TEST	LIVE-TEST
Update To:	[# of Books]/12	[Cost of Books]*"/12"

Run the query. Answer the prompt by selecting the **Yes** button.

Here is the table with the new data.

ID field	Last Name	First Name	Books	# of Books	Cost of Book
1	Cederoth	Katherine	Yes	64	$4,732.35
2	Yeaoman	Mike	No	0	$0.00
3	Yeaoman	Shirley	Yes	42	$649.06
4	Dionne	Tom	Yes	3	$56.53
5	Lawrence	Anderson	Yes	0	$1.86
6	Lawrence	Motherbee	Yes	5	$462.96
7	Lawrence	Fatherbee	Yes	4	$370.37
8	Lawrence	Sisterbee	Yes	1	$6.48
9	Deenoyer	Tony	Yes	3	$38.04

Both of the above functions could have had Round, Fix or Int functions used. For Anderson Lawrence, 4 divided by 12 does not equal 0, but the [# of Books] field is an Integer field and does not show decimals. It is not possible to have 1/3 of a book so this feature was appropriate when the table was designed. Sisterbee Lawrence also has a decimal value when divided by 12 and Access rounds up to 1. Other records are also rounded up or down based upon the decimal value returned after the division. So please remember the display of decimal you can control.

Not displaying decimals may affect visual expectations of calculation. If you were to multiply the new [# of Books] field by 100, the record for Anderson Lawrence would show a value. The expectation that multiplying 0 by 100 should be 0 would not be met. Remember Access is displaying values based upon formatting and behind the visual presentation a field may have a different value.

The [Cost of Books] could also have any of these three functions added to handle the decimal.

Chapter 7 - Date functions – Update queries.

Queries which use Date functions to Update data are explained in this chapter. These same functions can be used on Forms and Reports as well as with the queries. These functions are explained in chapter 4 and again in 10.

The LIVE-TEST table is shown below (some fields have been hidden).

ID field	Last Name	First Name	Birthday	Books	# of Books	Cost of Books
1	Cederoth	Katherine	6/15/1957	Yes	64	$4,732.35
2	Yeaoman	Mike	12/14/1958	No	0	$0.00
3	Yeaoman	Shirley	6/22/1957	Yes	42	$649.06
4	Dionne	Tom	12/1/1977	Yes	3	$56.53
5	Lawrence	Anderson	3/15/1999	Yes	0	$1.86
6	Lawrence	Motherbee	5/15/1969	Yes	5	$462.96
7	Lawrence	Fatherbee	5/22/1967	Yes	4	$370.37
8	Lawrence	Sisterbee	7/22/1997	Yes	1	$6.48
9	Deenoyer	Tony	2/29/1996	Yes	3	$38.04

An Update query to add 1 to the [Birthday] field is shown below (remember this is an UPDATE query). The formula is **[Birthday] + 1.**

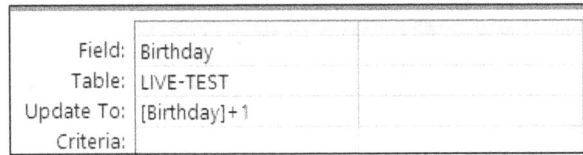

The query is executed and the prompt below displays.

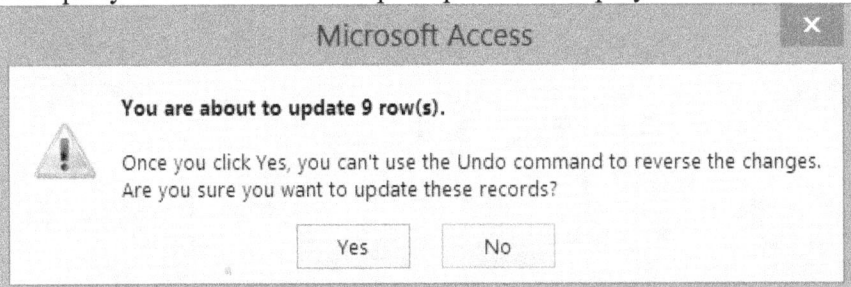

Select the [Yes] button to run the query. Notice, all 9 rows will be changed (the order of the fields displayed have been alteed).

Functioning with Access – 2013
Chapter 7 – Date functions – Update queries

The LIVE-TEST table is updated as shown below.

ID field	Last Name	First Name	Birthday	Books	# of Books	Cost of Books
1	Cederoth	Katherine	6/16/1957	Yes	64	$4,732.35
2	Yeaoman	Mike	12/15/1958	No	0	$0.00
3	Yeaoman	Shirley	6/23/1957	Yes	42	$649.06
4	Dionne	Tom	12/2/1977	Yes	3	$56.53
5	Lawrence	Anderson	3/16/1999	Yes	0	$1.86
6	Lawrence	Motherbee	5/16/1969	Yes	5	$462.96
7	Lawrence	Fatherbee	5/23/1967	Yes	4	$370.37
8	Lawrence	Sisterbee	7/23/1997	Yes	1	$6.48
9	Deenoyer	Tony	3/1/1996	Yes	3	$38.04

This update query has changed the day. For the 1st record the value of the [Birthday] field changed from 6/15/1957 to 6/16/1957.

Adding 365 to the [Birthday] field will increment the day segment of the field. The formula is **[Birthday] + 365.**

The query is executed Answer the prompt by selecting the Yes button.

Here is the table with the changed values. Record #1 has changed to 6/16/1958. However, notice that records #5 and #7 are 1 day less than expected, this is due to Leap day adding 1 day to the year.

ID field	Last Name	First Name	Birthday	Books	# of Books	Cost of Books
1	Cederoth	Katherine	6/16/1958	Yes	64	$4,732.35
2	Yeaoman	Mike	12/15/1959	No	0	$0.00
3	Yeaoman	Shirley	6/23/1958	Yes	42	$649.06
4	Dionne	Tom	12/2/1978	Yes	3	$56.53
5	Lawrence	Anderson	3/15/2000	Yes	0	$1.86
6	Lawrence	Motherbee	5/16/1970	Yes	5	$462.96
7	Lawrence	Fatherbee	5/22/1968	Yes	4	$370.37
8	Lawrence	Sisterbee	7/23/1998	Yes	1	$6.48
9	Deenoyer	Tony	3/1/1997	Yes	3	$38.04

Using this method to update date fields is not always effective. The DataAdd functions can be used to do the work efficiently. These functions are presented on the following pages.

DateAdd function explained.

Starting with the same initial values in the LIVE-TEST table, a query will add two months to the [Birthday] field. Here are the interval arguments (from Access help).

Setting	Description
yyyy	Year
q	Quarter
m	Month
y	Day of year
d	Day
w	Weekday
ww	Week
h	Hour
n	Minute
s	Second

Here is the original data.

ID field	Last Name	First Name	Birthday	Books	# of Books	Cost of Books
1	Cederoth	Katherine	6/15/1957	Yes	64	$4,732.35
2	Yeaoman	Mike	12/14/1958	No	0	$0.00
3	Yeaoman	Shirley	6/22/1957	Yes	42	$649.06
4	Dionne	Tom	12/1/1977	Yes	3	$56.53
5	Lawrence	Anderson	3/15/1999	Yes	0	$1.86
6	Lawrence	Motherbee	5/15/1969	Yes	5	$462.96
7	Lawrence	Fatherbee	5/22/1967	Yes	4	$370.37
8	Lawrence	Sisterbee	7/22/1997	Yes	1	$6.48
9	Deenoyer	Tony	2/29/1996	Yes	3	$38.04

Here is the Update query, the formula is **DateAdd("m",2,[Birthday])**.

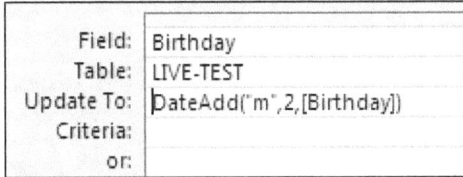

(Notice the double quotes, not single quotes)

When you run the query, you are prompted. Select the [Yes] button.

DateAdd function (continued).

Here is the updated table.

ID field	Last Name	First Name	Birthday	Books	# of Books	Cost of Book
1	Cederoth	Katherine	8/15/1957	Yes	768	$56,788.22
2	Yeaoman	Mike	2/14/1959	No	0	$0.00
3	Yeaoman	Shirley	8/22/1957	Yes	500	$7,788.76
4	Dionne	Tom	2/1/1978	Yes	35	$678.30
5	Lawrence	Anderson	5/15/1999	Yes	4	$22.30
6	Lawrence	Motherbee	7/15/1969	Yes	55	$5,555.55
7	Lawrence	Fatherbee	7/22/1967	Yes	44	$4,444.44
8	Lawrence	Sisterbee	9/22/1997	Yes	7	$77.77
9	Deenoyer	Tony	4/29/1996	Yes	34	$456.44

The month portion of the Birthday field has been incremented by 2.

The next query will update the day by 10 days. The values have not been restored to the initial values.

This next formula will increase the number of days by 10.
The formula is: **DateAdd("d",10,[Birthday]).**

Field:	Birthday
Table:	LIVE-TEST
Update To:	DateAdd("d",10,[Birthday])

When you run the query, you are prompted. Select the **Yes** button.

Here is the table with these changes.

ID field	Last Name	First Name	Birthday	Books	# of Books	Cost of Book
1	Cederoth	Katherine	8/25/1957	Yes	768	$56,788.22
2	Yeaoman	Mike	2/24/1959	No	0	$0.00
3	Yeaoman	Shirley	9/1/1957	Yes	500	$7,788.76
4	Dionne	Tom	2/11/1978	Yes	35	$678.30
5	Lawrence	Anderson	5/25/1999	Yes	4	$22.30
6	Lawrence	Motherbee	7/25/1969	Yes	55	$5,555.55
7	Lawrence	Fatherbee	8/1/1967	Yes	44	$4,444.44
8	Lawrence	Sisterbee	10/2/1997	Yes	7	$77.77
9	Deenoyer	Tony	5/9/1996	Yes	34	$456.44

All of the records have had the day portion of the Birthday increased by 10.

DateAdd function (continued).

The next query will subtract 5 years from the Birthday. NOTE: The data has not been refreshed.

The formula is: **DateAdd("yyyy",-5,[Birthday])**.

Field:	Birthday
Table:	LIVE-TEST
Update To:	DateAdd("yyyy",-5,[Birthday])

When you run the query, you are prompted. Select the Yes button.

This is the table after the query is complete.

ID field	Last Name	First Name	Birthday	Books	# of Books	Cost of Book
1	Cederoth	Katherine	8/25/1952	Yes	768	$56,788.22
2	Yeaoman	Mike	2/24/1954	No	0	$0.00
3	Yeaoman	Shirley	9/1/1952	Yes	500	$7,788.76
4	Dionne	Tom	2/11/1973	Yes	35	$678.30
5	Lawrence	Anderson	5/25/1994	Yes	4	$22.30
6	Lawrence	Motherbee	7/25/1964	Yes	55	$5,555.55
7	Lawrence	Fatherbee	8/1/1962	Yes	44	$4,444.44
8	Lawrence	Sisterbee	10/2/1992	Yes	7	$77.77
9	Deenoyer	Tony	5/9/1991	Yes	34	$456.44

The **DateAdd** function allows you to determine how you are adding to a Date, whether it be a Month, Year, Week or a Day.

You can use the **DateAdd** function to add or subtract a specified time interval from a date. For example, you can use **DateAdd** to calculate a date 30 days from today or a time 45 minutes from now. To add days to [Birthday], you can use Day of Year ("y"), Day ("d"), or Weekday ("w"). The **DateAdd** function won't return an invalid date. The following example adds one month to January 31: **DateAdd("m", 1, "31-Jan-95")**. In this case, **DateAdd** returns 28-Feb-95, not 31-Feb-95.

DateDiff function explained.

Another function mentioned elsewhere is the **DateDiff** function; it can also be used to update values. If you are updating the difference between two dates, this function is very effective.

Here, the difference between the [Birthday] field and today's date (Now()) is calculated and placed into the [Date difference between Birthday and 8/30/2013] field.
Here is the formula: **DateDiff("yyyy",[Birthday],Now()).**

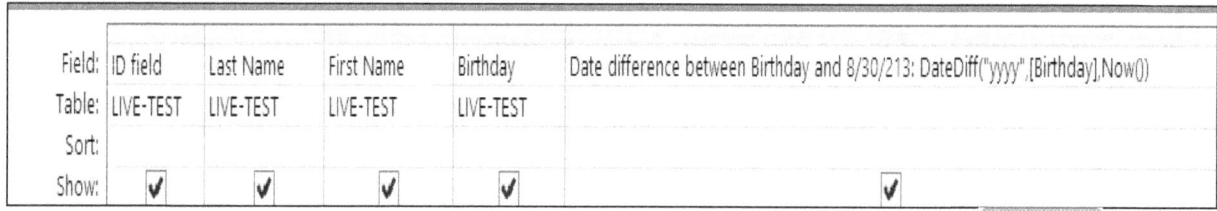

Now is 08/30/2013. When you run the query, you are prompted. Select the Yes button.

After the query runs, here is the table. The values are the number of years between the Birthday and 8/30/2013 (the day this query was created).

ID field	Last Name	First Name	Birthday	Date difference between Birthday and 8/30/213
1	Cederoth	Katherine	8/25/1952	61
2	Yeaoman	Mike	2/24/1954	59
3	Yeaoman	Shirley	9/1/1952	61
4	Dionne	Tom	2/11/1973	40
5	Lawrence	Anderson	5/25/1994	19
6	Lawrence	Motherbee	7/25/1964	49
7	Lawrence	Fatherbee	8/1/1962	51
8	Lawrence	Sisterbee	10/2/1992	21
9	Deenoyer	Tony	5/9/1991	22

Here are the interval arguments.

Setting	Description	Setting	Description
yyyy	Year	Q	Quarter
m	Month	Ww	Week
h	Hour	N	Minute
y	Day of year	D	Day
s	Second	W	Weekday

This function can be used in accounting applications and would enable you to keep the data in tables current for fields that use a date difference calculations.

Chapter 8 - Character functions – Append queries.

If your reporting needs require data to be altered in some manner, using a query, which has character functions, may help with your reporting presentation. Taking original data, manipulating it and placing this data in a table used just for reporting is a very viable way to insure the data meets your formatting requirements. These functions are explained in chapter 2, and again in 5.

Text (Character) functions that Append data to another table are explained in this chapter. To illustrate some of these functions, another table will be created.

Copy the LIVE-TEST table into a new table called LIVE-STORAGE. Delete all of the data in the LIVE-STORAGE table. In the table design, remove the Auto number from the [ID field] definition.

The next step is to create a new query. Go to the Query part of Access, create a new query, insert the LIVE-TEST table. To populate LIVE-STORAGE table with selected values from LIVE-TEST table, this query must be changed from a Select query to an Append query.

From the query you created above, select ![Append] for Query type.

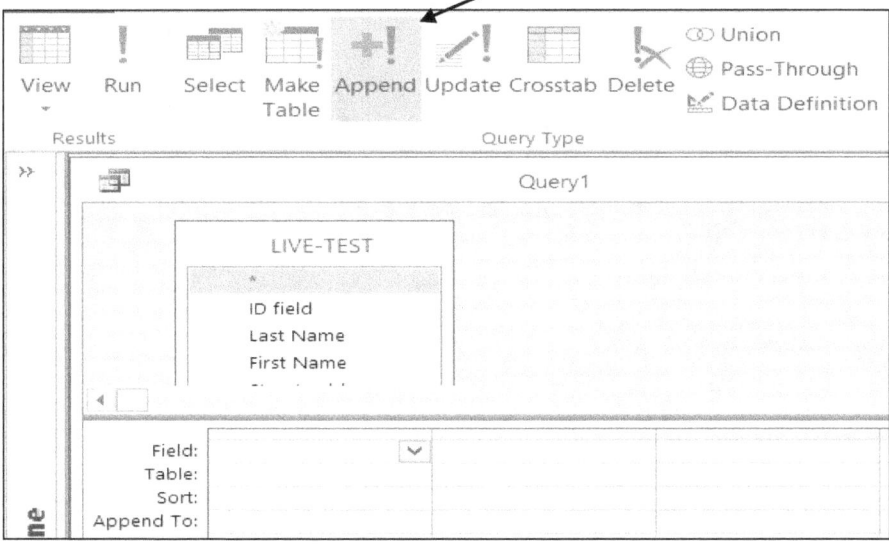

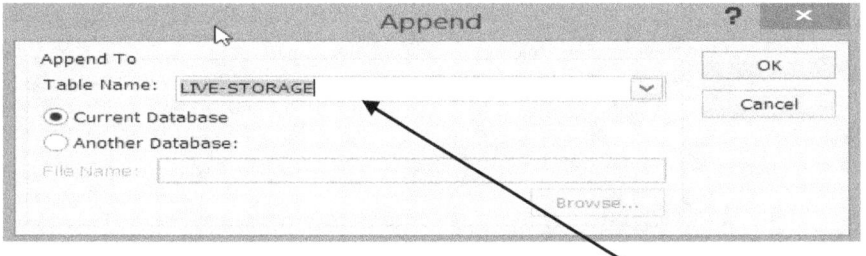

This will provide you with a prompt to select the table you will Append To.

A new **Append To** row will appear as shown below.

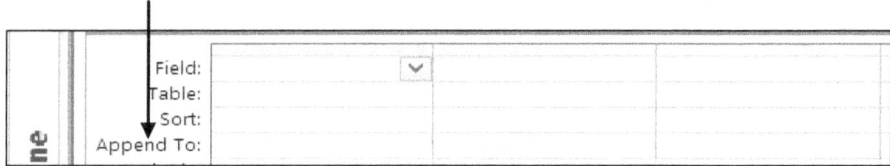

The first task will be to append to the LIVE-STORAGE table, all of the records from the LIVE-TEST table.

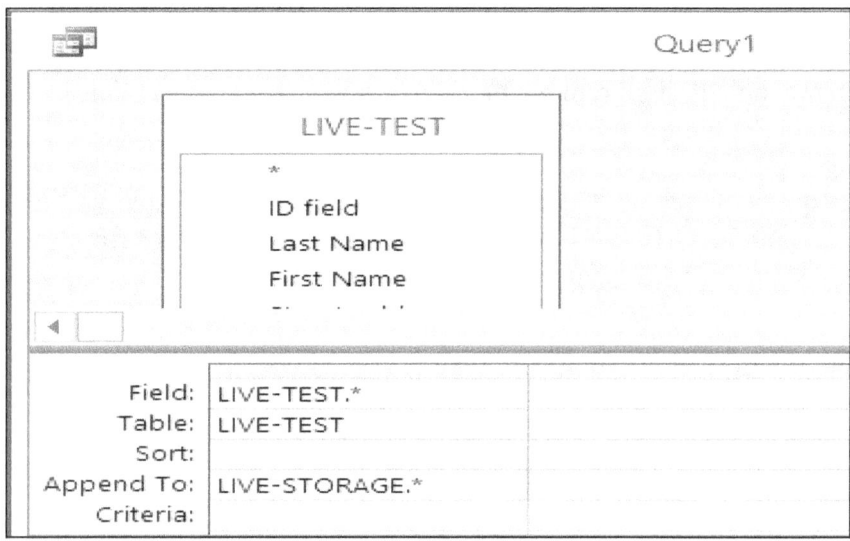

The above query will prompt you for confirmation.

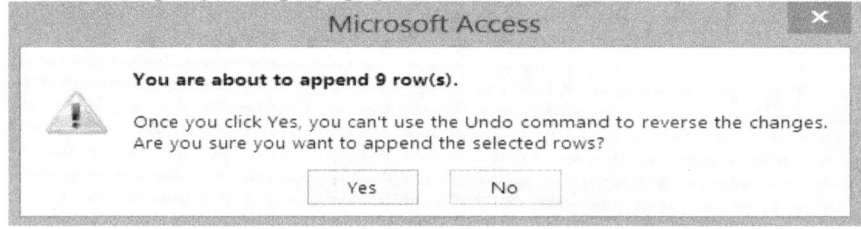

Select the 'Yes' button. All of the data is now in the LIVE-STORAGE table.

ID field	Last Name	First Name	Street-address	City	State	Color	Birthday
1	Cederoth	Katherine	141 Grant	Chicago	Illinois	Tan	8/25/1952
2	Yeaoman	Mike	322 Sheffield	San Francisco	California	Orange	2/24/1954
3	Yeaoman	Shirley	1112 Canada	San Antonio	Texas	Easter Pink	9/1/1952
4	Dionne	Tom	Route 4, 277 W	Onarga	Wisconsin	Milatary Green	2/11/1973
5	Lawrence	Anderson	PO box 12A79, s	Grand Prarie	Texas	Burnt Orange	5/25/1994
6	Lawrence	Motherbee	PO box 12A79, s	Grand Prarie	Texas	Scarlet Red	7/25/1964
7	Lawrence	Fatherbee	PO box 12A79, s	Grand Prarie	Texas	Green	8/1/1962
8	Lawrence	Sisterbee	PO box 12A79, s	Grand Prarie	Texas	Pink	10/2/1992
9	Deenoyer	Tony	1456 Bad Ax	St Francis	Oklahoma	Blue	5/9/1991

NOTE: not all fields are shown.

Functioning with Access – 2013
Chapter 8 – Text functions – Append queries

We desire to select the records of anyone who has the [Last Name] of Lawrence and copy these records in the LIVE-STORAGE table. This query will append just the Lawrence family to the bottoms of the LIVE-STORAGE table. Here is the query that limits the records selected.

NOTE: nothing in 'Append To' row for the 2nd column.

Field:	LIVE-TEST.*	Last Name
Table:	LIVE-TEST	LIVE-TEST
Sort:		
Append To:	LIVE-STORAGE.*	
Criteria:		"Lawrence"

Here is the confirmation prompt. There are 4 records that match the criteria.

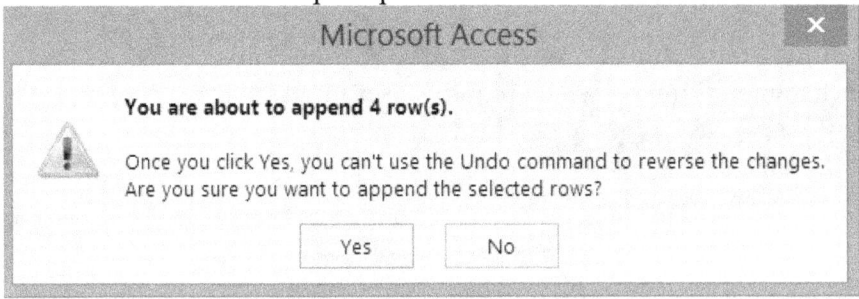

Select the "Yes" button.

Here is the LIVE-STORAGE table (NOTE: not all fields are shown).

ID field	Last Name	First Name	Street-address	City	State	Color	Birthday
1	Cederoth	Katherine	141 Grant	Chicago	Illinois	Tan	8/25/1952
2	Yeaoman	Mike	322 Sheffield	San Francisco	California	Orange	2/24/1954
3	Yeaoman	Shirley	1112 Canada	San Antonio	Texas	Easter Pink	9/1/1952
4	Dionne	Tom	Route 4, 277 We	Onarga	Wisconsin	Milatary Green	2/11/1973
5	Lawrence	Anderson	PO box 12A79, s	Grand Prarie	Texas	Burnt Orange	5/25/1994
6	Lawrence	Motherbee	PO box 12A79, s	Grand Prarie	Texas	Scarlet Red	7/25/1964
7	Lawrence	Fatherbee	PO box 12A79, s	Grand Prarie	Texas	Green	8/1/1962
8	Lawrence	Sisterbee	PO box 12A79, s	Grand Prarie	Texas	Pink	10/2/1992
9	Deenoyer	Tony	1456 Bad Ax	St Francis	Oklahoma	Blue	5/9/1991
5	Lawrence	Anderson	PO box 12A79, s	Grand Prarie	Texas	Burnt Orange	5/25/1994
6	Lawrence	Motherbee	PO box 12A79, s	Grand Prarie	Texas	Scarlet Red	7/25/1964
7	Lawrence	Fatherbee	PO box 12A79, s	Grand Prarie	Texas	Green	8/1/1962
8	Lawrence	Sisterbee	PO box 12A79, s	Grand Prarie	Texas	Pink	10/2/1992

The four Lawrence records have been appended to this table. The Append query will not overwrite records, this type of query just adds to table.

The Character functions learned in an earlier chapter can also be used. On the next page, a prompt will ask the user for the 1st 3 characters of the [Last Name]. Once typed in, those, which satisfy the criteria, are added to the LIVE-STORAGE table.

Using Append with the Left function.

(Before doing this query, delete the records from the LIVE-STORAGE table.)
The following query will return to the screen a prompt for the first 3 characters of the [Last Name]. You need to include 'Like' in the criteria along with an asterisk (*). The formula is:
Like (Left([Enter the 1st three characters of the Last Name field to append them to the LIVE-STORAGE table],3)) & "*".

This prompt appears (this is a 'Parameter' query, which requires user input).

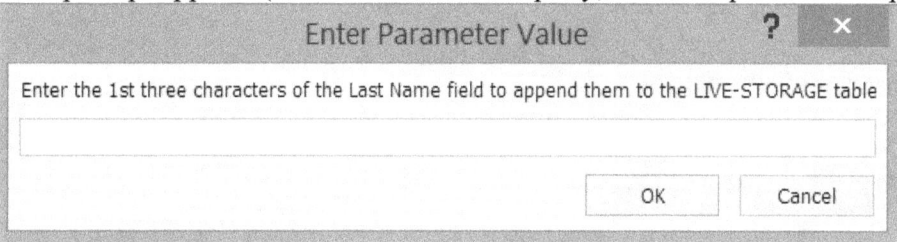

Type in **Yea**, and press the OK button. This message appears to insure you want to change the records. It found 4 that met the criteria.

Press the Yes button. Here is the output; the two records for the Yeaoman family have been appended to the bottom of the LIVE-STORAGE table (not all records or all fields are shown).

9	Deenoyer	Tony	1456 Bad Ax	St Francis	Oklahoma	Blue
5	Lawrence	Anderson	PO box 12A79, s	Grand Prarie	Texas	Burnt Orange
6	Lawrence	Motherbee	PO box 12A79, s	Grand Prarie	Texas	Scarlet Red
7	Lawrence	Fatherbee	PO box 12A79, s	Grand Prarie	Texas	Green
8	Lawrence	Sisterbee	PO box 12A79, s	Grand Prarie	Texas	Pink
2	Yeaoman	Mike	322 Sheffield	San Francisco	California	Orange
3	Yeaoman	Shirley	1112 Canada	San Antonio	Texas	Easter Pink

Using Append with the Right function.

(Before doing this query, delete the records from the LIVE-STORAGE table.)
The following query will return to the screen a prompt for the last 3 characters of the [First Name]. You need to include 'Like' in the criteria along with an asterisk(*). The formula is:
Like ("*" & Right([Enter the last three characters of the First Name field to append records to the LIVE-STORAGE table],3)).

The 'Like' function must be included because there are characters to the left of the 'bee'.

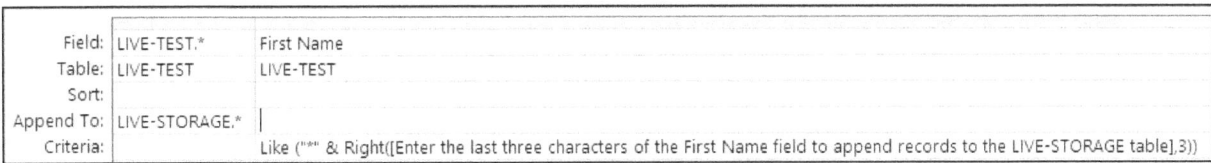

Run this query and the following prompt appears. Enter 'bee'.

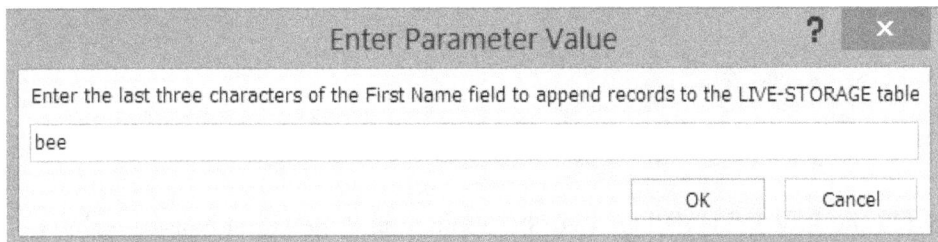

Click on the "OK" button and you will be prompted again,

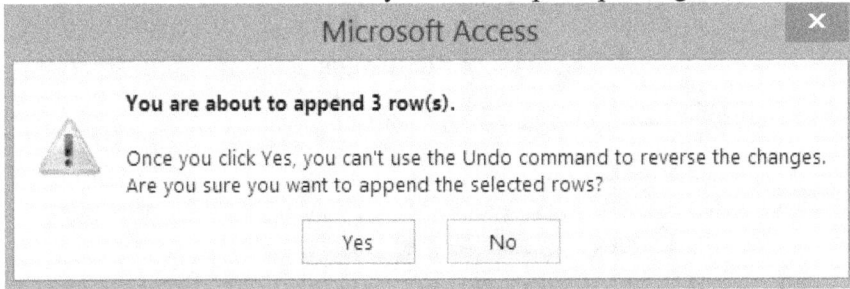

Select the "Yes" button. The LIVE-STORAGE table will have 3 records added.

8	Lawrence	Sisterbee	PO box 12A79, s	Grand Prarie	Texas	Pink
2	Yeaoman	Mike	322 Sheffield	San Francisco	California	Orange
3	Yeaoman	Shirley	1112 Canada	San Antonio	Texas	Easter Pink
6	Lawrence	Motherbee	PO box 12A79, s	Grand Prarie	Texas	Scarlet Red
7	Lawrence	Fatherbee	PO box 12A79, s	Grand Prarie	Texas	Green
8	Lawrence	Sisterbee	PO box 12A79, s	Grand Prarie	Texas	Pink

The Character functions explained in Chapter 2 can be used with Append queries. Refer to that chapter to develop appropriate queries.

Using Append with the Mid function.

The **Mid** function can be used to retrieve portions of a field. Below is an Append query which selects all data and takes 3 characters of the [First Name] field, starting from position 3, and places these into the [First Name] field in the LIVE-STORAGE table.

The text in the query is: **Name: Mid([First Name],3,3).** Notice in the first column there is no entry in the 'Table' row. You may have to edit this query to get it to work.

Field:	Name: Mid([First Name],3,3)	ID field	Last Name	Street-address	City
Table:		LIVE-TEST	LIVE-TEST	LIVE-TEST	LIVE-TEST
Sort:					
Append To:	First Name	ID field	Last Name	Street-address	City

Execute the query and this prompt will appear.

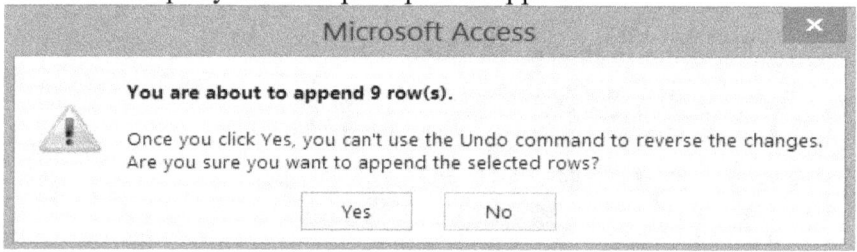

Select the "Yes" button and the LIVE-STORAGE will be updated and the [First Name] field is populated with the segment of text as defined by the Mid function above.

9	Cederoth	the	141 Grant	Chicago	Illinois	Tan
10	Yeaoman	ke	322 Sheffield	San Francisco	California	Orange
11	Yeaoman	irl	1112 Canada	San Antonio	Texas	Easter Pink
12	Dionne	m	Route 4, 277 W	Onarga	Wisconsin	Milatary Green
13	Lawrence	der	PO box 12A79, s	Grand Prarie	Texas	Burnt Orange
14	Lawrence	the	PO box 12A79, s	Grand Prarie	Texas	Scarlet Red
15	Lawrence	the	PO box 12A79, s	Grand Prarie	Texas	Green
16	Lawrence	ste	PO box 12A79, s	Grand Prarie	Texas	Pink
17	Deenoyer	ny	1456 Bad Ax	St Francis	Oklahoma	Blue

NOTE: not all fields are shown.

This Mid function query illustrates that data can be manipulated and placed into another table.

Using Append with the Replace function.

The Replace function can also be used in the same manner. The next query will replace the values in the [First Name] field with the word "Secret" in the LIVE-STORAGE table. Working through this as with other functions, you will find that it **does NOT work.**

The following query was created using this formula:
Name: Replace([First Name],"*","Secret"). Note: not all fields are shown.

Field:	Name: Replace([First Name],"*","Secret")	ID field	Last Name
Table:		LIVE-TEST	LIVE-TEST
Sort:			
Append To:	First Name	ID field	Last Name

The prompt for confirmation appears; select the "Yes" button.

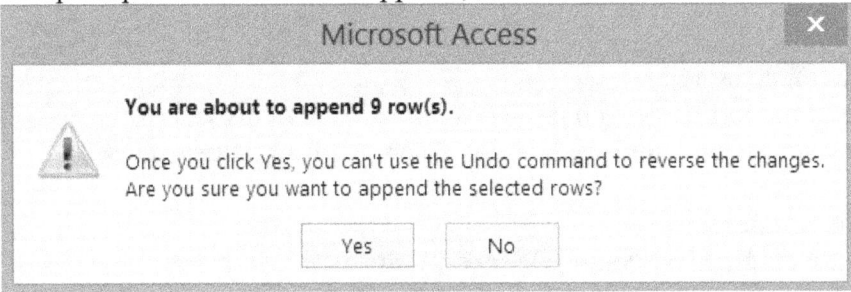

After answering the prompt, the table is updated as shown (only newly append rows are shown).

ID field	Last Name	First Name	Street-address	City	State
1	Cederoth	Katherine	141 Grant	Chicago	Illinois
2	Yeaoman	Mike	322 Sheffield	San Francisco	California
3	Yeaoman	Shirley	1112 Canada	San Antonio	Texas
4	Dionne	Tom	Route 4, 277 West	Onarga	Wisconsin
5	Lawrence	Anderson	PO box 12A79, slot 7	Grand Prarie	Texas
6	Lawrence	Motherbee	PO box 12A79, slot 8	Grand Prarie	Texas
7	Lawrence	Fatherbee	PO box 12A79, slot 9	Grand Prarie	Texas
8	Lawrence	Sisterbee	PO box 12A79, slot 10	Grand Prarie	Texas
9	Deenoyer	Tony	1456 Bad Ax	St Francis	Oklahoma

The [First Name] field is not updated as was expected. The query ran and appended as designed, but the data was not changed. **After trying other combinations of wildcards, a formula that works is shown on the next page.** The Replace function operates slightly different than other functions; it requires a specific text string to replace. Previously " ." was used.

Using Append with the Replace function(continued).

From Access Help the following is found: **Replace(***expression, find, replace*[, *start*[, *count*[, *compare*]]]**)**

Part	Description
The **Replace** function syntax has these named arguments:	
expression	Required. String expression containing substring to replace.
find	Required. Substring being searched for.
replace	Required. Replacement substring.
start	Optional. Position within *expression* where substring search is to begin. If omitted, 1 is assumed.
count	Optional. Number of substring substitutions to perform. If omitted, the default value is –1, which means make all possible substitutions.
compare	Optional. Numeric value indicating the kind of comparison to use when evaluating substrings. See Settings section for values.

In this example:
   expression is the field name [First Name].
   find is the text string we are trying to find (which in this example is the fields value)
   replace is the text value we want to insert into the position where the **find** value occurs.

The formula required to do this update is:
   Name: Replace([First Name],[First Name],"Secret"), this is shown below.

Field:	Name: Replace([First Name],[First Name],"Secret")	ID field	Last Name
Table:		LIVE-TEST	LIVE-TEST
Sort:			
Append To:	First Name	ID field	Last Name

After answering **Yes** to the prompt, the table is populated as shown below (only newly inserted records are shown and not all fields are shown).

Cederoth	Secret	141 Grant	Chicago	Illinois	Tan
Yeaoman	Secret	322 Sheffield	San Francisco	California	Orange
Yeaoman	Secret	1112 Canada	San Antonio	Texas	Easter Pink
Dionne	Secret	Route 4, 277 W(	Onarga	Wisconsin	Milatary Green
Lawrence	Secret	PO box 12A79, s	Grand Prarie	Texas	Burnt Orange
Lawrence	Secret	PO box 12A79, s	Grand Prarie	Texas	Scarlet Red
Lawrence	Secret	PO box 12A79, s	Grand Prarie	Texas	Green
Lawrence	Secret	PO box 12A79, s	Grand Prarie	Texas	Pink
Deenover	Secret	1456 Bad Ax	St Francis	Oklahoma	Blue

In your work with Access, you may never have a need to replace the entire contents of a field with a text string. Hopefully, this example and the error made initially will guide you in making fewer mistakes.

Using Append with the Len function.

The Len function in the next query will be used to populate the LIVE-STORAGE table with all of the records and change the value in the [First Name] field to the number of characters of the [Last Name].

The query formula is: **Name: Len([Last Name]).**

Here is the query.

Field:	Name: Len([Last Name])	ID field	Last Name	Street-address
Table:		LIVE-TEST	LIVE-TEST	LIVE-TEST
Sort:				
Append To:	First Name	ID field	Last Name	Street-address

After answering the prompt, by selecting the [Yes] button, the table is updated as shown (only new rows are shown).

The LIVE-STORAGE table is populated with the values from LIVE-TEST table and the [First Name] field is updated with a number that is the length of the [Last Name] field.

ID field	Last Name	First Name	Street-address	City	State
1	Cederoth	8	141 Grant	Chicago	Illinois
2	Yeaoman	7	322 Sheffield	San Francisco	California
3	Yeaoman	7	1112 Canada	San Antonio	Texas
4	Dionne	6	Route 4, 277 West	Onarga	Wisconsin
5	Lawrence	8	PO box 12A79, slot 7	Grand Prarie	Texas
6	Lawrence	8	PO box 12A79, slot 8	Grand Prarie	Texas
7	Lawrence	8	PO box 12A79, slot 9	Grand Prarie	Texas
8	Lawrence	8	PO box 12A79, slot 10	Grand Prarie	Texas
9	Deenoyer	8	1456 Bad Ax	St Francis	Oklahoma

You may have noticed that in these Append queries, it is not important, in the queries, how you arrange your fields. The software looks for the name of the field that is updated and makes the changes regardless of their location in the query.

Using Append with the InStr function.

The InStr function in the next query will be used to change the value in the [First Name] field to the position of the letter 'e' in the [Last Name] field. The position of a character inside of a longer character is often needed. If you are working with data that has a common character in it (like a comma or a space or a dash), you can find out what position the character is occupying. In this example the letter 'e' is being used.

The query formula is: **Name: InStr([Last Name],'e').**

Here is the query.

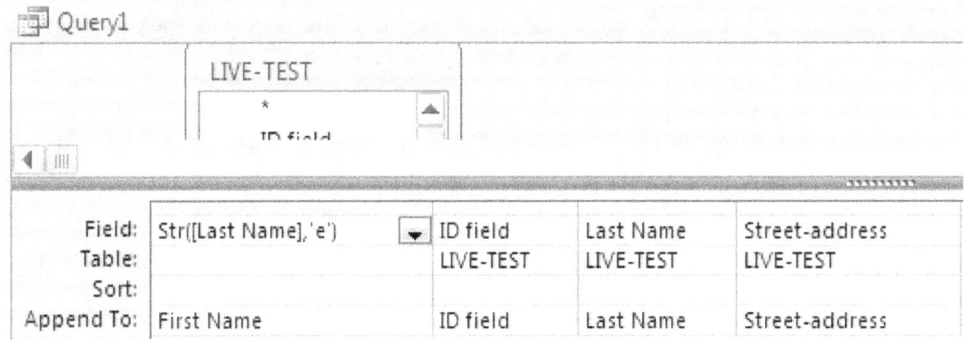

After answering the prompt, by selecting the Yes button, the table is updated as shown (only new rows are shown).

The LIVE-STORAGE table is populated with the values from LIVE-TEST table and the [First Name] field is updated with a number that is the position of the character 'e' (1st occurrence) in the [Last Name] field.

Last Name	First Name	Street-address	City	State	Color
Cederoth	2	141 Grant	Chicago	Illinois	Tan
Yeaoman	2	322 Sheffield	San Francisco	California	Orange
Yeaoman	2	1112 Canada	San Antonio	Texas	Easter Pink
Dionne	6	Route 4, 277 W	Onarga	Wisconsin	Milatary Green
Lawrence	5	PO box 12A79, s	Grand Prarie	Texas	Burnt Orange
Lawrence	5	PO box 12A79, s	Grand Prarie	Texas	Scarlet Red
Lawrence	5	PO box 12A79, s	Grand Prarie	Texas	Green
Lawrence	5	PO box 12A79, s	Grand Prarie	Texas	Pink
Deenoyer	2	1456 Bad Ax	St Francis	Oklahoma	Blue

Please remember that these records are being added to the bottom of the table. These records are not replacing current records. To update the current records, you would have to use an UPDATE style of query.

Using Append with the Ltrim & Trim functions.

The Ltrim function is useful to remove unwanted leading spaces. In the query below, the data in the LIVE-TEST table has had spaces added to the [First Name] field. The query will remove the leading spaces and place the appropriate text in the LIVE-STORAGE table.

The LIVE-TEST table is modified to add leading spaces to some of the [First Name] and [Last Name] fields. This is shown below.

ID field	Last Name	First Name	Street-address	City
1	Cederoth	Katherine	141 Grant	Chicago
2	Yeaoman	Mike	322 Sheffield	San Francisco
3	Yeaoman	Shirley	1112 Canada	San Antonio
4	Dionne	Tom	Route 4, 277 West	Onarga
5	Lawrence	Anderson	PO box 12A79, slot 7	Grand Prarie
6	Lawrence	Motherbee	PO box 12A79, slot 8	Grand Prarie
7	Lawrence	Fatherbee	PO box 12A79, slot 9	Grand Prarie
8	Lawrence	Sisterbee	PO box 12A79, slot 10	Grand Prarie
9	Deenoyer	Tony	1456 Bad Ax	St Francis

The new query will use the Trim and Ltrim function to remove the spaces from the records and place the values in the LIVE-STORAGE table.

Here are the formulas: **First: LTrim([First Name])** for the [First Name] field.
Last: Trim([Last Name]) for the [Last Name] field.

NOTE: not all fields are shown.

Field:	First: LTrim([First Name])	Last: Trim([Last Name])	ID field
Table:			LIVE-TEST
Sort:			
Append To:	First Name	Last Name	ID field

Execute the query and answer the prompt. The output will have no leading spaces.

ID field	Last Name	First Name	Street-address	City
1	Cederoth	Katherine	141 Grant	Chicago
2	Yeaoman	Mike	322 Sheffield	San Francisco
3	Yeaoman	Shirley	1112 Canada	San Antonio
4	Dionne	Tom	Route 4, 277 West	Onarga
5	Lawrence	Anderson	PO box 12A79, slot 7	Grand Prarie
6	Lawrence	Motherbee	PO box 12A79, slot 8	Grand Prarie
7	Lawrence	Fatherbee	PO box 12A79, slot 9	Grand Prarie
8	Lawrence	Sisterbee	PO box 12A79, slot 10	Grand Prarie
9	Deenoyer	Tony	1456 Bad Ax	St Francis

NOTE: only the new records are shown.

Chapter 9 - Math functions – Append queries.

Math functions can append aggregate values to other tables. In chapter 6 an attempt to update a field in a current table to an aggregate value was not allowed by Access. Average, Count and other aggregate math functions are explained in this chapter as the values are used in Append queries. The table below indicates the functions in this chapter. The LIVE-TEST table has been refreshed with the qry-MAKE-LIVE-TEST query. These functions are explained in chapter 3, and again in 6.

Function Name	Function format	Function use – why use it?
Average	Avg([field name])	To place the average of a set of values into another field/table.
Count	Count([field name])	To place a Count of a set of values into another field/table.
Max	Max([field name])	To place the Maximum of a set of values into another field/table.
Min	Min([field name])	To place the Minimum of a set of values into another field/table.
Sum	Sum([field name])	To place the Sum of a set of values into another field/table.

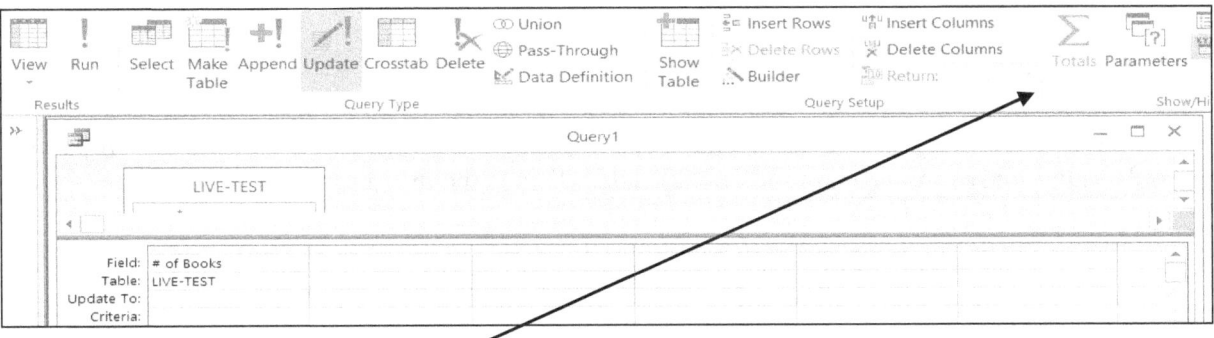

An Update query does not allow you to use this Aggregate function, notice the Totals button is disabled. This query is change to an Append query; you must provide the table that will receive the values.

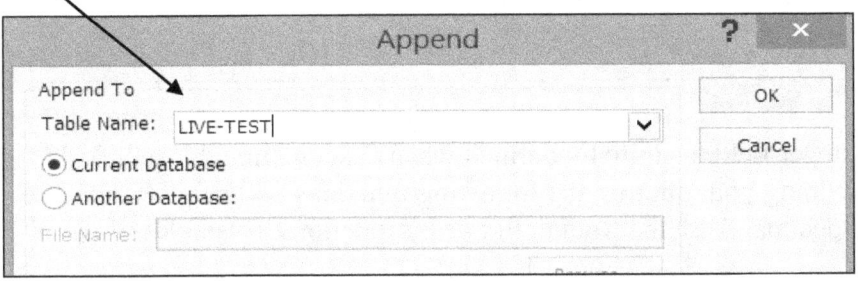

Using Append with the Avg function.

Below is the query that will run. This is an Append query.

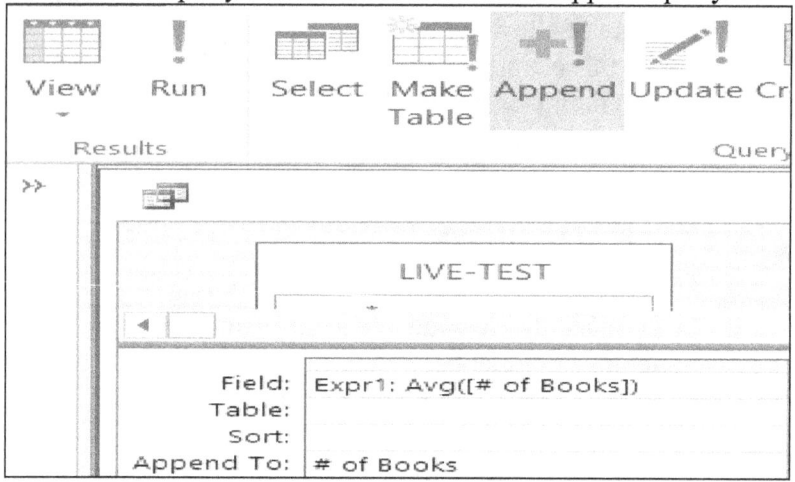

Here is the prompt as you execute the query.

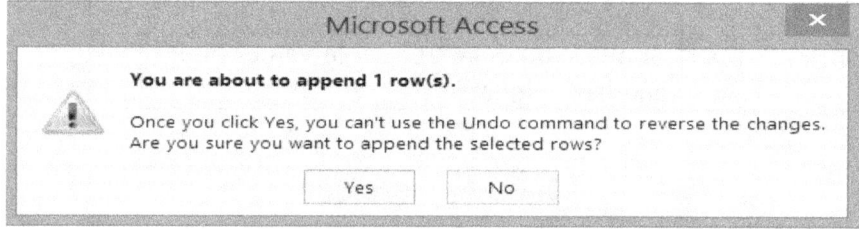

Select the "Yes" button. A new record has been added to the LIVE-TEST table as shown below; the only value for record #10 is [# of Books] field. This is the average.

ID field	Last Name	First Name	Street-address	City	# of Books	Cost of Book
1	Cederoth	Katherine	141 Grant	Chicago	768	$56,788.22
2	Yeaoman	Mike	322 Sheffield	San Francisco	0	$0.00
3	Yeaoman	Shirley	1112 Canada	San Antonio	500	$7,788.76
4	Dionne	Tom	Route 4, 277 W	Onarga	35	$678.30
5	Lawrence	Anderson	PO box 12A79, s	Grand Prarie	4	$22.30
6	Lawrence	Motherbee	PO box 12A79, s	Grand Prarie	55	$5,555.55
7	Lawrence	Fatherbee	PO box 12A79, s	Grand Prarie	44	$4,444.44
8	Lawrence	Sisterbee	PO box 12A79, s	Grand Prarie	7	$77.77
9	Deenoyer	Tony	1456 Bad Ax	St Francis	34	$456.44
10					161	

The [# of Books] field is an Integer field (as initially defined when first creating this table). If decimals appear when you are doing your queries, the following functions will help to eliminate them. To limit the number of decimals, use the Round, Fix or Int functions. Examples of these follow.

Functioning with Access – 2013
Chapter 9 – Math functions – Append queries

Using Append with the Round, Fix or Int functions.

The first formula is: **Expr1: Round(Avg([# of Books]))**. Access supplies the text **Expr1**: this does not impact the work we are doing. This formula controls decimals.

Field:	Expr1: Round(Avg([# of Books]))
Table:	
Sort:	
Append To:	# of Books

The formula is: **Expr1: Fix(Avg([# of Books]))**. This formula controls decimals.

Field:	Expr1: Fix(Avg([# of Books]))
Table:	
Sort:	
Append To:	# of Books

The formula is: **Expr1: Int(Avg([# of Books]))**. This formula controls decimals.

Field:	Expr1: Int(Avg([# of Books]))
Table:	
Sort:	
Append To:	# of Books

Here is the LIVE-TEST table after the four queries.

ID field	Last Name	First Name	Street-address	City	# of Books	Cost of Book
1	Cederoth	Katherine	141 Grant	Chicago	768	$56,788.22
2	Yeaoman	Mike	322 Sheffield	San Francisco	0	$0.00
3	Yeaoman	Shirley	1112 Canada	San Antonio	500	$7,788.76
4	Dionne	Tom	Route 4, 277 W	Onarga	35	$678.30
5	Lawrence	Anderson	PO box 12A79, s	Grand Prarie	4	$22.30
6	Lawrence	Motherbee	PO box 12A79, s	Grand Prarie	55	$5,555.55
7	Lawrence	Fatherbee	PO box 12A79, s	Grand Prarie	44	$4,444.44
8	Lawrence	Sisterbee	PO box 12A79, s	Grand Prarie	7	$77.77
9	Deenoyer	Tony	1456 Bad Ax	St Francis	34	$456.44
10					161	
11					161	
12					160	
13					160	

In summary, record #10 is without any functions, record #11 has **Fix**, record #12 has **Round** and record #13 has **Int**.

Using Append with Count, Min, Max or Sum functions.

The Append query added a new row to the table; however, it does not indicate that the value is an average. The same will happen if you use the Count, Max, Min or other aggregate functions.

To save the data, a new table is created to hold these aggregates; this table will be called TOTAL-HOLDER. Each field is appropriately made with the proper number of decimals (2 for averages and currency). Below is the table design.

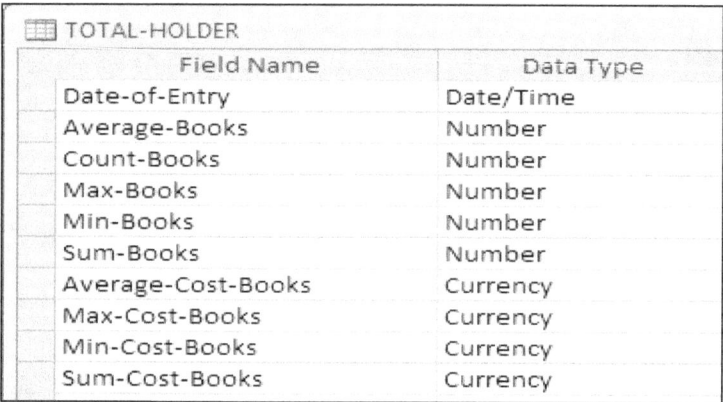

The query below was made to Append data to the TOTAL-HOLDER table. To do this, the query type is Append. When you create an Append query, the prompt below appears for you to indicate what table you wish to append.

Select TOTAL-HOLDER from the drop down selector, then click 'OK' button.

When this query is run, the aggregates will be added to the TOTAL-HOLDER table, not to the LIVE-TEST table.

A date field was added to allow capturing of the date when the table was updated by executing this query.

Functioning with Access – 2013
Chapter 9 – Math functions – Append queries

Using Append with Count, Min, Max or Sum functions (continued).

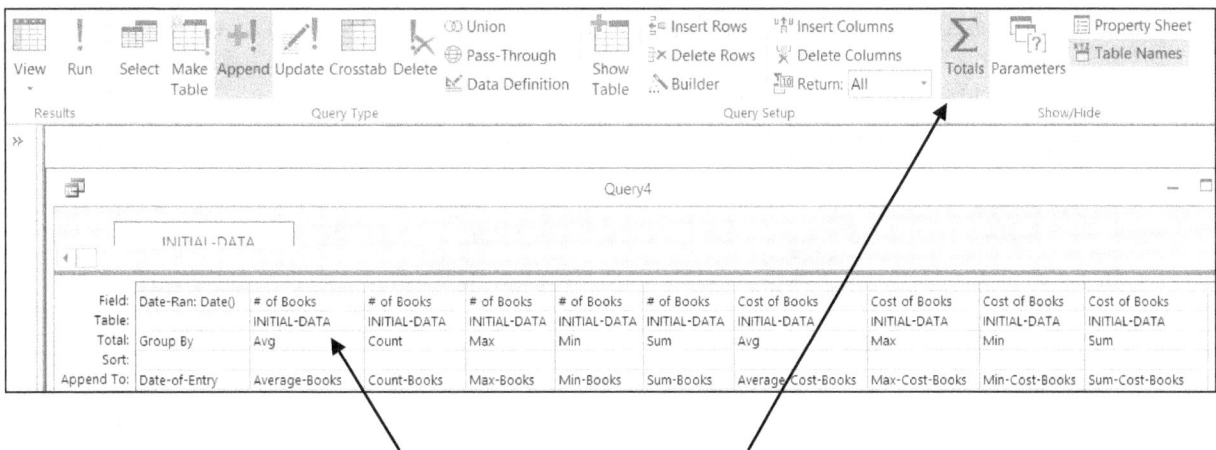

The query uses the fields from INITIAL-DATA table. The Totals button is enabled which creates the Total row in the query.

When executed, this prompt appears.

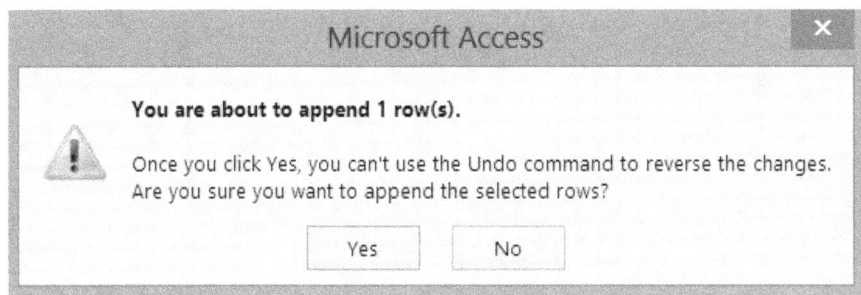

Select the 'Yes' button and the Totals will be added to the bottom of the TOTAL-HOLDER table. Below is the table broken up into two parts for better visibility.

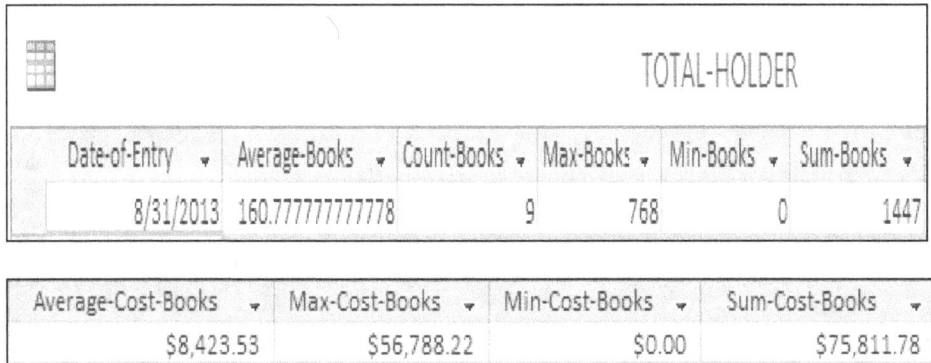

Using Append with Count, Min, Max or Sum functions (continued).

More data was entered into the INITIAL-DATA table and the query was ran again on September 1
Here is the same table after a 2nd day of entry

Date-of-Entry	Average-Books	Count-Books	Max-Books	Min-Books	Sum-Books
8/31/2013	160.777777777778	9	768	0	1447
9/1/2013	116.333333333333	9	600	4	1047

Average-Cost-Books	Max-Cost-Books	Min-Cost-Books	Sum-Cost-Books
$8,423.53	$56,788.22	$0.00	$75,811.78
$16,274.64	$67,788.76	$22.30	$146,471.78

This table can be used to retain these values every day for a time period. New tables could be created to hold a month's data. After a year, all of these monthly tables could be combined (using more Append queries) and totals for the year could be found as well as the other mathematical functions.

Chapter 10 - Date functions – Append queries.

The usage of Date functions in Append queries is explained in this chapter. In referring to Date fields or functions, these can be interpreted as minutes, hours, days, months or many other time measurements. The queries here will show how while using the Date functions, a table can have appended many different values for Date/Time. These functions are explained in chapter 4, and again in 7.

A new table is created which is called DATE-HOLDER. The design of this empty table is shown below.

Field Name	Data Type
ID field	Text
Last Name	Text
First Name	Text
Birthday	Date/Time
DateInfo1	Text
DateInfo2	Text
DateInfo3	Text
DateInfo4	Text

The following functions will be illustrated using the Birthday field and the Now. DateDiff, DateAdd, DatePart, Year, Day, WeekDay, WeekDayName, Month, and Year functions.

Data will be entered into this table from other table through the use of Append queries.

==

Below are the Date functions available in 2013. On the following pages, some of these will be explained.

Expression Values
CDate
CVDate
Date
Date$
DateAdd
DateDiff
DatePart
DateSerial
DateValue
Day
Hour
IsDate

Minute
Month
MonthName
Now
Second
Time
Time$
Timer
TimeSerial
TimeValue
Weekday
WeekdayName
Year

Functioning with Access – 2013
Chapter 10 – Date functions – Append queries

Using DateDiff function in an Append query.

To see how this function works, two date fields are required. Access has a variable called Now() which returns today's Date/Time. Create a new query, as shown below, that includes the LIVE-TEST table. Here is the DATA-HOLDER table that I created.

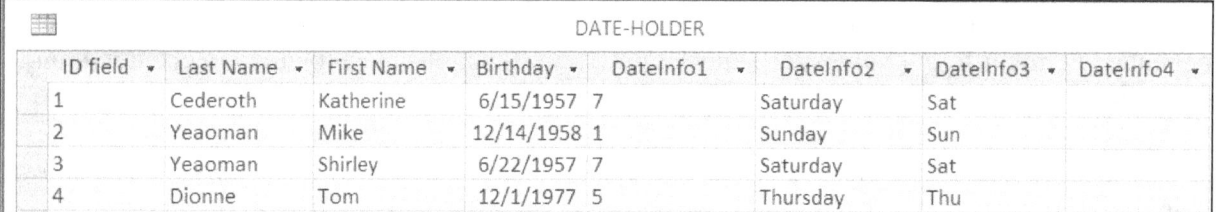

Here is the start of creating the query.
Select the first 3 fields [ID field], [Last Name] & [First Name].

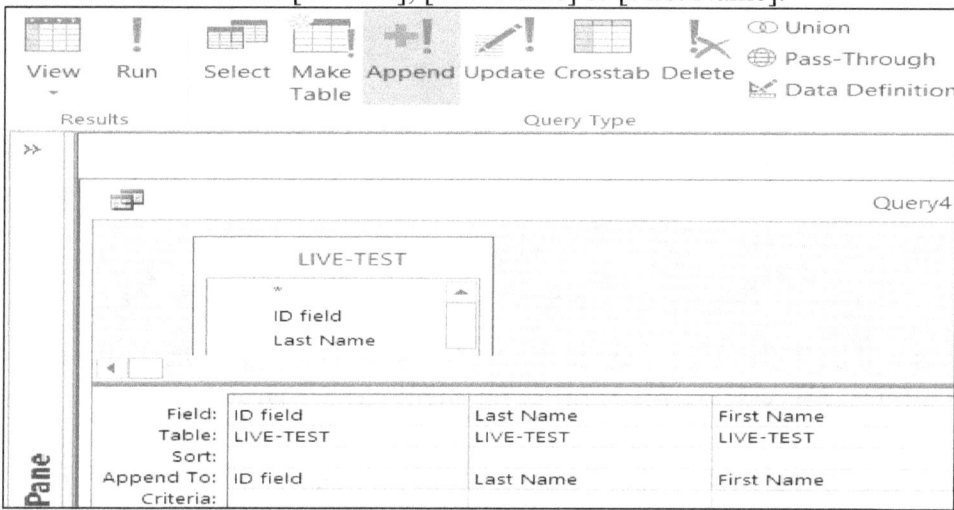

You will be prompted to indicate what table to Append To (shown below). Select DATE-HOLDER.

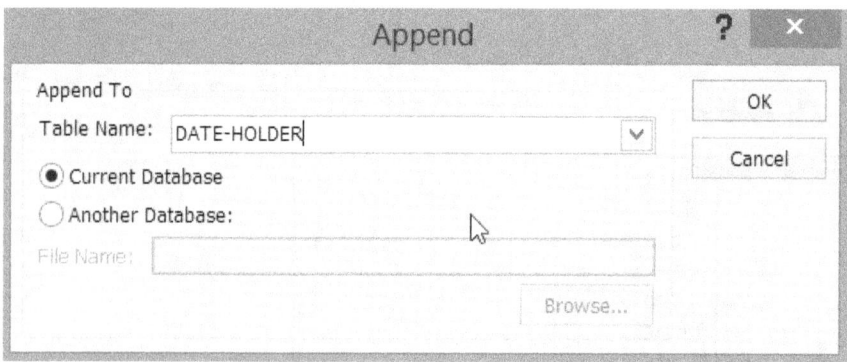

Using DateDiff function in an Append query (continued).

Using the [Birthday] field and Now() function, this query will append to the DATE-HOLDER table the [ID field], [Last Name], [First Name] and the [Birthday]. Also this query will append to the [DateInfo1] field the difference between these two dates in Years, in the [DateInfo2] field will go the difference in Months, in the [DateInfo3] field will go the difference in Days and in the [DateInfo4] field will go the difference in hours.

A new append query is created (as shown below). Select the following fields: [ID field], [Last Name], [First Name] and [Birthday]. To populate the [DateInfo] fields, formulas will be made and are shown below.

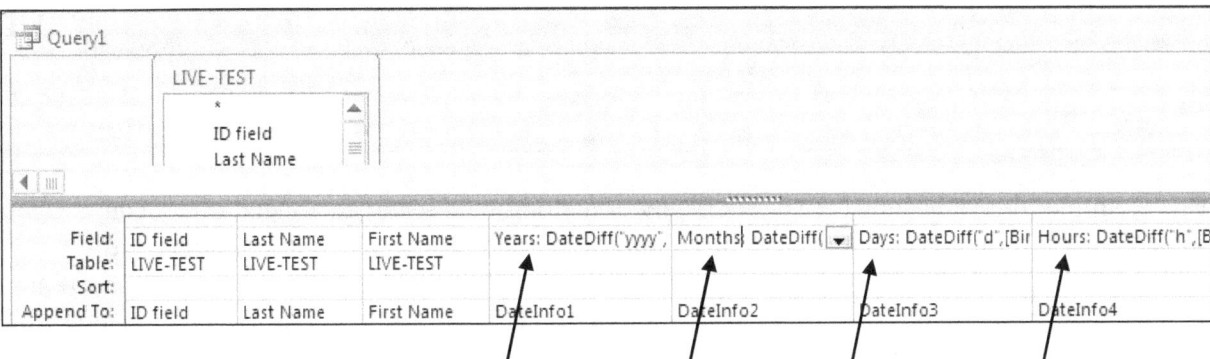

The formulas for the DateInfo fields are:
DateInfo1: **Years: DateDiff("yyyy",[Birthday],Now()) & " Years"**
DateInfo2: **Months: DateDiff("m",[Birthday],Now()) & " Months"**
DateInfo3: **Days: DateDiff("d",[Birthday],Now()) & " Days"**
DateInfo4: **Hours: DateDiff("h",[Birthday],Now()) & " Hours"**.

In each one of these fields, text (Years, Months, Days or Hours) was added to indicate the time period being shown.

This query is broken into two for better display of the formulas.

Field:	ID field	Last Name	First Name	Years: DateDiff("yyyy",[Birthday],Now()) & " Years"
Table:	LIVE-TEST	LIVE-TEST	LIVE-TEST	
Sort:				
Append To:	ID field	Last Name	First Name	DateInfo1

Field:	Months: DateDiff("m",[Birthday],Now()) & " Months"	Days: DateDiff("d",[Birthday],Now()) & " Days"	Hours: DateDiff("h",[Birthday],Now()) & " Hours"
Table:			
Sort:			
Append To:	DateInfo2	DateInfo3	DateInfo4

Run the query and select the "Yes" button.

Using DateDiff function in an Append query (continued).

The Now() function will return its default value, which includes the date and time and will be same value for every record. This query was run on 8/31/2013 at 7PM.

ID field	Last Name	First Name	Birthday	DateInfo1	DateInfo2	DateInfo3	DateInfo4
1	Cederoth	Katherine		56 Years	674 Months	20531 Days	492755 Hours
2	Yeaoman	Mike		55 Years	656 Months	19984 Days	479627 Hours
3	Yeaoman	Shirley		56 Years	674 Months	20524 Days	492587 Hours
4	Dionne	Tom		36 Years	428 Months	13057 Days	313379 Hours
5	Lawrence	Anderson		14 Years	173 Months	5283 Days	126803 Hours
6	Lawrence	Motherbee		44 Years	531 Months	16179 Days	388307 Hours
7	Lawrence	Fatherbee		46 Years	555 Months	16903 Days	405683 Hours
8	Lawrence	Sisterbee		16 Years	193 Months	5884 Days	141227 Hours
9	Deenoyer	Tony		17 Years	210 Months	6393 Days	153443 Hours

This example illustrates how the DateDiff function along with using an append query can populate a table with information. In the example above, text was added to indicate the time period. If you need to determine a time period difference (an example may be determining if an invoice is 30, 60 or 90 days overdue), use this function and place the output in a number field. Then test the values to determine what grouping they belong.

Using DateAdd function in an Append query.

To add to a date field, many options are available. The query has been change to use the DateAdd function. To the [Birthday] the same four functions will be used, 2 will be added to each. As the append query works, 2 years, 2 months, 2 days and 2 hours will be added to the [Birthday] value and will populate [DateInfo1-4] fields.

Below is the query (1st 4 fields are not shown).
Here are the formulas:
Years: DateAdd("yyyy",2,[Birthday])
Months: DateAdd("m",2,[Birthday])
Days: DateAdd("d",2,[Birthday])
Hours: DateAdd("h",2,[Birthday]).

Last 4 fields.

Field:	Years: DateAdd("yyyy",2,[Birthday])	Months: DateAdd("m",2,[Birthday])	Days: DateAdd("d",2,[Birthday])	Hours: DateAdd("h",2,[Birthday])
Table:				
Sort:				
Append To:	DateInfo1	DateInfo2	DateInfo3	DateInfo4

Execute the query,

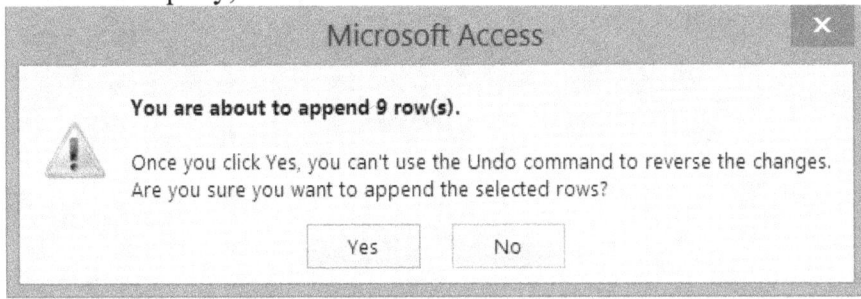

Select the "Yes" button to append to the DATE-HOLDER table.

Using DateAdd function in an Append query (continued).

ID field	Last Name	First Name	Birthday	DateInfo1	DateInfo2	DateInfo3	DateInfo4
1	Cederoth	Katherine	6/15/1957	56 Years	674 Months	20531 Days	492755 Hours
2	Yeaoman	Mike	12/14/1958	55 Years	656 Months	19984 Days	479627 Hours
3	Yeaoman	Shirley	6/22/1957	56 Years	674 Months	20524 Days	492587 Hours
4	Dionne	Tom	12/1/1977	36 Years	428 Months	13057 Days	313379 Hours
5	Lawrence	Anderson	3/15/1999	14 Years	173 Months	5283 Days	126803 Hours
6	Lawrence	Motherbee	5/15/1969	44 Years	531 Months	16179 Days	388307 Hours
7	Lawrence	Fatherbee	5/22/1967	46 Years	555 Months	16903 Days	405683 Hours
8	Lawrence	Sisterbee	7/22/1997	16 Years	193 Months	5884 Days	141227 Hours
9	Deenoyer	Tony	2/29/1996	17 Years	210 Months	6393 Days	153443 Hours
1	Cederoth	Katherine	6/15/1957	6/15/1959	8/15/1957	6/17/1957	6/15/1957 2:00:00 AM
2	Yeaoman	Mike	12/14/1958	12/14/1960	2/14/1959	12/16/1958	12/14/1958 2:00:00 AM
3	Yeaoman	Shirley	6/22/1957	6/22/1959	8/22/1957	6/24/1957	6/22/1957 2:00:00 AM
4	Dionne	Tom	12/1/1977	12/1/1979	2/1/1978	12/3/1977	12/1/1977 2:00:00 AM
5	Lawrence	Anderson	3/15/1999	3/15/2001	5/15/1999	3/17/1999	3/15/1999 2:00:00 AM
6	Lawrence	Motherbee	5/15/1969	5/15/1971	7/15/1969	5/17/1969	5/15/1969 2:00:00 AM
7	Lawrence	Fatherbee	5/22/1967	5/22/1969	7/22/1967	5/24/1967	5/22/1967 2:00:00 AM
8	Lawrence	Sisterbee	7/22/1997	7/22/1999	9/22/1997	7/24/1997	7/22/1997 2:00:00 AM
9	Deenoyer	Tony	2/29/1996	2/28/1998	4/29/1996	3/2/1996	2/29/1996 2:00:00 AM

Because the fields were initially formatted as text, the different formats of values displays correctly (numbers with text (41 years or 499 months) and the Date values (6/22/1999 or 8/22/1957)).

The output from this query illustrates that using the DateAdd function will return a different value based upon the parameter provided. Adding 2 in various ways will add years, months, days or hours to a midnight reference point.

Using DatePart function in an Append query.

DatePart function will return the value specified from a date. Below the year, month, day and hour are pulled from the [Birthday] field and appended to the DATE-STORAGE table in the [DateInfo1-4] fields.

Field:	Year: DatePart("yyyy",[Birthday]) & " Birth year"	Month: DatePart("m",[Birthday]) & " Birth month"
Table:		
Sort:		
Append To:	DateInfo1	DateInfo2

Here are the last two fields

Field:	Day: DatePart("d",[Birthday]) & " Birth day"	Hours: DatePart("h",[Birthday]) & " Birth hour"
Table:		
Sort:		
Append To:	DateInfo3	DateInfo4

The formulas are: **Year: DatePart("yyyy",[Birthday]) & " Birth year"**
Month: DatePart("m",[Birthday]) & " Birth month"
Day: DatePart("d",[Birthday]) & " Birth day"
Hours: DatePart("h",[Birthday]) & " Birth hour".

Text is added at the end of the field to indicate the value returned.

The data is deleted from the DATE-HOLDER table and the query is executed.

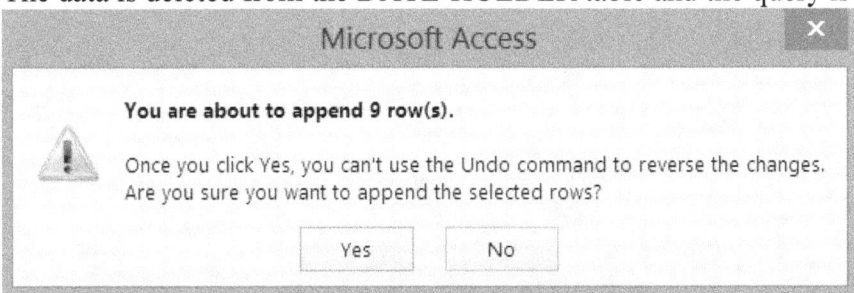

The prompt appears; select the "Yes" button.

On the next page is the table after it has been updated.

Functioning with Access – 2013
Chapter 10 – Date functions – Append queries

Using DatePart function in an Append query (continued).

Here is the DATE-HOLDER table after values have been appended.

1	Cederoth	Katherine	6/15/1957	1957 Birth year	6 Birth month	15 Birth day	0 Birth hour
2	Yeaoman	Mike	12/14/1958	1958 Birth year	12 Birth month	14 Birth day	0 Birth hour
3	Yeaoman	Shirley	6/22/1957	1957 Birth year	6 Birth month	22 Birth day	0 Birth hour
4	Dionne	Tom	12/1/1977	1977 Birth year	12 Birth month	1 Birth day	0 Birth hour
5	Lawrence	Anderson	3/15/1999	1999 Birth year	3 Birth month	15 Birth day	0 Birth hour
6	Lawrence	Motherbee	5/15/1969	1969 Birth year	5 Birth month	15 Birth day	0 Birth hour
7	Lawrence	Fatherbee	5/22/1967	1967 Birth year	5 Birth month	22 Birth day	0 Birth hour
8	Lawrence	Sisterbee	7/22/1997	1997 Birth year	7 Birth month	22 Birth day	0 Birth hour
9	Deenoyer	Tony	2/29/1996	1996 Birth year	2 Birth month	29 Birth day	0 Birth hour

This table shows how to remove segments of a date field. Also illustrated is the technique to incorporate text with data from a Date field.

Using the WeekDay and WeekDayName functions in an Append query.

The WeekDay function will return from a Date/Time field the day of the week.
The coding to do this is: **WeekDay([Birthday]).**

The WeekDayName function will return from a Date/Time field the name of the day of the week. The coding to do this is: **WeekDayName(WeekDay([Birthday])).**

A variation of the WeekDayName function will return an abbreviation of the day.
The coding to do this is: **WeekDayName((Weekday([Birthday]),1).**

Here is an example of a query that will do all three functions.

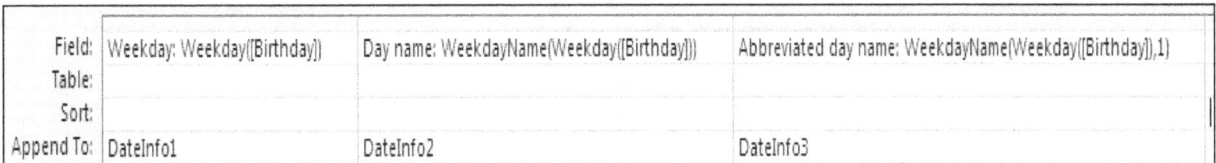

Here are the formulas:
Weekday: Weekday([Birthday])
Day name: WeekdayName(Weekday([Birthday]))
Abbreviated day name: WeekdayName(Weekday([Birthday]),1).

The query is executed and the following prompt appears.

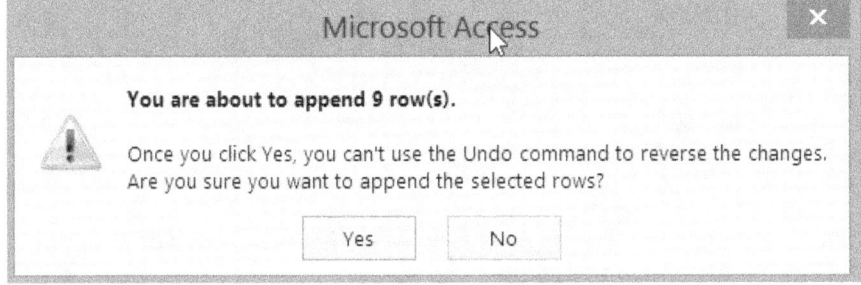

Select the "Yes" button to append these records to the DATE-HOLDER table.

The output from the query follows on the next page.

Using the WeekDay and WeekDayName functions in an Append query.

1	Cederoth	Katherine	6/15/1957	7	Saturday	Sat
2	Yeaoman	Mike	12/14/1958	1	Sunday	Sun
3	Yeaoman	Shirley	6/22/1957	7	Saturday	Sat
4	Dionne	Tom	12/1/1977	5	Thursday	Thu
5	Lawrence	Anderson	3/15/1999	2	Monday	Mon
6	Lawrence	Motherbee	5/15/1969	5	Thursday	Thu
7	Lawrence	Fatherbee	5/22/1967	2	Monday	Mon
8	Lawrence	Sisterbee	7/22/1997	3	Tuesday	Tue
9	Deenoyer	Tony	2/29/1996	5	Thursday	Thu

The 5th column (DateInfo1 field) has the number day of the week (1-7).
The 6th column (DateInfo2) shows the day name.
The 7th column (DateInfo3) displays an abbreviation of the day name.

This illustrates the power of functions to retrieve information from a Date field and present it to you in ways that you control.

From Microsoft Help:

WeekdayName Function

Description: Returns a string indicating the specified day of the week.

Syntax: **WeekdayName**(*weekday*, *abbreviate*, *firstdayofweek*)

The **WeekdayName** function syntax has these parts:

Part	Description
weekday	Required. The numeric designation for the day of the week. Numeric value of each day depends on setting of the *firstdayofweek* setting.
abbreviate	Optional. **Boolean** value that indicates if the weekday name is to be abbreviated. If omitted, the default is **False**, which means that the weekday name is not abbreviated.
firstdayofweek	Optional. Numeric value indicating the first day of the week. See Settings section for values.

The abbreviate is Boolean, so by placing a 1 after the weekday value, it is set to True.

Chapter 11 - Parameter Queries.

Using text functions along with Parameter queries will enable a user to select unique records by answering a prompt. The following queries are Select queries, not Update.

Using the Left function to find records.

The 1st step is to create a new Select query. Go to the Query part of Access, create a new query, insert the LIVE-TEST table, and select the [ID field], [Last Name] and [First Name] fields. In the Last Name column, enter code for the criteria, type in the following code:
Left([Last Name],3)=([1st 3 characters of Last Name]).

This code will prompt you for the 1st three characters of the [Last Name]. The user will then enter the 1st three characters. This value will be compared to **Left([Last Name],3).** If they match, then records will be returned. If you type in over 3 characters, it will not work because the software will compare only three characters.
The '1st 3 characters of Last Name' text is not the name of any field in the table.

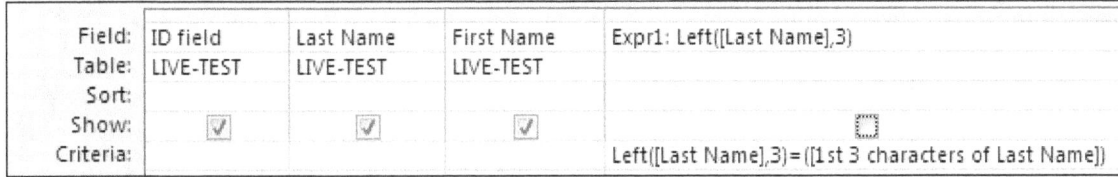

Here is the input to the prompt. Enter **Yea**.

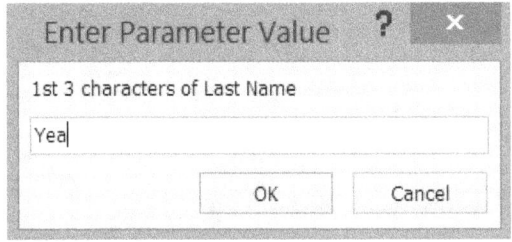

Select the OK button.

Here is the output.

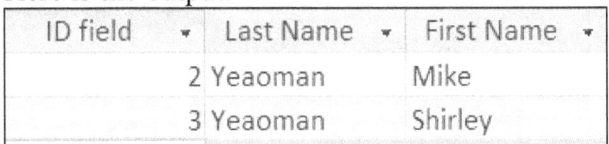

Using the Left function to find records (continued).

Here the query done again and the length is changed to 6. Notice that a new column is created and the filed is not shown.

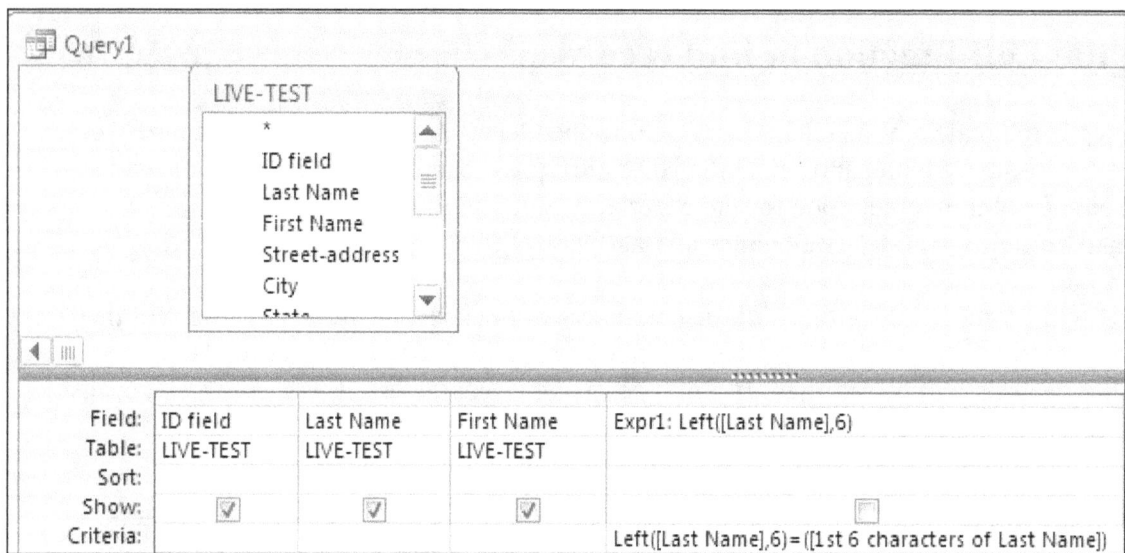

Here is the formula: **Left([Last Name],6)=([1st 6 characters of Last Name])**.

Here is the prompt (after the text was changed to 6 characters). Type in **Lawren**.

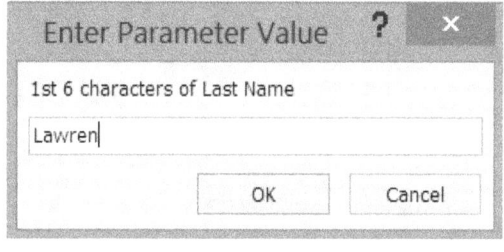

Select the OK button.

Here is the output.

Functioning with Access – 2013
Chapter 11 – Parameter query examples

Using the Left function to exclude records.

The Right function can also be used to exclude records. The same steps used with the Left function to exclude records can be used with the Right function. Using the same formula for the Right function, modify it by changing the '=' to '<>' as follows.
Left([Last Name],3)<>([Enter first 3 characters of Last Name to exclude]).

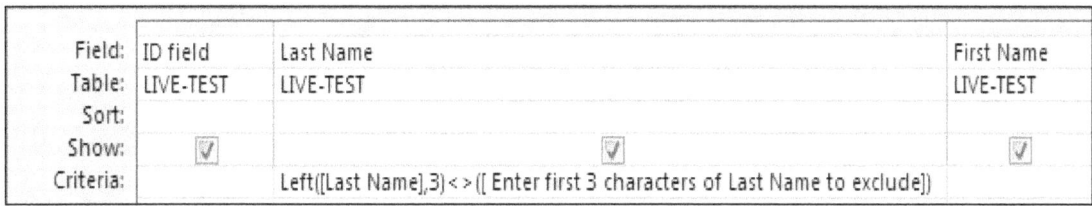

The above query will return to the screen the [ID field], the [Last Name] field and the [First Name] field. These values are returned for all records where the 3 rightmost characters of the [Last Name] field do not match the input from the user. Here I sthe prompt. Enter in **Yea**.

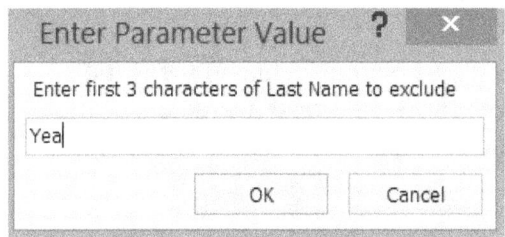

Select the OK button
Here are the records returned by answering the prompt with **Yea**.

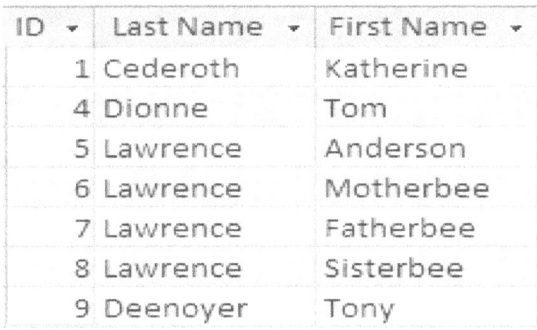

This can be very effective in finding records that do not match particular criteria.

- 153 -

Using the Right function to find records.

The same steps used with the Left function to find records can be used with the Right function. Using your query created for the Left function, change the query to the following to search for records where the last 3 characters match a pattern.

Here is the formula: **Right([Last Name],3)=([Last 3 characters of Last Name]).**

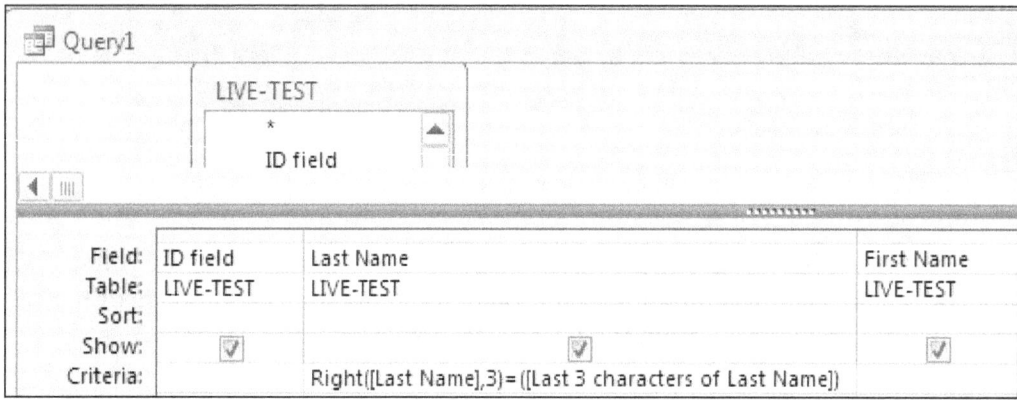

The above query will return to the screen the [ID field], the [Last Name] field and the [First Name] field. These values are returned for all records where the 3 rightmost characters of the [Last Name] field match the input from the user. Here is the prompt. Enter **nce**. Select the OK button and run the query.

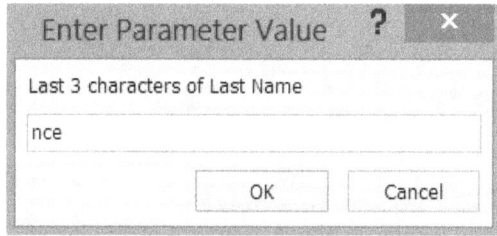

Here are the records returned by answering the prompt with **nce**.

ID	Last Name	First Name
5	Lawrence	Anderson
6	Lawrence	Motherbee
7	Lawrence	Fatherbee
8	Lawrence	Sisterbee

Using the Right function to find records (continued).

Here the query done again and the length is changed to 6.
Here is the formula: **Right([Last Name],6)=([Last 6 characters of Last Name]).**

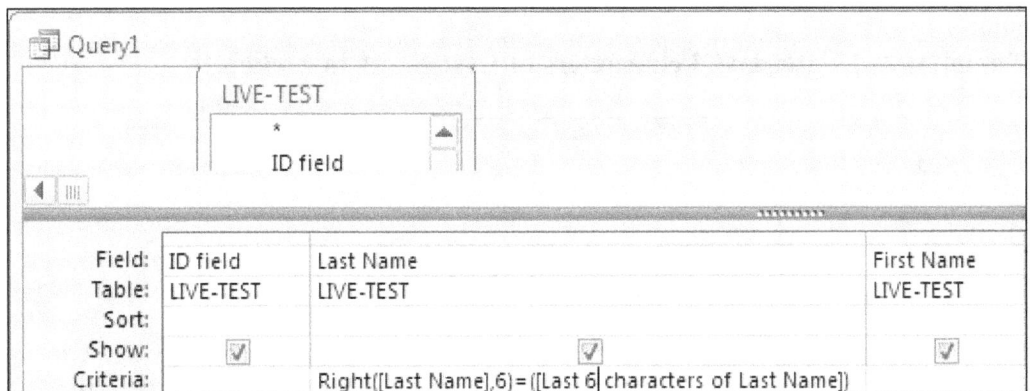

Here is the prompt. Enter in **wrence**. Select the OK button and run the query

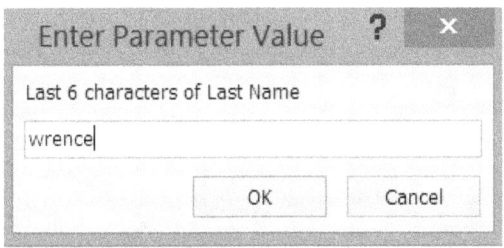

Here is the output.

ID	Last Name	First Name
5	Lawrence	Anderson
6	Lawrence	Motherbee
7	Lawrence	Fatherbee
8	Lawrence	Sisterbee

The use of the Right or Left functions can be very useful if the data has patterns of text at the beginning or end of a field.

Using the Right function to exclude records.

The Right function can also be used to exclude records. The same steps used with the Left function to exclude records can be used with the Right function. Using the same formula for the Right function, modify it by changing the '=' to '<>' as follows.
Here is the formula:

Right([Last Name],3)<>([Enter last 3 characters of Last Name to exclude]).

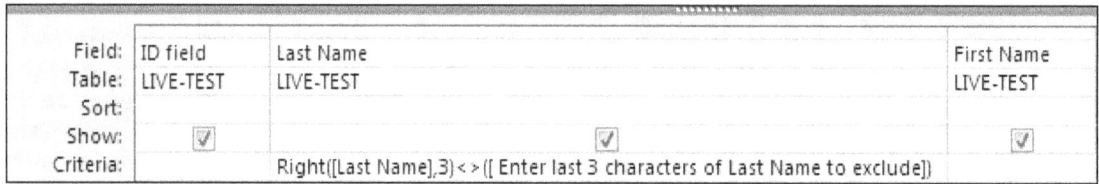

The above query will return to the screen the [ID field], the [Last Name] field and the [First Name] field. These values are returned for all records where the 3 rightmost characters of the [Last Name] field do not match the input from the user. Enter **nce** into the prompt.

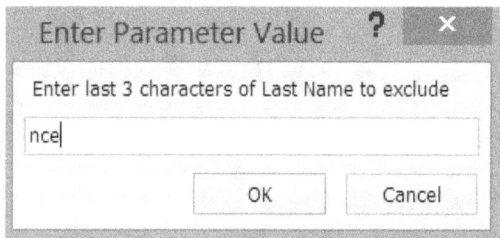

Run the query by clicking on the [OK] button.

Here are the records returned by answering the prompt with 'nce'.

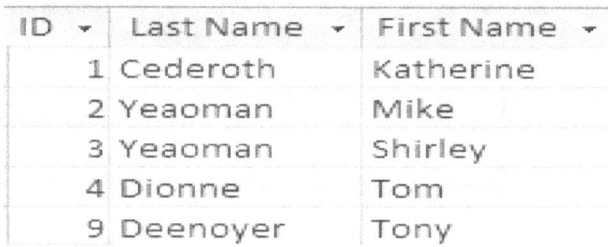

This can be very effective in finding records that do not match particular criteria.

Using the Mid function to find records.

Both the Left and Right functions are useful to find exact matches of text a pattern at the start or end of a field. The Mid function will allow you to search for specific character strings in larger character strings; however you must know where to start the search and how long the character string is. If the data that you have is organized, then it can be very useful. If the data is not organized then this function may never work for you.

The 1st step is to create a new Select query (or modify the query used for the Right function).

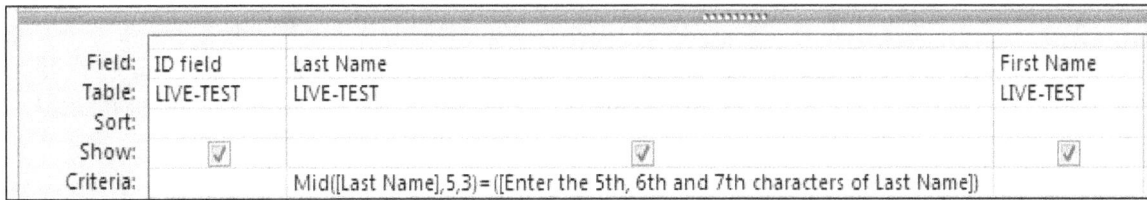

The above query will return to the screen the [ID field], [Last Name] and the [First Name] fields. These values are returned for all records where the 5th, 6th and 7th characters in the [Last Name] field match what the user entered.
The formula for this is:
   Mid([Last Name],5,3)=([Enter the 5th, 6th and 7th characters of Last Name]).

Here is the prompt, will be checking for the characters **enc**.

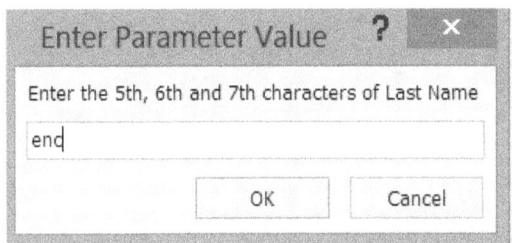

Run the query by clicking on the OK button.

Here are the records returned

ID	Last Name	First Name
5	Lawrence	Anderson
6	Lawrence	Motherbee
7	Lawrence	Fatherbee
8	Lawrence	Sisterbee

This can be a very useful function in some instances; it depends upon the data you are using with your queries.

Functioning with Access – 2013
Chapter 11 – Parameter query examples

Using the Mid function to exclude records.

The Mid function will allow you to search for specific character strings in larger character strings and exclude them. If the data that you have is organized, then it can be very useful. If the data is not organized then this function may never work for you.

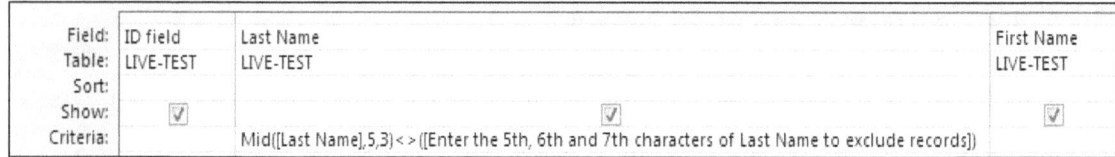

The above query will return to the screen the [ID field], [Last Name] and the [First Name] fields. These values are returned for all records where the 5th, 6th and 7th characters in the [Last Name] field does not match what the user entered
The formula for this is:
Mid([Last Name],5,3)<>([Enter the 5th, 6th and 7th characters of Last Name to exclude records]).

Here is the prompt. Enter in **enc**.

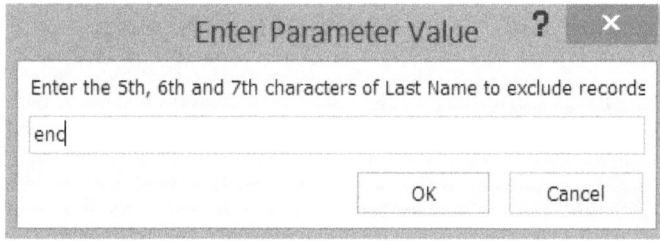

Run the query by clicking on the [OK] button.

Here are the records returned. All records that do not have **enc** in the 5th, 6th and 7th character positions are returned.

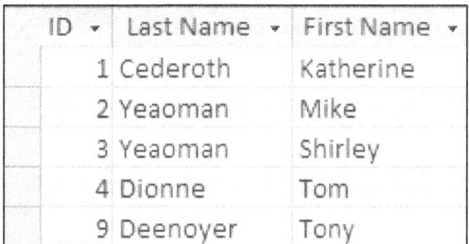

This can be a very useful function in some instances; it depends upon the data you are using with your queries.

- 158 -

Functioning with Access – 2013
Chapter 11 – Parameter query examples

Using the Len function to find records.

How many characters is the data in a field? Some of the field sizes in this database are 50 characters. The maximum number of characters the field will hold is 50, but the field may not contain that many characters. [Street-address] is such a field. Each record DOES NOT have a 50 character long street address.

If you want to find the records based upon the length of a field's content, the Len function can be used. If a field should always have 5 or 6 characters in it, this function can be useful to find data entry errors. The following will give examples of returning records based upon the number of characters entered in the [Last Name] field.

The formula is: **Len([Last Name])=([Enter the number of characters for Last Name]).**

Here is the query

Field:	ID field	Last Name	First Name
Table:	LIVE-TEST	LIVE-TEST	LIVE-TEST
Sort:			
Show:	✓	✓	✓
Criteria:		Len([Last Name])=([Enter the number of characters for Last Name])	

Here is the prompt, which will be looking for Last Names that are 8 characters long.

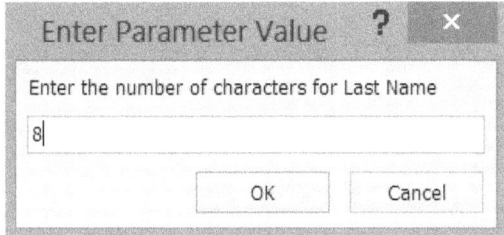

Run the query by clicking on the OK button.

Here is the output.

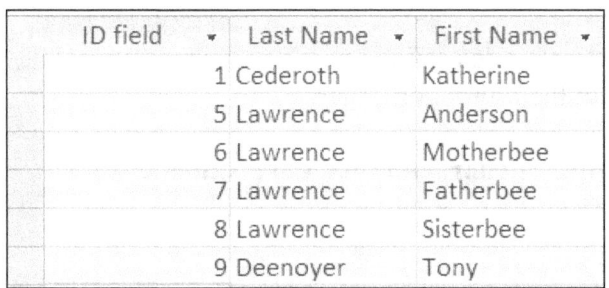

Only the records which have exactly 8 characters are returned.

- 159 -

Using the Len function to find records (continued).

If you are looking to return the records that have under a specified number of characters, the formula can be slightly changed. In the following example, the formula has been changed. The new formula is:

Len([Last Name])<=([Enter the maximum number of characters for Last Name]).

The main change is instead of using '=' between the fields, use '<='. The wording was also changed. The Maximum number of characters is 7.

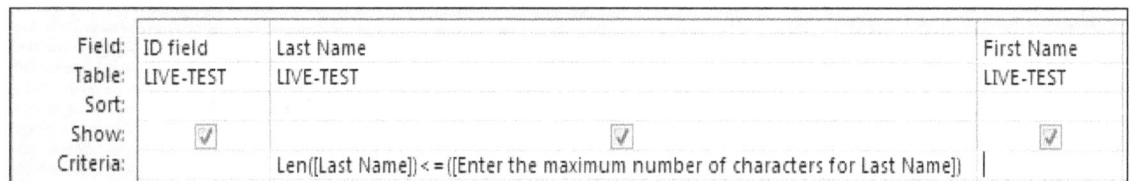

Here is the prompt, will be returning records where the [Last Name] is under 8 characters.

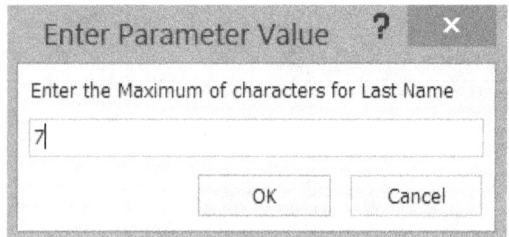

Run the query by clicking on the OK button.

Here are the records returned.

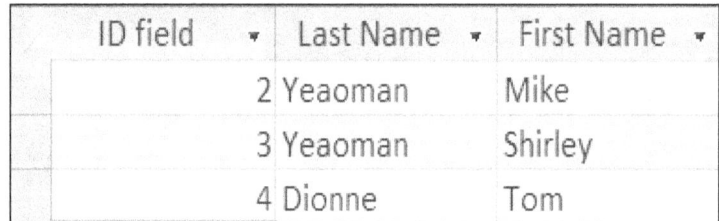

The formula can be change to find records that are over a determined number of characters. The following formula will return the number entered in the prompt or larger.

Len([Last Name])>=([Enter the minimum number of characters for Last Name]).

Functioning with Access – 2013
Chapter 11 – Parameter query examples

Using the Len function to exclude records.

If you want to find the records that, do not match the length of a field's content, the Len function can be used. If a field should never have only 8 characters in it, this function can be useful to find data entry errors. The following will give examples of returning records based upon the number of characters entered in the [Last Name] field.

The formula is:
Len([Last Name])<>([Enter an incorrect number of characters for Last Name]).

Here is the query

Field:	ID field	Last Name	First Name
Table:	LIVE-TEST	LIVE-TEST	LIVE-TEST
Sort:			
Show:	✓	✓	✓
Criteria:		Len([Last Name])<>([Enter an incorrect number of characters for Last Name])	

Here is the prompt and the value entered is 8. Run the query by clicking on the 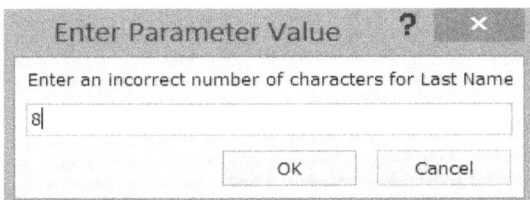 button.

Here is the output.

ID field	Last Name	First Name
2	Yeaoman	Mike
3	Yeaoman	Shirley
4	Dionne	Tom

Only the records which do not have exactly 8 characters are returned.

This query is done again; the prompt value entered is 7. Below is the output.

ID field	Last Name	First Name
1	Cederoth	Katherine
4	Dionne	Tom
5	Lawrence	Anderson
6	Lawrence	Motherbee
7	Lawrence	Fatherbee
8	Lawrence	Sisterbee
9	Deenoyer	Tony

Only the records which do not have exactly 7 characters are returned.

Using the InStr function to find records.

The most useful function to find records that have text in a particular field is done by using the InStr field. The formula will test if the character string exists in another string. If the text is found, the query will return all records meeting the criteria.

Here is the formula: **InStr([Last Name],[Enter a string to search for])>"0"**.

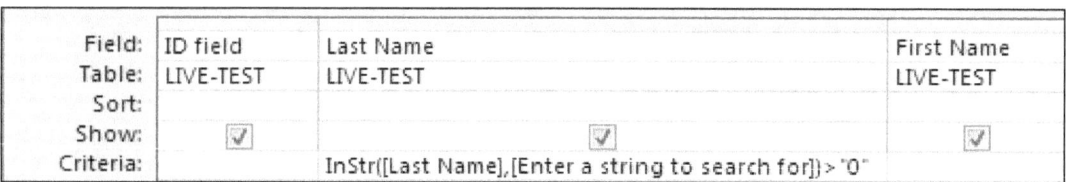

The query will search for any [Last Name] that has contains the text 'der'.

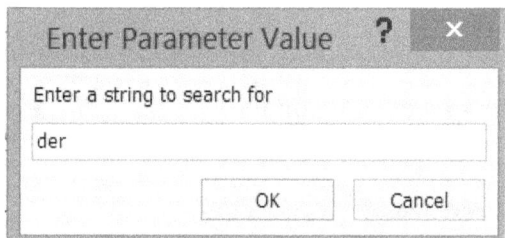

Run the query by clicking on the 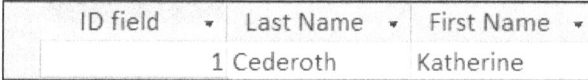 button. Here is the record found.

ID field	Last Name	First Name
1	Cederoth	Katherine

Run the query again, looking for records with 'en' in the [Last Name].

ID field	Last Name	First Name
5	Lawrence	Anderson
6	Lawrence	Motherbee
7	Lawrence	Fatherbee
8	Lawrence	Sisterbee
9	Deenoyer	Tony

Run the query again, looking for records with 'o' in the [Last Name].

ID field	Last Name	First Name
1	Cederoth	Katherine
2	Yeaoman	Mike
3	Yeaoman	Shirley
4	Dionne	Tom
9	Deenoyer	Tony

This formula can be used to find text, numbers or any patterns.

Using the InStr function to exclude records.

Sometimes you need to find all records that **do not** have a text pattern. The formula can be changed (along with the prompt) to bring back those that do not have the text string. The formula is: **InStr([Last Name],[Enter a string to exclude])="0"**.

The formula checks each record and those that fail (the formula returns 0) are returned.

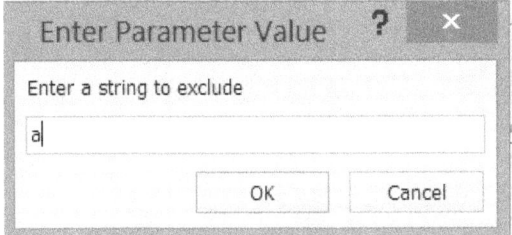

Here is the prompt which is excluding all records with an 'a' in the [Last Name].

Here are the records that do not have an 'a' in the [Last Name] field.

ID field	Last Name	First Name
1	Cederoth	Katherine
4	Dionne	Tom
9	Deenoyer	Tony

This last example illustrates the varied way that you can use functions to return or to exclude records. These were done with a Select query, but could be done with an Append query to place into another table

Functioning with Access – 2013
Chapter 12 – Using Help,
Wild cards and Input masks

Chapter 12 - Using Help.

The information in this chapter is from Microsoft help.

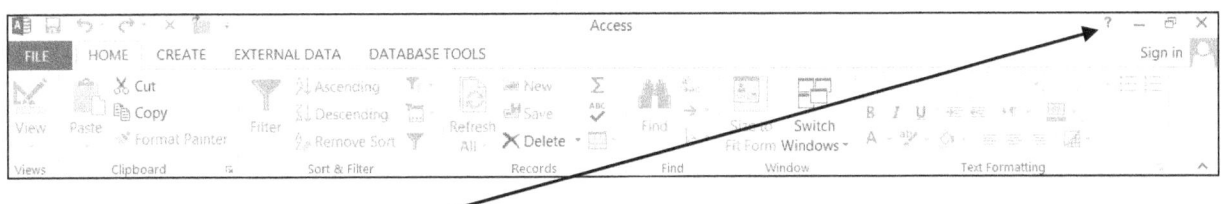

Select the Help icon

The following will display. Access will look for information out on the web, much of the help is in articles or Videos.

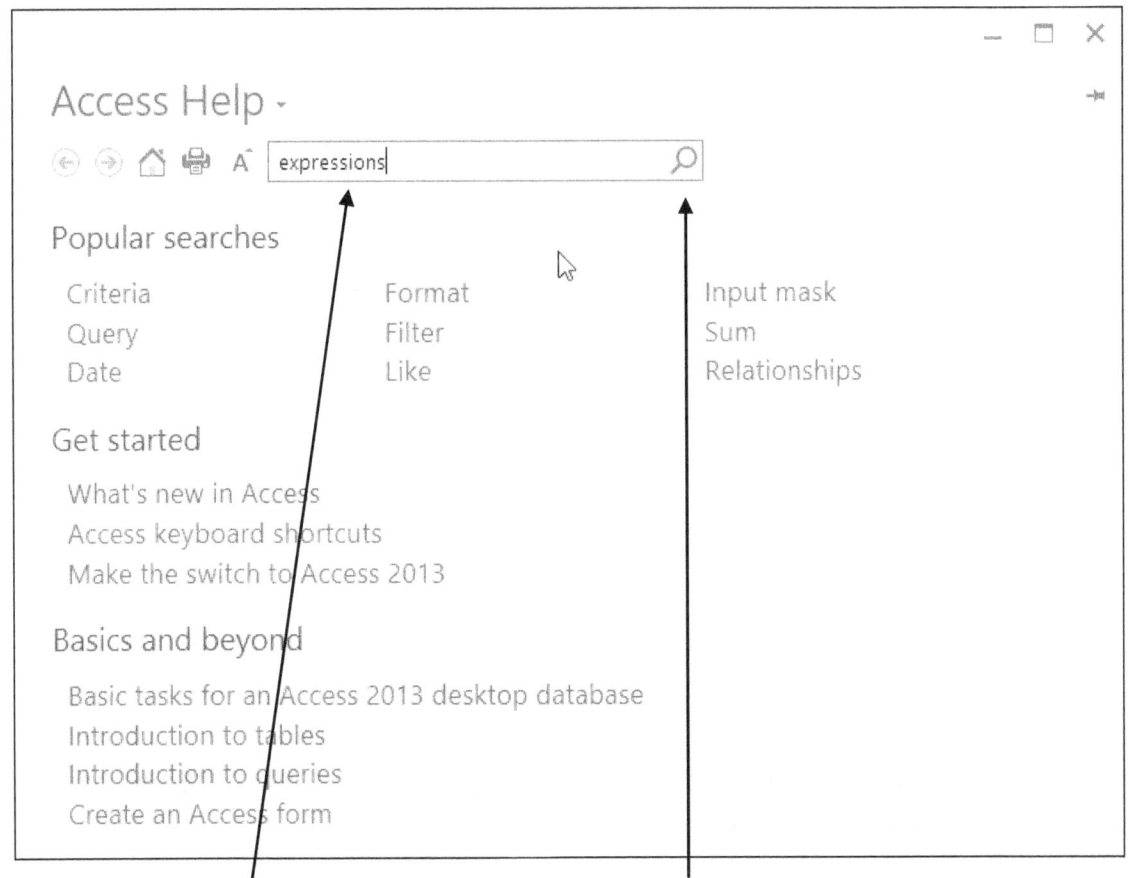

Enter in Expressions and press the magnifying glass.

- 165 -

Here are some of the references to Expressions that are available.

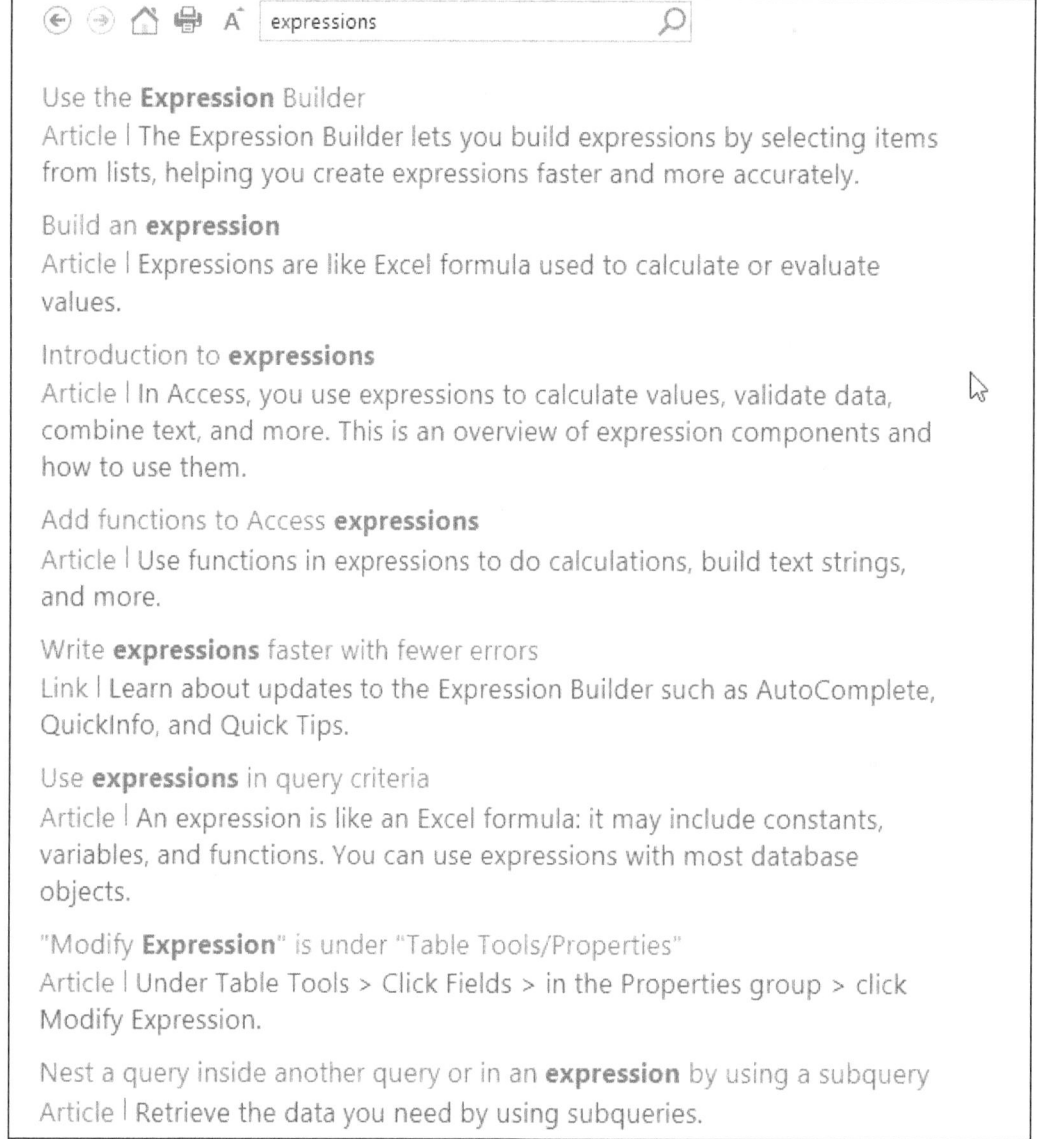

Expressions, Macros and Programming are powerful sources of direction for anyone wanting to increase their knowledge beyond this or any book.

Expressions are what this book are focussing on. On each page a function is used in an Expression.

Functioning with Access – 2013
Chapter 12 – Using Help, Wild cards and Input masks

More expressions are available if you scroll down and press NEXT

|◄ PREV | NEXT

If...Then...Else Statement
Link | Use the If-Then-Else statement in Visual Basic for Applications (VBA) to execute statements depending on the value of an expression.

Learn the differences between Is Null and IsNull()
Link | Should you use Is Null or IsNull to determine if an expression contains a null value? Depends on the context.

CDate function
Link | Use CDate to convert any valid date expression to the Date/Time data type.

Video: Stop a query from asking for input
Video | How to remove parameters and fix a common problem in expressions.

Use the COUNT function
Article | Calculate aggregate values by using the COUNT function in expressions.

If...Then...Else Macro Block
Link | Use the If macro block to conditionally execute a group of actions, depending on the value of an expression.

Stop a query from asking for input
Training | How to remove parameters and fix a common problem in expressions.

Create a make table query
Article | Use a make table query to convert the results of a select query to a table.

Why does Access want me to enter a parameter value?
Article | Learn why Access displays the Enter Parameter Value dialog box.

Functioning with Access – 2013
Chapter 12 – Using Help,
Wild cards and Input masks

And here is the information in Help if you serach on Functions

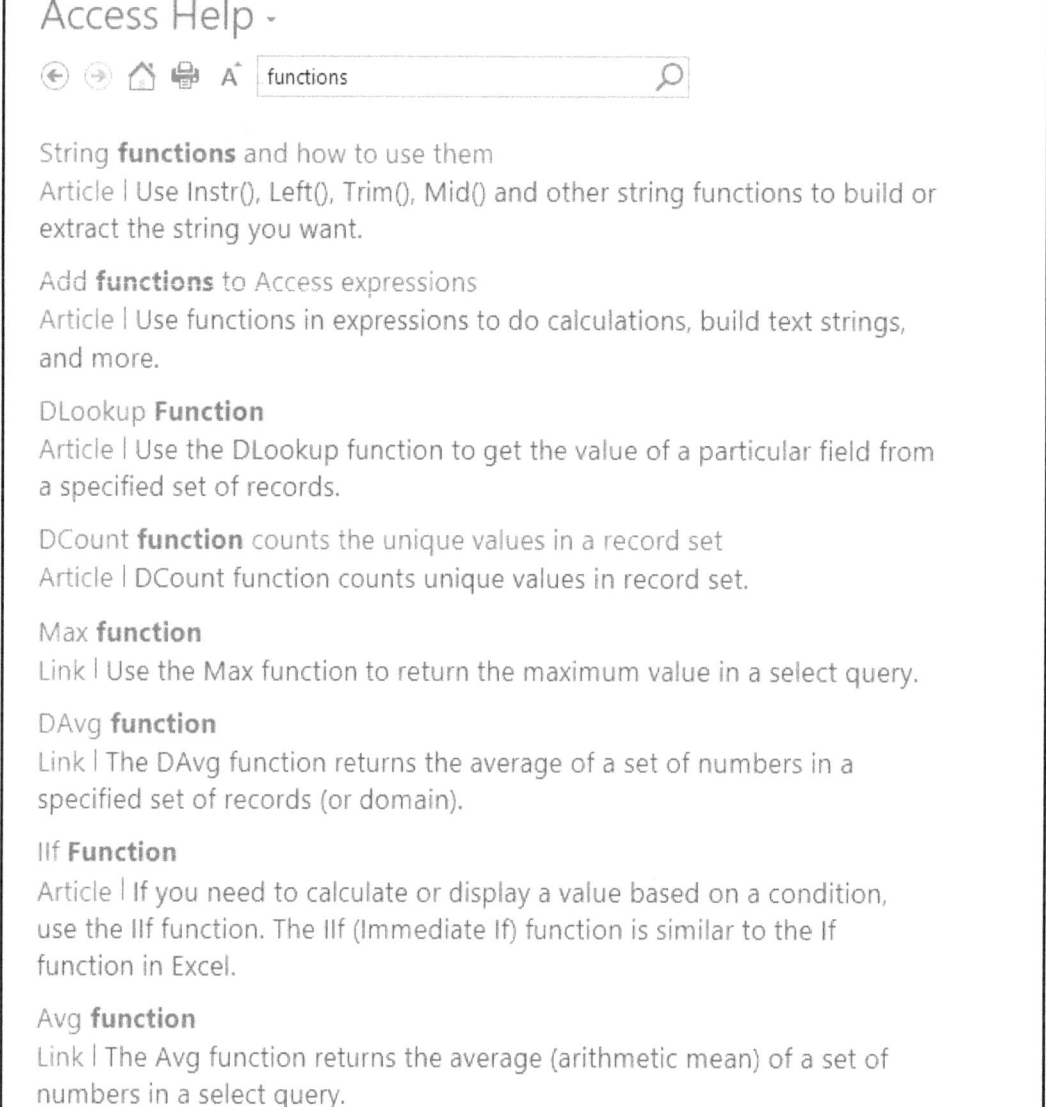

Using Wildcard Characters in String Comparisons (from Access Help).

Built-in pattern matching provides a versatile tool for making string comparisons. The following table shows the wildcard characters you can use with the **Like** operator and the number of digits or strings they match.

Character(s) in *pattern*	Matches in *expression*
? or _ (underscore)	Any single character
* or %	Zero or more characters
#	Any single digit (0 — 9)
[*charlist*]	Any single character in *charlist*
[!*charlist*]	Any single character not in *charlist*

You can use a group of one or more characters (*charlist*) enclosed in brackets ([ ]) to match any single character in *expression,* and *charlist* can include almost any characters in the ANSI character set, including digits. You can use the special characters opening bracket ([ ), question mark (?), number sign (#), and asterisk (*) to match themselves directly only if enclosed in brackets. You cannot use the closing bracket ( ]) within a group to match itself, but you can use it outside a group as an individual character.

In addition to a simple list of characters enclosed in brackets, *charlist* can specify a range of characters by using a hyphen (-) to separate the upper and lower bounds of the range. For example, using [A-Z] in *pattern* results in a match if the corresponding character position in *expression* contains any of the uppercase letters in the range A through Z. You can include multiple ranges within the brackets without delimiting the ranges. For example, [a-zA-Z0-9] matches any alphanumeric character.

It is important to note that the ANSI SQL wildcards (%) and (_) are only available with Microsoft® Jet version 4.X and the Microsoft OLE DB Provider for Jet. They will be treated as literals if used through Microsoft Access or DAO.

Other important rules for pattern matching include the following:

- An exclamation mark (!) at the beginning of *charlist* means that a match is made if any character except those in *charlist* are found in *expression*. When used outside brackets, the exclamation mark matches itself.
- You can use the hyphen (-) either at the beginning (after an exclamation mark if one is used) or at the end of *charlist* to match itself. In any other location, the hyphen identifies a range of ANSI characters.
- When you specify a range of characters, the characters must appear in ascending sort order (A-Z or 0-100). [A-Z] is a valid pattern, but [Z-A] is not.
- The character sequence [ ] is ignored; it is considered to be a zero-length string ("").

Like Operator explained.

Compares a string expression to a pattern in an SQL expression.

Syntax: *expression* Like *"pattern"*

The **Like** operator syntax has these parts:

Part	Description
expression	SQL expression used in a WHERE clause.
pattern	String or character string literal against which *expression* is compared.

Remarks

You can use the **Like** operator to find values in a field that match the pattern you specify. For *pattern*, you can specify the complete value (for example, Like "Smith"), or you can use wildcard characters to find a range of values (for example, Like "Sm*").
In an expression, you can use the **Like** operator to compare a field value to a string expression. For example, if you enter Like "C*" in an SQL query, the query returns all field values beginning with the letter C. In a parameter query, you can prompt the user for a pattern to search for.
The following example returns data that begins with the letter P followed by any letter between A and F and three digits:
Like "P[A-F]###"
The following table shows how you can use **Like** to test expressions for different patterns.

Kind of match	Pattern	Match (returns True)	No match (returns False)
Multiple characters	a*a	aa, aBa, aBBBa	aBC
	ab	abc, AABB, Xab	aZb, bac
Special character	a[*]a	a*a	aaa
Multiple characters	ab*	abcdefg, abc	cab, aab
Single character	a?a	aaa, a3a, aBa	aBBBa
Single digit	a#a	a0a, a1a, a2a	aaa, a10a
Range of characters	[a-z]	f, p, j	2, &
Outside a range	[!a-z]	9, &, %	b, a
Not a digit	[!0-9]	A, a, &, ~	0, 1, 9
Combined	a[!b-m]#	An9, az0, a99	abc, aj0

Functioning with Access – 2013
Chapter 12 – Using Help,
Wild cards and Input masks

Valid input mask characters.

Microsoft Access interprets characters in the first part of the **InputMask** property definition as shown in the following table. To define a literal character, enter any character other than those shown in the table, including spaces and symbols. To define one of the following characters as a literal character, precede that character with a \.

Character	Description
0	Digit (0 through 9, entry required; plus [+] and minus [-] signs not allowed).
9	Digit or space (entry not required; plus and minus signs not allowed).
#	Digit or space (entry not required; blank positions converted to spaces, plus and minus signs allowed).
L, ?	Letter (A through Z, entry required).
A, a	Letter or digit (entry required).
&	Any character or a space (entry required).
C	Any character or a space (entry optional).
. , : ; - /	Decimal placeholder and thousands, date, and time separators. (The actual character used depends on the regional settings specified by double-clicking Regional Settings in the Windows Control Panel.)
<	Causes all characters that follow to be converted to lowercase.
>	Causes all characters that follow to be converted to uppercase.
!	Causes the input mask to display from right to left, rather than from left to right. Characters typed into the mask always fill it from left to right. You can include the exclamation point anywhere in the input mask.
\	Causes the character that follows to be displayed as a literal character. Used to display any of the characters listed in this table as literal characters (for example, \A is displayed as just A).
""	Characters enclosed in double quotation marks will be displayed literally.
Password	Setting the **InputMask** property to the word **Password** creates a password entry text box. Any character typed in the text box is stored as the character but is displayed as an asterisk (*).

Examples of input masks.

An input mask is used in fields (in tables and queries) and in text boxes and combo boxes (in forms) to format data and provide some control over what values can be entered. An input mask consists of literal characters (such as spaces, dots, dashes, and parentheses) that separate blanks to fill in. The **InputMask** property setting consists of literal characters along with special characters that determine the kind of value that can be entered into the blank in that position. Input masks are primarily used in Text and Date/Time fields, but can also be used in Number or Currency fields.

This topic provides reference information about: Examples of input masks

The following table shows some useful input mask definitions and examples of values you can enter into them. Refer to the table at the end of this topic for details on the codes used to create input mask definitions.

Input mask definition	Examples of values
(000) 000-0000	(206) 555-0248
(999) 999-9999!	(206) 555-0248
	( ) 555-0248
(000) AAA-AAAA	(206) 555-TELE
#999	-20
	2000
>L????L?000L0	GREENGR339M3
	MAY R 452B7
>L0L 0L0	T2F 8M4
00000-9999	98115-
	98115-3007
>L<?????????????	Maria
	Pierre
ISBN 0-&&&&&&&&&-0	ISBN 1-55615-507-7
	ISBN 0-13-964262-5
>LL00000-0000	DB51392-0493

Defining input masks.

The input mask definition can contain up to three sections separated by semicolons; for example, (999) 000-0000!;0;" ".

Section	Meaning
First	The input mask itself.
Second	Determines whether to store the literal display characters. 0 = store literal characters with the value entered 1 or leave blank = store only characters entered in blanks
Third	Character that is displayed for blanks in the input mask. You can use any character; type " " (double quotation marks, space, double quotation marks) to display a space. If you leave this section blank, the underscore (_) is used.

Choose Function Example

You can use the Choose function to create a calculated control whose value is determined by the value of a field in a table in your database. For example, suppose you have a Shippers table that contains a field called ShipperID. You could create a calculated control on a form to display a text name for the shipper based on the value of the ShipperID field.

=**Choose**([ShipperID], "Speedy", "United", "Federal")

Chapter 13 - Character set information.

Character Set (0 – 127) these can be used with Char() function

0	☐	32	[space]	64	@	96	`
1	☐	33	!	65	A	97	A
2	☐	34	"	66	B	98	B
3	☐	35	#	67	C	99	C
4	☐	36	$	68	D	100	D
5	☐	37	%	69	E	101	e
6	☐	38	&	70	F	102	f
7	☐	39	'	71	G	103	g
8	**	40	(	72	H	104	h
9	**	41	)	73	I	105	i
10	**	42	*	74	J	106	j
11	☐	43	+	75	K	107	k
12	☐	44	,	76	L	108	l
13	**	45	-	77	M	109	m
14	☐	46	.	78	N	110	n
15	☐	47	/	79	O	111	o
16	☐	48	0	80	P	112	p
17	☐	49	1	81	Q	113	q
18	☐	50	2	82	R	114	r
19	☐	51	3	83	S	115	s
20	☐	52	4	84	T	116	t
21	☐	53	5	85	U	117	u
22	☐	54	6	86	V	118	v
23	☐	55	7	87	W	119	w
24	☐	56	8	88	X	120	x
25	☐	57	9	89	Y	121	y
26	☐	58	:	90	Z	122	z
27	☐	59	;	91	[	123	{
28	☐	60	<	92	\	124	|
29	☐	61	=	93	]	125	}
30	☐	62	>	94	^	126	~
31	☐	63	?	95	_	127	☐

The values in the table above are the Windows default.
However, values in the ANSI character set above 127 (next page) are determined by the code page specific to your operating system.
(this information is from Microsoft)

Character Set (128 – 255)

128	€	160	[space]	192	À	224	à
129	€	161	¡	193	Á	225	á
130	€	162	¢	194	Â	226	â
131	€	163	£	195	Ã	227	ã
132	€	164	¤	196	Ä	228	ä
133	€	165	¥	197	Å	229	å
134	€	166	¦	198	Æ	230	æ
135	€	167	§	199	Ç	231	ç
136	€	168	¨	200	È	232	è
137	€	169	©	201	É	233	é
138	€	170	ª	202	Ê	234	ê
139	€	171	«	203	Ë	235	ë
140	€	172	¬	204	Ì	236	ì
141	€	173		205	Í	237	í
142	€	174	®	206	Î	238	î
143	€	175	¯	207	Ï	239	ï
144	€	176	°	208	Ð	240	ð
145	€	177	±	209	Ñ	241	ñ
146	€	178	²	210	Ò	242	ò
147	€	179	³	211	Ó	243	ó
148	€	180	´	212	Ô	244	ô
149	€	181	µ	213	Õ	245	õ
150	€	182	¶	214	Ö	246	ö
151	€	183	·	215	×	247	÷
152	€	184	¸	216	Ø	248	ø
153	€	185	¹	217	Ù	249	ù
154	€	186	º	218	Ú	250	ú
155	€	187	»	219	Û	251	û
156	€	188	¼	220	Ü	252	ü
157	€	189	½	221	Ý	253	ý
158	€	190	¾	222	Þ	254	þ
159	€	191	¿	223	ß	255	ÿ

These characters (128 to 256) are not supported by Microsoft Windows.

(This information is from Microsoft)

ASCII Characters for MPE Users

The ASCII character set defines 128 characters (0 to 127 decimal, 0 to FF hexadecimal, and 0 to 177 octal). This character set is a subset of many other character sets with 256 characters, including the ANSI character set of MS Windows, the Roman-8 character set of HP systems, and the IBM PC Extended Character Set of DOS, and the ISO Latin-1 character set used by Web browsers. They are not the same as the EBCDIC character set used on IBM mainframes.

The Control Characters

The first 32 values are non-printing **control characters**, such as *Return* and *Line feed*. You generate these characters on the keyboard by holding down the Control key while you strike another key. For example, Bell is value 7, Control plus G, often shown in documents as ^G. Notice that 7 is 64 less than the value of G (71); the Control key subtracts 64 from the value of the keys that it modifies.
For the text version of the following tables, click Control Characters and Printing Characters.

This information retrieved from http://www.robelle.com/library/smugbook/ascii.html
(9/17/13)

Functioning with Access – 2013
Chapter 13 – Character set info

Control Characters

Char	Oct	Dec	Hex	Control-Key	Control Action
NUL	0	0	0	^@	Null character
SOH	1	1	1	^A	Start of heading, = console interrupt
STX	2	2	2	^B	Start of text, maintenance mode on HP console
ETX	3	3	3	^C	End of text
EOT	4	4	4	^D	End of transmission, not the same as ETB
ENQ	5	5	5	^E	Enquiry, goes with ACK; old HP flow control
ACK	6	6	6	^F	Acknowledge, clears ENQ logon hand
BEL	7	7	7	^G	Bell, rings the bell...
BS	10	8	8	^H	Backspace, works on HP terminals/computers
HT	11	9	9	^I	Horizontal tab, move to next tab stop
LF	12	10	a	^J	Line Feed
VT	13	11	b	^K	Vertical tab
FF	14	12	c	^L	Form Feed, page eject
CR	15	13	d	^M	Carriage Return
SO	16	14	e	^N	Shift Out, alternate character set
SI	17	15	f	^O	Shift In, resume defaultn character set
DLE	20	16	10	^P	Data link escape
DC1	21	17	11	^Q	XON, with XOFF to pause listings; ":okay to send".
DC2	22	18	12	^R	Device control 2, block-mode flow control
DC3	23	19	13	^S	XOFF, with XON is TERM=18 flow control
DC4	24	20	14	^T	Device control 4
NAK	25	21	15	^U	Negative acknowledge
SYN	26	22	16	^V	Synchronous idle
ETB	27	23	17	^W	End transmission block, not the same as EOT
CAN	30	24	17	^X	Cancel line, MPE echoes !!!
EM	31	25	19	^Y	End of medium, Control-Y interrupt
SUB	32	26	1a	^Z	Substitute
ESC	33	27	1b	^[	Escape, next character is not echoed
FS	34	28	1c	^\	File separator
GS	35	29	1d	^]	Group separator
RS	36	30	1e	^^	Record separator, block-mode terminator
US	37	31	1f	^_	Unit separator

Functioning with Access – 2013
Chapter 13 – Character set info

Printing Characters (continued on next 2 pages)

Char	Dec	Description	Octal	Hex
SP	32	Space	40	20
!	33	Exclamation mark	41	21
"	34	Quotation mark (" in HTML)	42	22
#	35	Cross hatch (number sign)	43	23
$	36	Dollar sign	44	24
%	37	Percent sign	45	25
&	38	Ampersand	46	26
`	39	Closing single quote (apostrophe)	47	27
(	40	Opening parentheses	50	28
)	41	Closing parentheses	51	29
*	42	Asterisk (star, multiply)	52	2a
+	43	Plus	53	2b
,	44	Comma	54	2c
-	45	Hyphen, dash, minus	55	2d
.	46	Period	56	2e
/	47	Slant (forward slash, divide)	57	2f
0	48	Zero	60	30
1	49	One	61	31
2	50	Two	62	32
3	51	Three	63	33
4	52	Four	64	34
5	53	Five	65	35
6	54	Six	66	36
7	55	Seven	67	37
8	56	Eight	70	38
9	57	Nine	71	39
:	58	Colon	72	3a
;	59	Semicolon	73	3b
<	60	Less than sign (< in HTML)	74	3c
=	61	Equals sign	75	3d
>	62	Greater than sign (> in HTML)	76	3e
?	63	Question mark	77	3f
@	64	At-sign	100	40

Printing Characters (continued on next page)

Char	Dec	Description	Octal	Hex
A	65	Uppercase A	101	41
B	66	Uppercase B	102	42
C	67	Uppercase C	103	43
D	68	Uppercase D	104	44
E	69	Uppercase E	105	45
F	70	Uppercase F	106	46
G	71	Uppercase G	107	47
H	72	Uppercase H	110	48
I	73	Uppercase I	111	49
J	74	Uppercase J	112	4a
K	75	Uppercase K	113	4b
L	76	Uppercase L	114	4c
M	77	Uppercase M	115	4d
N	78	Uppercase N	116	4e
O	79	Uppercase O	117	4f
P	80	Uppercase P	120	50
Q	81	Uppercase Q	121	51
R	82	Uppercase R	122	52
S	83	Uppercase S	123	53
T	84	Uppercase T	124	54
U	85	Uppercase U	125	55
V	86	Uppercase V	126	56
W	87	Uppercase W	127	57
X	88	Uppercase X	130	58
Y	89	Uppercase Y	131	59
Z	90	Uppercase Z	132	5a
[	91	Opening square bracket	133	5b
\	92	Reverse slant (Backslash)	134	5c
]	93	Closing square bracket	135	5d
^	94	Caret (Circumflex)	136	5e
_	95	Underscore	137	5f

Printing Characters

Char	Dec	Description	Octal	Hex
`	96	Opening single quote	140	60
a	97	Lowercase a	141	61
b	98	Lowercase b	142	62
c	99	Lowercase c	143	63
d	100	Lowercase d	144	64
e	101	Lowercase e	145	65
f	102	Lowercase f	146	66
g	103	Lowercase g	147	67
h	104	Lowercase h	150	68
i	105	Lowercase i	151	69
j	106	Lowercase j	152	6a
k	107	Lowercase k	153	6b
l	108	Lowercase l	154	6c
m	109	Lowercase m	155	6d
n	110	Lowercase n	156	6e
o	111	Lowercase o	157	6f
p	112	Lowercase p	160	70
q	113	Lowercase q	161	71
r	114	Lowercase r	162	72
s	115	Lowercase s	163	73
t	116	Lowercase t	164	74
u	117	Lowercase u	165	75
v	118	Lowercase v	166	76
w	119	Lowercase w	167	77
x	120	Lowercase x	170	78
y	121	Lowercase y	171	79
z	122	Lowercase z	172	7a
{	123	Opening curly brace	173	7b
|	124	Vertical line	174	7c
}	125	Cloing curly brace	175	7d
~	126	Tilde (approximate)	176	7e
DEL	127	Delete (rubout), cross-hatch box	177	7f

Functioning with Access – 2013
Chapter 13 – Character set info

Extended ASCII (characters 128 – 256) from http://www.ascii-code.com/ (3/22/07)
These are the codes from 128 to 187 (continued on next page)

Code	Char	Name	Code	Char	Name	Code	Char	Name
128	€	unused	148	"	close double quote	168	¨	diaeresis
129	•	unused	149	•	bullet (large)	169	©	copyright
130	,	baseline single quote	150	–	en dash	170	ª	feminine ordinal
131	ƒ	florin	151	—	em dash	171	«	left double guillemet
132	„	baseline double quote	152	~	tilde	172	¬	not
133	…	ellipsis	153	™	unregistered trademark	173		soft hyphen
134	†	dagger (single)	154	š	s caron	174	®	registered trademark
135	‡	dagger (double)	155	›	right single guillemet	175	¯	macron
136	ˆ	circumflex	156	œ	oe ligature	176	°	ring (also degrees)
137	‰	per mil	157	•	unused	177	±	plus/minus
138	Š	S caron	158	ž	unused	178	²	superscript 2
139	‹	left single guillemet	159	Ÿ	Y diaeresis	179	³	superscript 3
140	Œ	OE ligature	160		non-breaking space	180	´	acute
141	•	unused	161	¡	Spanish inverted !	181	µ	micro symbol (or mu)
142	Ž	unused	162	¢	cents	182	¶	pilcrow (paragraph symbol)
143	•	unused	163	£	pounds	183	·	bullet (small)
144	•	unused	164	¤	intl. monetary symbol	184	¸	cedilla
145	'	open single quote	165	¥	yen	185	¹	superscript 1
146	'	close single quote	166	¦	broken bar	186	º	masculine ordinal
147	"	open double quote	167	§	section symbol	187	»	right double guillemet

Functioning with Access – 2013
Chapter 13 – Character set info

Extended ASCII (characters 128 – 256) from http://www.ascii-code.com/ (3/22/07)

These are the codes from 188 to 255

Code	Char	Name	Code	Char	Name	Code	Char	Name
188	¼	one-fourth	210	Ò	O grave	232	è	e grave
189	½	one-half	211	Ó	O acute	233	é	e acute
190	¾	three-fourths	212	Ô	O circumflex	234	ê	e circumflex
191	¿	Spanish inverted ?	213	Õ	O tilde	235	ë	e diaeresis
192	À	A grave	214	Ö	O diaeresis	236	ì	i grave
193	Á	A acute	215	×	multiply symbol	237	í	i acute
194	Â	A circumflex	216	Ø	O with oblique stroke	238	î	i circumflex
195	Ã	A tilde	217	Ù	U grave	239	ï	i diaeresis
196	Ä	A diaeresis	218	Ú	U acute	240	ð	Icelandic eth
197	Å	A ring	219	Û	U circumflex	241	ñ	n tilde
198	Æ	AE ligature	220	Ü	U diaeresis	242	ò	o grave
199	Ç	C cedilla	221	Ý	Y acute	243	ó	o acute
200	È	E grave	222	Þ	Icelandic Thorn	244	ô	o circumflex
201	É	E acute	223	ß	German sharp s	245	õ	o tilde
202	Ê	E circumflex	224	à	a grave	246	ö	o diaeresis
203	Ë	E diaeresis	225	á	a acute	247	÷	divide symbol
204	Ì	I grave	226	â	a circumflex	248	ø	o with oblique stroke
205	Í	I acute	227	ã	a tilde	249	ù	u grave
206	Î	I circumflex	228	ä	a diaeresis	250	ú	u acute
207	Ï	I diaeresis	229	å	a ring	251	û	u circumflex
208	Ð	Icelandic Eth	230	æ	ae ligature	252	ü	u diaeresis
209	Ñ	N tilde	231	ç	c cedilla	253	ý	y acute
						254	þ	Icelandic thorn
						255	ÿ	y diaeresis

ASCII - The **A**merican **S**tandard **C**ode for **I**nformation **I**nterchange is a standard seven-bit code that was proposed by ANSI in 1963, and finalized in 1968. Other sources also credit much of the work on ASCII to work done in 1965 by Robert W. Bemer (www.bobbemer.com). ASCII was established to achieve compatibility between various types of data processing equipment. Later-day standards that document ASCII include ISO-14962-1997 and ANSI-X3.4-1986(R1997).

ASCII, pronounced "ask-key", is the common code for microcomputer equipment. The standard ASCII character set consists of 128 decimal numbers (7-bits) ranging from zero through 127 assigned to letters, numbers, punctuation marks, and the most common special characters. The Extended ASCII Character Set also consists of 128 decimal numbers and ranges from 128 through 255 (using the full 8-bits of the byte) representing additional special, mathematical, graphic, and foreign characters. (Downloaded from http://www.idevelopment.info/data/Programming/ascii_table/PROGRAMMING_ascii_table.shtml)

Appendix

Function()/Steps	Page(s)
Adding to Date	67, 68, 117, 118, 121, 146
AND queries	4
Avg()	49-52, 136-137
Concatenation	32-34, 102-104, 108
Count()	53, 138-140
DateAdd()	67-69, 119-121, 145-146
DateDiff()	62-66, 68, 122, 142-144
DatePart()	70-71, 147-148
Day()	75, 85, 147-148
Expression Builder	7-11, 22, 47, 59, 61
Fix()	52, 111-112, 137
Format()	62-64
Hour()	74, 85, 143, 145, 147-148
Input Masks	171-173
InStr()	36-39, 100-101, 105, 132, 162-164
Int()	52, 111, 137
LCase()	42, 107-108
Left()	23-25, 33-34, 88-91, 108, 126, 151-153
Len()	35, 99, 108, 131, 159-161
Like operator	89, 92, 96, 97, 126-127, 170
LTrim()	40-42, 102-104, 133
Math operators	113-115
Max()	54, 138-140
Mid()	29-31, 95-97, 128, 157-158
Min()	55, 138-140
Minute()	73, 85
Month()	81, 86, 143, 145, 147-148

Function()/Steps	Page(s)
Now()	62-63, 66, 72-74, 83, 122, 141-144
OR queries	4
Parameter	89, 93, 95, 126-127, 151-164
Replace()	43-45, 97-98, 104-105, 129-130
Right()	26-28, 33-34, 38, 92-94, 108, 127, 154-156
Round()	51-52, 110, 136-137
RTrim()	40-42, 102-104
Second()	72, 85
SQL	46
Sum()	56, 138-140
Timer()	83-84, 86
Trim()	40-42, 102-104, 133
UCase()	42, 106, 108
VBA Code	85, 86
WeekDay()	76-78, 86, 149-150
WeekDayName()	79-80, 149-150
Wildcards	96, 169
Year()	82, 86, 143, 145, 147-148

www.ingramcontent.com/pod-product-compliance
Lightning Source LLC
Chambersburg PA
CBHW080910170526

45158CB00008B/2068